Communications
in Computer and Information Science 75

G.S. Tomar   William I. Grosky
Tai-hoon Kim   Sabah Mohammed
Sanjoy Kumar Saha (Eds.)

Ubiquitous Computing and Multimedia Applications

International Conference, UCMA 2010
Miyazaki, Japan, June 23-25, 2010
Proceedings

Volume Editors

G.S. Tomar
VITM, Indore, India
E-mail: gstomar@rediffmail.com

William I. Grosky
University of Michigan, Dearborn, MI, USA
E-mail: wgrosky@umich.edu

Tai-hoon Kim
Hannam University, Daejeon, South Korea
E-mail: taihoonn@hnu.kr

Sabah Mohammed
Lakehead University, Thunder Bay, Ontario, Canada
E-mail: sabah.mohammed@lakeheadu.ca

Sanjoy Kumar Saha
Jadavpur University, Calcutta, India
E-mail: sks_ju@yahoo.co.in

Library of Congress Control Number: 2010928114

CR Subject Classification (1998): I.5, I.2, I.4, F.1, H.3, H.4

ISSN   1865-0929
ISBN-10   3-642-13466-1 Springer Berlin Heidelberg New York
ISBN-13   978-3-642-13466-1 Springer Berlin Heidelberg New York

springer.com

© Springer-Verlag Berlin Heidelberg 2010
Printed in Germany

Typesetting: Camera-ready by author, data conversion by Scientific Publishing Services, Chennai, India
Printed on acid-free paper   06/3180   5 4 3 2 1 0

Foreword

Advanced Science and Technology, Advanced Communication and Networking, Information Security and Assurance, Ubiquitous Computing and Multimedia Applications are conferences that attract many academic and industry professionals. The goal of these co-located conferences is to bring together researchers from academia and industry as well as practitioners to share ideas, problems and solutions relating to the multifaceted aspects of advanced science and technology, advanced communication and networking, information security and assurance, ubiquitous computing and multimedia applications.

This co-located event included the following conferences: AST 2010 (The second International Conference on Advanced Science and Technology), ACN 2010 (The second International Conference on Advanced Communication and Networking), ISA 2010 (The 4th International Conference on Information Security and Assurance) and UCMA 2010 (The 2010 International Conference on Ubiquitous Computing and Multimedia Applications).

We would like to express our gratitude to all of the authors of submitted papers and to all attendees, for their contributions and participation. We believe in the need for continuing this undertaking in the future.

We acknowledge the great effort of all the Chairs and the members of advisory boards and Program Committees of the above-listed events, who selected 15% of over 1,000 submissions, following a rigorous peer-review process. Special thanks go to SERSC (Science & Engineering Research Support soCiety) for supporting these co-located conferences.

We are grateful in particular to the following speakers who kindly accepted our invitation and, in this way, helped to meet the objectives of the conference: Hojjat Adeli (The Ohio State University), Ruay-Shiung Chang (National Dong Hwa University), Adrian Stoica (NASA Jet Propulsion Laboratory), Tatsuya Akutsu (Kyoto University) and Tadashi Dohi (Hiroshima University).

We would also like to thank Rosslin John Robles and Maricel O. Balitanas, graduate students of Hannam University, who helped in editing the material with great passion.

April 2010   Tai-hoon Kim

Preface

We would like to welcome you to the proceedings of the 2010 International Conference on Ubiquitous Computing and Multimedia Applications (UCMA 2010), which was held on June 23–25, 2010, at Sheraton Grande Ocean Resort, in Miyazaki, Japan.

UCMA 2010 focused on various aspects of advances in ubiquitous computing and multimedia applications with computational sciences, mathematics and information technology. It provided a chance for academic and industry professionals to discuss recent progress in the related areas. We expect that the conference and its publications will be a trigger for further related research and technology improvements in this important subject. We would like to acknowledge the great effort of all the Chairs and members of the Program Committee. Out of around 150 submissions to UCMA 2010, we accepted 22 papers to be included in the proceedings and presented during the conference. This gives an acceptance ratio firmly below 15%. Eight of the papers accepted for UCMA 2010 were published in a special volume, LNCS 6059, by Springer. The remaining 14 accepted papers can be found in this CCIS volume.

We would like to express our gratitude to all of the authors of submitted papers and to all attendees, for their contributions and participation. We believe in the need for continuing this undertaking in the future.

Once more, we would like to thank all the organizations and individuals who supported this event as a whole and, in particular, helped in the success of UCMA 2010.

April 2010

G.S. Tomar
William I. Grosky
Tai-hoon Kim
Sabah Mohammed
Sanjoy Kumar Saha

Organization

Organizing Committee

Honorary Chair	Hojjat Adeli (The Ohio State University, USA)
General Co-chairs	G.S. Tomar (VITM, India) William I. Grosky (University of Michigan - Dearborn, USA)
Program Co-chairs	Tai-hoon Kim (Hannam University, Korea) Sabah Mohammed (Lakehead University, Canada) Sanjoy Kumar Saha (Jadavpur University, India)
Workshop Co-chairs	Muhammad Khurram Khan (King Saud University, Kingdom of Saudi Arabia) Seok-soo Kim (Hannam University, Korea)
International Advisory Board	Cao Jiannong (The Hong Kong Polytechnic University, Hong Kong) Frode Eika Sandnes (Oslo University College, Norway) Schahram Dustdar (Vienna University of Technology, Austria) Andrea Omicini (Università di Bologna, Italy) Lionel Ni (The Hong Kong University of Science & Technology, Hong Kong) Rajkumar Buyya (University of Melbourne, Australia) Hai Jin (Huazhong University of Science and Technology, China) N. Jaisankar (VIT University, India)
Publicity Co-chairs	Paolo Bellavista (Università di Bologna, Italy) Ing-Ray Chen (Virginia Polytechnic Institute and State University, USA) Yang Xiao (University of Alabama, USA) J.H. Abawajy (Deakin University, Australia) Muhammad Khurram Khan (King Saud University, Kingdom of Saudi Arabia) Ching-Hsien Hsu (Chung Hua University, Taiwan) Deepak Laxmi Narasimha (University of Malaya, Malaysia) Prabhat K. Mahanti (University of New Brunswick, Canada) Soumya Banerjee (Birla Institute of Technology, India)
Publication Chair	Bongen Gu (Chungju National University, Korea)
Local Arrangements Co-chairs	G.S. Tomar (VITM, India) Debnath Bhattacharyya (Heritage Institute of Technology, India)

Program Committee

Alexander Loui
Biplab K. Sarker
Brian King
Chantana Chantrapornchai
Claudia Linnhoff-Popien
D. Manivannan
Dan Liu
Eung Nam Ko
Georgios Kambourakis
Gerard Damm
Han-Chieh Chao
Hongli Luo
Igor Kotenko
J. H. Abawajy
Jalal Al-Muhtadi

Javier Garcia-Villalba
Khaled El-Maleh
Khalil DRIRA
Larbi Esmahi
Liang Fan
Mahmut Kandemir
Malrey Lee
Marco Roccetti
Mei-Ling Shyu
Ming Li
Pao-Ann Hsiung
Paolo Bellavista
Rami Yared
Rainer Malaka
Robert C. Hsu

Robert G. Reynolds
Rodrigo Mello
Schahram Dustdar
Seung-Hyun Seo
Seunglim Yong
Stefano Ferretti
Stuart J Barnes
Su Myeon Kim
Swapna S. Gokhale
Taenam Cho
Tony Shan
Toshihiro Tabata
Wanquan Liu
Wenjing Jia
Yao-Chung Chang

Table of Contents

System Requirement Analyses for Ubiquitous Environment Management System

Sang Boem Lim[1], Kyung Jun Gil[1], Ho Rim Choe[2], and Yang Dam Eo[1,*]

[1] Department of Advanced Technology Fusion at Konkuk University
Seoul, Korea
{sblim,sn1079,eoandrew}@konkuk.ac.kr
[2] TOIP Inc.,
Seoul, Korea
horimchoe@hotmail.com

Abstract. We are living in new stage of society. U-City introduces new paradigm that cannot be archived in traditional city to future city. Korea is one of the most active countries to construct U-City based on advances of IT technologies—especially based on high-speed network through out country [1]. Peoples are realizing ubiquitous service is key factor of success of U-City. Among the U-services, U-security service is one of the most important services. Nowadays we have to concern about traditional threat and also personal information. Since apartment complex is the most common residence type in Korea. We are developing security rules and system based on analyses of apartment complex and assert of apartment complex. Based on these analyses, we are developing apartment complex security using various technologies including home network system. We also will discuss basic home network security architecture.

Keywords: Apartment Complex Requirement Analyses, Home Network, Apartment Complex Management.

1 Introduction

Currently, we are facing new type of city named U-City (Ubiquitous City). U-City introduces new paradigm that cannot be archived in traditional city to future city. Basis of U-City is ubiquitous computing technologies that introduced by Mark Weiser in late 80's. Peoples are applying ubiquitous technologies as infrastructure of city and constructing U-City as new model of future city. U-City [2] is the envisioned futuristic one integrating IT infrastructures and ubiquitous services into the urban space. Also, this aims at offering a high quality of life for residents in terms of security, welfare and convenience. Korea is one of the most active countries to construct U-City based on advances of IT technologies—especially based on high-speed network through out country [1].

---

* Corresponding author.

G.S. Tomar et al. (Eds.): UCMA 2010, CCIS 75, pp. 1–10, 2010.
© Springer-Verlag Berlin Heidelberg 2010

Most important and hard to achieve to construct U-City is not constructing city with many IT technologies. To find killer application for U-City is the most important and hard job to do. Definition of U-service [3] is all the activities that are served using U-City infrastructure and ubiquitous technology to get information and contents. These services must available at anytime, anywhere to residences, companies, and government.

One of the most important U-services is ubiquitous security service. By the society is becoming more complicated, peoples are more and more concerning about security. We need to protect ourselves not only from traditional threat but also personal identity stealing. By utilizing information and communication technologies, city problem due to urbanization such as security issue can be handled. It can resolve stagnation, dense and over population matters within the city and it can enhance citizen's quality of life [1].

U-security (Ubiquitous-security) is designed to prevent form anxiety and concern about security and to protect personal information and form traditional threat in U-City. Basic idea of U-security service is to build integrated security management system based on high-speed network. This security system should have good defense from intelligent crime and should be nature-friendly to have harmony with environmental design. This system also has to have functionality integration with existing security systems. In order to provide security and comfortless of residence, this system should provides various useful services.

Apartment complex is the most common residence type in Korea. Traditionally, securities of apartment complex mainly depend on human resources. There are few apartment complexes that are using surveillance equipments. Even in these apartment complexes, still human resources are most important and dependable resource in security. However, human has limitations. They are mainly depend on five senses and pre-define situations based old custom and habit. There are always possibility human's are miss leading the situation. We need cutting edge surveillance system to make up for the weak point. Human resources are still very important fact on security. The human resources and surveillance system must have cooperative relationship to get better security system.

Currently, there are many kinds of manned security systems and unmanned security systems. People try to integrate these systems using automated security systems like CCTV. However, integration of these systems cannot prevent intelligent crime like system hacking. We need more intelligent security system for current environment. U-security service is one of the alternatives of this problem.

In this paper, we will categorize apartment complex and asserts to identify security level of each area and asserts. Based on these analyses, we are developing apartment complex security using various technologies including home network system. We also will discuss basic home network security architecture.

2   Related Works

A voice captures sensor network system for a secure ubiquitous home environment [4] has been studied. In this paper, they applied new voice capture sensor network to build secure ubiquitous home environment. By the result of this experience, authors are proposed the development of efficient voice-based smart home application roadmap. They also provide a solution to low-cost alternative to solving real world problem in WSN (Wireless Sensor Network) area. This study is used in HCI (Human Computer Interaction) area.

Some studies are proposed user identification method for personal security in ubiquitous environment for example [5]. Authors are proposed a method and an agent system to protect personal information. Main target of this research is to provide protection on the ID and password when users are using some applications or services in ubiquitous environment. They are also using Grid computing technology to provide same functionalities in the heterogeneous environment.

Privacy and personal information protection in ubiquitous environment is one of the big issues. There are many studies in this area like [7] [9]. These papers tried to define boundaries and limitations of surveillance, security and privacy in ubiquitous society. Authors concerned about too much of surveillance that is infringement of citizen's privacy. In order to give maximum securities and to protect privacy, they are proposed new model of surveillance in ubiquitous society.

Ubiquitous society produces new kind of threats. Traditional applications are not ready for these threats. One report [6] proposed new application-level security policy languages. Author argued that this policy could be applied to both existing applications and future applications. One interesting study in this report is author modeled the world to provide security model.

In our research, we are providing resource and hierarchy of space modeling in order to build more secure apartment complex. We define security level of each resources based on these modeling. These modeling are described in the following section in depth.

3 System Requirement Analysis

In this chapter, we describe resource analysis and hierarchy of space analysis to define resources and spaces in apartment complex. These analyses are used to improve safety and comfortable environment of apartment complex.

3.1 Resource Analysis

We categorize apartment complex resources into eight asset areas and each asset area has its own value rating (see Table 1). Eight asset areas are residents, vehicles, high-value items, equipments, subsidiary facilities, buildings, equipment offices, and information assets. For the value rating, we divide into five levels--VH (Very High), H (High), M (Moderate), L (Low), and VL (Very Low). Based on these categories and value ratings, we are setting privileges and securities and providing most accurate services.

Among the eight assets, we have five HV value rating: residents, vehicles, high-value items, equipment offices, and information assets, one H value rating: equipments, one M value rating: subsidiary facilities, and one L value rating: building.

Table 1. Apartment asserts and value rating

Assets	Objects	Value Rating
Residents	**Identity**: VIP, foreigner, celebrity, and ordinary citizen. **Age**: Senior citizen, teenager, and children.	VH
Vehicles	Resident vehicle, guest vehicle, and maintenance vehicle	VH
High-value Items	**Inside of house**: cashes, computers, jewels, credit cards, resident card, home appliances, and antiques. **Outside of house**: leisure equipments, vehicles, bicycles, and motorcycles.	VH
Equipments	Machinery devices, electronic devices, electricity devices, facility devices, and network devices	H
Subsidiary Facilities	Health club, driving range, playground, and senior citizens' center	M
Buildings	Main entrance and storages	L
Equipment Offices	Security office, machine room, and boiler room	VH
Information	Personal ID number, internet baking information, id and password, and important DB	VH

Residents have VH value rating because residents are most important resources in apartment complex. We divide residents into two categories based on identity and age. Resident identities include VIP, foreigner, celebrity, and ordinary citizen. Senior-citizen, teenager, and children are member of age identities. It is very important to identify each resident to provide right services and securities.

Vehicles have VH value rating because of the security reasons. It is essential to identify each vehicle and control them based on vehicles category. In the vehicle categories, we have resident vehicle, guest vehicle, and maintenance vehicle. High-value items are also ranked in VH value rating because it is important to protect resident properties. High-valued items can be located inside of the house or outside of the house. Items such as cash, computer, jewel, credit card, resident card, home appliance, and antique are located inside of the house. In the outside of house, we have leisure equipments, vehicles, bicycles, and motorcycles. We should identify and protect these items because these high-valued items are target of thief.

Many types of equipment are installed in apartment complex to support residence's quality of life. In this paper, we assume machinery devices, electronic devices, electricity devices, facility devices, and network devices. These devices and subsidiary facilities are basic devices for comfortable life in apartment complex. Nowadays, people are more and more concerning about quality of life. In this reason, apartment complex requires more subsidiary facility spaces like health club, driving range, playground, and senior citizens' center. Subsidiary facilities have M value rating because security of subsidiary facilities is not directly impact to the residence's life.

We have two building related resources; apartment buildings and equipment offices. Apartment building contains main entrance and storages. Equipment offices are including security office, machine room, and boiler room. These offices are managing and controlling the entire apartment complex. We give the VH value rating for equipment offices.

Protecting information is one of the most important matters these days. Lots of personal information exists inside of apartment complex to protect. Personal ID number, Internet baking information, id and password, and important DB are examples of information resources. We classify information assert as VH value rating. It is essential to design and implement good apartment complex network and home network security. Network security on home network is discussed in chapter 4 in depth.

3.2 Hierarchy of Space Analysis

In this analysis, we divide apartment complex into five domains (see Fig. 1): private domain, semi-private domain, semi-public domain, public domain, and facility management domain. Each domain has its own characteristics, services, and security level. For example, the most important concern of private domain is personal privacy, meanwhile public domain have to have accessibility by everyone.

Private and semi-private domains are located in the apartment complex and used mainly by apartment residences. We need higher security standards for these areas.

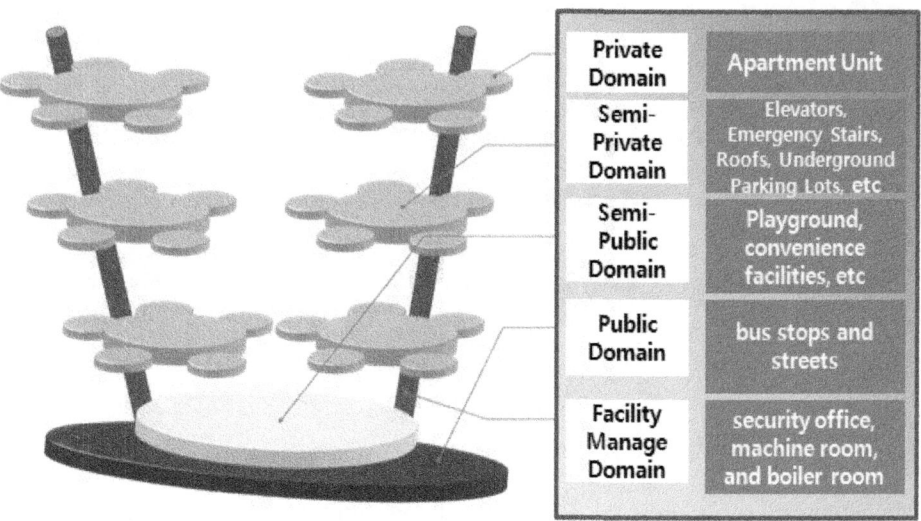

Fig. 1. Hierarchy of Space

Apartment unite is the most private space in the apartment complex. We categorized each apartment unit as private domain. We have to provide enough securities to protect personal privacy. Facilities that are used mainly by apartment residences are listed as semi-private domain. In this domain, we include elevators, emergency stairs, roofs, underground parking lots, etc. We also have to maintain some securities in semi-private domain to protect apartment residences.

Both apartment residences and general public use semi-public and public domains. Securities and management of most public domain facilities are outside of apartment complex's scope. Semi-public domain is located in apartment complex. However, it is opened to both apartment residences and public. Playground, convenience facilities, etc. are listed under semi-public domain. Everyone can access public domain that includes bus stops and streets, freely.

Facility management domain is used to control, manage, and maintain apartment complex. We decoupled this domain with other domains because facility management domain needs unique securities and management level. Facility management domain includes offices and rooms that are needed for apartment complex management such as security office, machine room, and boiler room.

3.3 Define Security Level Based on Analysis

We categorize level of security risk of each asset area from resource analysis and each domain from hierarchy of space analysis (See fig. 2). This information is very important base data to install security equipment on apartment complex. We frame security equipment installation plan and emergency respond process based on level of security risk. Among these securities, we will discuss in depth about network and home securities on next section.

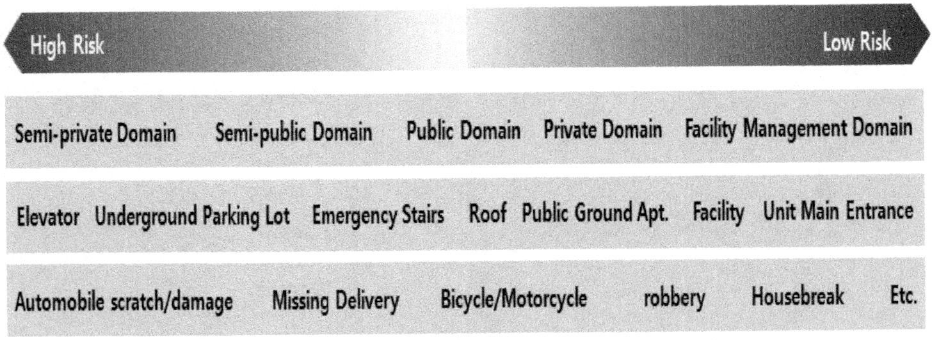

High Risk				Low Risk
Semi-private Domain	Semi-public Domain	Public Domain	Private Domain	Facility Management Domain
Elevator Underground Parking Lot	Emergency Stairs	Roof Public Ground Apt.	Facility	Unit Main Entrance
Automobile scratch/damage	Missing Delivery	Bicycle/Motorcycle	robbery	Housebreak Etc.

Fig. 2. Security Level

4   Communication System Design

Communication system is the core of ubiquitous cities and homes. In our project, all the apartment complexes are inter-connected with network to provide conveniences and securities to the residences. In this section, we will discuss about basic network concepts and home network systems in the apartment complex.

4.1 Network Concept

When we are designing network system (Fig. 3), we focused on three important matters: speed, convenience, and dedicated Internet connections. In order to provide seamless ubiquitous services, network speed is the essential fact. To achieve high-speed network connectivity, we lay the optical cables between apartments to provide high-speed network and reduce static. Fast Ethernet (100Mbps) interfaces and dedicated Internet lines are providing necessary bandwidth for ubiquitous services.

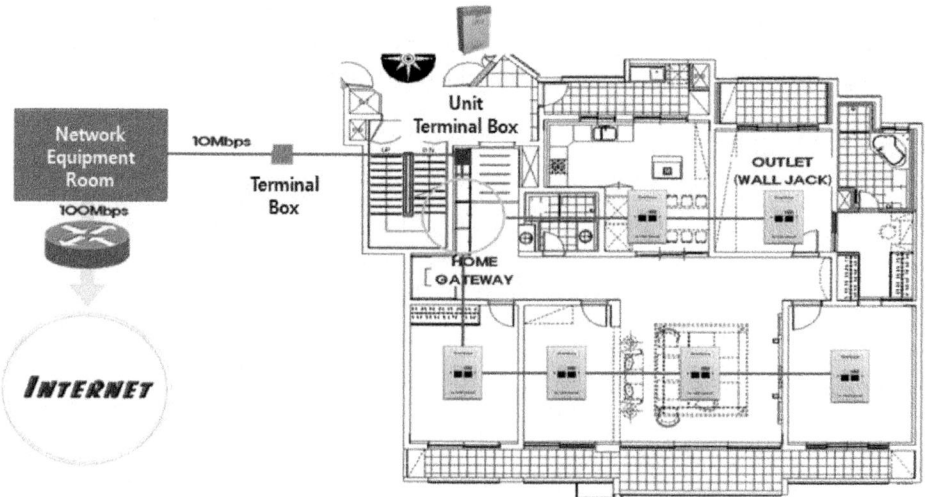

Fig. 3. Overview of Apartment Complex Network System

Popular technologies came with easy to use and conveniences. Even technically advanced products cannot survive without these facts. Convenience is one of the most important goals of our project. Apartment residences can use high-speed internet without any confusing configurations, can remotely control home appliances using network, can use convenience applications in the intranet, and can connect internet at anywhere in the apartment complex using wireless access points.

We can reduce security system building and management cost by using dedicated Internet connection, which provides same Internet interface to every apartments. We can apply same Internet security level or can outsource security service to security control center using this interface. This interface make possible to provide remote home appliance control service. Dedicated Internet line can be recovered faster than other Internet services from the failure. It is easy to add more services such as private domain name and mail, if we are using dedicated Internet connection.

4.2 Home Networking System

Main goal of home network system (Fig. 4) is to provide intelligent home management system. In order to provide easy to use and intelligent system, each unit has wireless connection and every home appliances and devices are interconnected with wireless or wired network. Every home appliances and devices has own services and maintenance rules. These services and rules are registered with home server. Home server manages services, devices, and network connectivity in a unit.

We provide mobile WEB-PAD that is using wireless network, to use and control various devices and services. We can use Internet, manage entrance door, control lights and home appliances, control security devices, and manage temperature and humidity by using mobile WEB-PAD. Not like built-in touchy screen in previous apartments, mobile WEB-PAD can provide more convenience to the user.

One of the great features of our home networking system is we can control home appliances and devices, communicate with visitor, and check the voice and video messages from anywhere using cellular phone, ordinary phone, and PC.

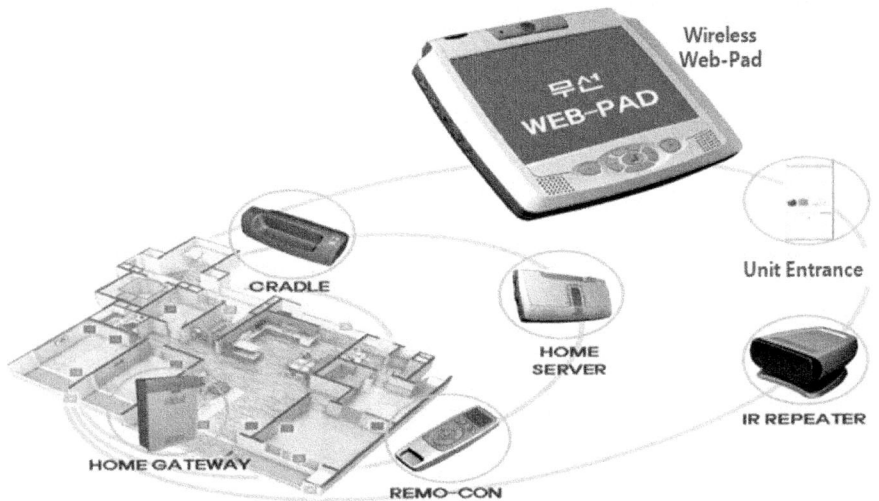

Fig. 4. Home Network System

5   Conclusion and Future Works

In this paper, we discussed system requirement analyses and network requirements to build intelligent apartment complex. System requirement analyses and home network system is core of safe and comfortable apartment complex.

For the system requirement analyses, we described resource analysis and hierarchy of space analysis to define resources and spaces in apartment complex. We also defined security level based on analyses. We categorized apartment complex resources into eight asset areas. Each asset area is assigned with its own value rating. We divide apartment complex into five domains for hierarchy of space analysis. Each domain has its own characteristics, services, and security level. We are designing apartment complex based on these analyses and security levels.

Communication system is the core of ubiquitous cities and homes. In our project, all the apartment complexes are inter-connected with network to provide conveniences and securities to the residences. We discussed basic network concepts and home network systems in the apartment complex. All apartment devices can be controlled with wireless WEB-PAD since all the devices are inter-connected with network. We also can control apartment devices from outside of apartment using cellular phone, ordinary phone, and PC.

Currently we are working on detailed design on home network, network security system design, and physical security system design. In order to provide better services, we need detail home network system. In this design, we will provide rules and service boundaries when we are providing home appliance control, other devices control, unit security, and unit network for residence devices.

Since security is one of the most concerning topic among apartment residences, we are researching on both network security and physical security. To protect valuable personal information, we are designing multi-layered network security system. Currently, our design has five layers to protect network. We are installing our design in the apartment complex to prove correctness of our system. In the future, we will modify our system according to operation results. Physical security is as important as network security. In this reason, we are spending our effort to provide better security system. For now, we are dealing with main gate security for vehicles, main entrance security system using biometric system, surveillance system, emergency call system, and security central station. We are installing our systems and adding more ideas in this area.

Acknowledgement

This work is financially supported by Korea Minister of Ministry of Land, Transport and Maritime Affairs (MLTM) as "U-City Master and Doctor Course Grant Program".

This research is supported by the project "Development of u-Eco City Business Service Platform" funded by the Ministry of Land, Transport and Maritime Affairs of Korea.

References

1. Kim, C.H.: MLTM's Ubiquitous City Strategic Planning. In: 2008 U-City international Conference, Seoul, Korea, October 30-31 (2008)
2. Jang, B.T.: Overview Telematics Core technology for U-City. In: 2008 U-City international Conference, Seoul, Korea, October 30-31 (2008)
3. Han, I.K., et al.: U-City Service Model, U-Eco City Textbook 04-U-City Management, Ubiquitous & Ecology City R&D Center, pp. 10–11, 53–60
4. Palafox, L.E., Antonio García-Macías, J.: Deploying a voice capture sensor network system for a secure ubiquitous home environment. International Journal of Communication Systems 22, 1199–1212 (2009)

5. Lee, E.-S., Lee, S.H.: Design of the Architecture for Agent of the Personality Security in the Ubiquitous Environment. In: Nguyen, N.T., Jo, G.-S., Howlett, R.J., Jain, L.C. (eds.) KES-AMSTA 2008. LNCS (LNAI), vol. 4953, pp. 444–453. Springer, Heidelberg (2008)
6. Scott, D.J.: Abstracting application-level security policy for ubiquitous computing, University of Cambridge Computer Laboratory (January 2005)
7. Albrechtslund, A.: The Postmodern Panopticon: Surveillance and Privacy in the Age of Ubiquitous Computing. In: Proceedings of CEPE 2005: Sixth international conference of computer ethics: Philosophical enquiry, Enschede, Netherlands, July 17-19 (2005)
8. Shin, D.H., Nah, Y.M., Lee, I.-S., Yi, W.S., Won, Y.J.: Security Protective measures for the Ubiquitous City Integrated Operation Center. In: Third International Conference on Broad-Band Communications, Information Technology & Biomedical Applications, pp. 239–244. IEEE Computer Society, Los Alamitos
9. Buennemeyer, T.K., Marchany, R.C., Tront, J.G.: Ubiquitous Security: Privacy versus Protection. In: Proc. of the 2006 International Conf. on Pervasive Systems, pp. 71–77 (2006)

Home Infotainment Platform – A Ubiquitous Access Device for Masses

Arpan Pal, M. Prashant, Avik Ghose, and Chirabrata Bhaumik

Innovation Labs – Kolkata, Tata Consultancy Services Limited, Bengal Intelligence Park,
4th Floor Unit-D, Block EP , Salt Lake Electronic Complex, Kolkata-700091
{arpan.pal,prashant1.m,avik.ghose,c.bhaumik}@tcs.com

Abstract. There is tremendous need for a low-cost Internet-Enabled Platform for developing countries like India that uses TV as the display medium and can connect to Internet using various available connectivity solutions. The paper presents how a generic framework middleware can be used to create a Home Infotainment Platform that can support variety of value-added applications. It also talks about the innovative designs employed to bring about the low-cost solution keeping in mind both the limitations of TV as a display and non-availability of high quality-of-service networks. Finally the social, economic and environmental implications of wide-spread deployment of the proposed solution are outlined.

Keywords: Infotainment, Set top Box, Connected TV, Interactive TV, Internet Access Device, On-screen Keyboard, Rate Adaptive QoS.

1 Introduction

In developing countries, computer adoption rate is pretty low as many consumers are unable to afford one and also because many of them lack basic computer skills. This drastically limits access to information and communication via the Internet. In India, out of 204.9 million households only 4.2 million households have a computer, whereas 110 million households have a TV with cable connection [1].

On the consumer usage front, India is not a strong performer in terms of Internet usage, with below 10 percent of the population regularly using the Internet. Additionally, broadband penetration in India is below 2 percent of households. Home Infotainment Platform aims to overcome this barrier of access to information through a familiar device i.e. the television set that most consumers already own.

By using standard Internet connection through 2G/3G wireless and ADSL, we propose a Home Infotainment Platform that provides consumers access to interactive services over the television at a reasonable cost. It is an information and communication platform that provides consumers with computer functionalities on a television set. The average computer user relies on a computer mainly for information access, entertainment and collaboration. The proposed solution offers the same functionality on a television set at a much lower cost compared to a traditional computer. The proposed solution prioritizes the requirements of a non technology savvy computer user on one hand and the price conscious user on the other.

G.S. Tomar et al. (Eds.): UCMA 2010, CCIS 75, pp. 11–19, 2010.

The average computer user relies on a computer mainly for information access, entertainment and collaboration. The HIP solution brings the same functionality on a television set using a low-cost Set Top Box.

The solution currently supports applications like Internet Browsing, Photo Viewer, Music Player, Video Player, SMS, Video Chat and Document Viewer. The core of the system is a novel robust and scalable framework that is flexible enough to deploy future applications like community gaming, home healthcare, distance education, digital video recording, place-shifting and IPTV. Therefore the platform can be seen as an enabler for next generation information access, healthcare and education for developing countries.

2   Solution Overview

The proposed solution uses a Set top Box like platform, where the existing TV broadcast is routed to the device via composite A/V in and output is given to the television via composite A/V out. The four USB ports in the box support devices such as keyboard, mouse, webcam, modem and flash drive. Headphones with microphone can be connected through sockets provided. In summary, the solution consists of a set of value-added information access, entertainment and collaboration applications on top of a proprietary middleware framework that runs on a Set top box device.

Fig. 1 provides the basic overview of the platform.

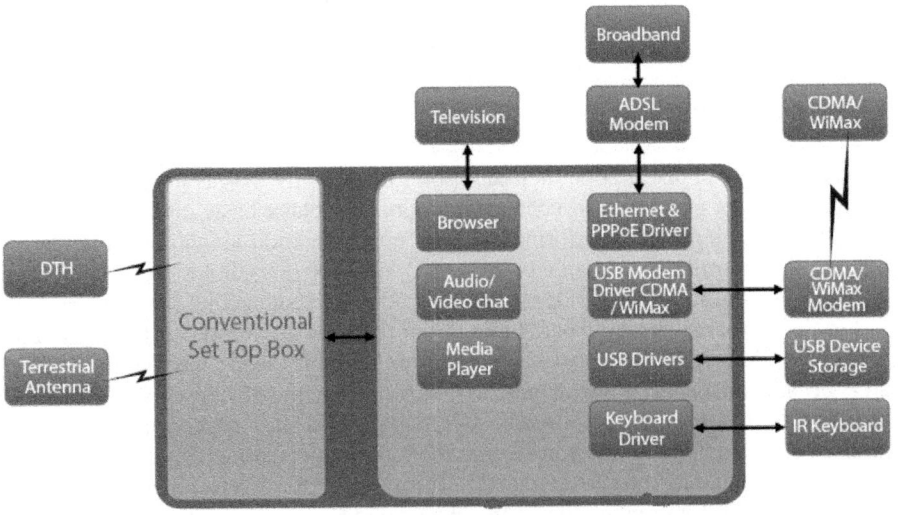

Fig. 1. HIP - Overview

Fig. 2 illustrates the basic connectivity details of the box. It is a robust and scalable platform that provides the flexibility of tweaking the framework to churn out solutions catering to different domains and verticals with a quick turn around time. For

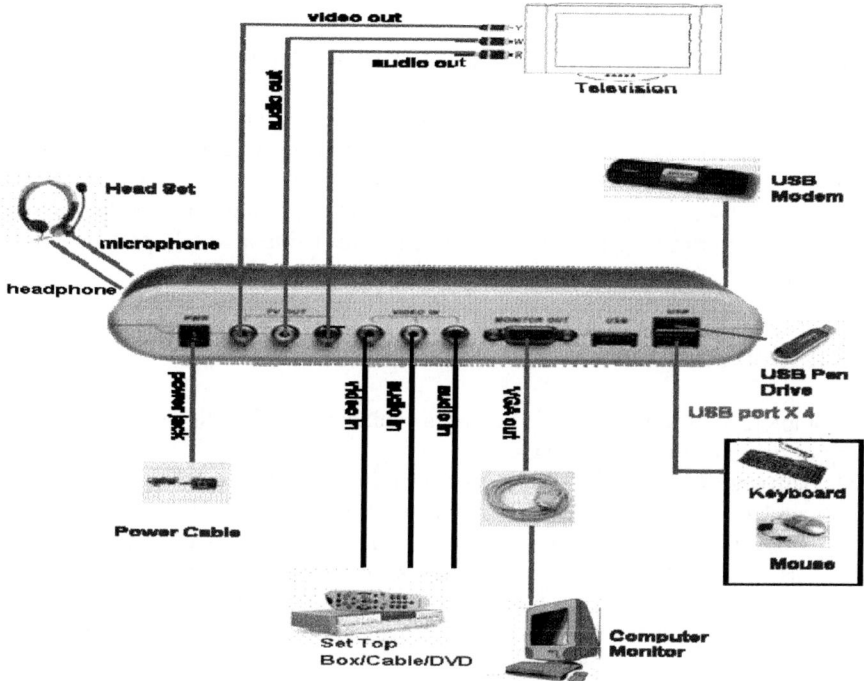

Fig. 2. HIP Connectivity Diagram

example, even though HIP was designed mainly keeping in the demands of the Consumer Infotainment, the same framework and platform has been used to build solutions like Telemedicine and Home Energy gateway.

3 Motivation

The motivation behind building the solution had been two-fold.

3.1 Social Motivation

- Reach the vast base of the pyramid market that seeks entertainment and benefit from information/ internet based services
- Produce a robust device that can enable infotainment as well as value added services
- Keep costs down to suit the small households in rural and urban population
- Use the popularity of television and cable connectivity across rural heartlands to provide more value
- Simplify and converge multiple devices and enrich user experience

3.2 Business Motivation

From business perspective, telecom operators in developing countries always find it very tough to increase the Average Revenue per User (ARPU). One of the channels to increase the ARPU is through Data Services. However, the main data access device, the Personal Computer has only about 2% penetration in Indian market and is not affordable to masses. So there is a business need for a low-cost access device which would help the service provider to exponentially increase their bandwidth sale on one hand and also to raise the demand for their modems using a widely prevalent medium like television.

4 Solution Architecture

The complete solution is designed using a scalable and flexible software framework on top of general purpose hardware.

The software framework adheres to embedded system design guidelines and constraints and is based on basic multimedia work-flow. The philosophy of the framework is that its processes are like perennial daemons which will always exist in the system and wait in their respective mailboxes for messages from a common controller which will be in the form of a library. The controller library is linked to the application GUI/CLI which can then be used to map various applications using the same framework.

Fig. 3 tries to show how this reconfigurable aspect of the framework can be used to create multiple and varied applications.

To bring in this reconfigurable aspect, all the processes are divided into three distinct but closely knit subsystems.

1. The source subsystem or SRC which defines from where the data has to be taken for processing
2. The processing subsystem or PROC which defines the kind of processing that needs to be done on the data to make it suitable for output
3. Finally the sink subsystem or SINK which defines where the data has to be put after it is processed

The controller library has been defined as the control subsystem of the framework which is the driving module for the other subsystems. The framework thus ensures that the same set of processes can be re-used at run-time to map into the various multimedia applications that could be expected from an embedded multimedia device.

Further, this framework has also been extended to sensor data as a source subsystem. This means that given a method to capture data from a sensor and a processing algorithm to convert the sensor data to meaningful information, it can be displayed, stored or uploaded as desired. This capability adds potential for applications in new dimensions like energy, medicine and communications, which are sensor-intensive.

Some of the solutions which have been derived from the framework are shown in Fig. 3. Each of these can be mapped into the framework, which brings out the flexibility feature of the framework.

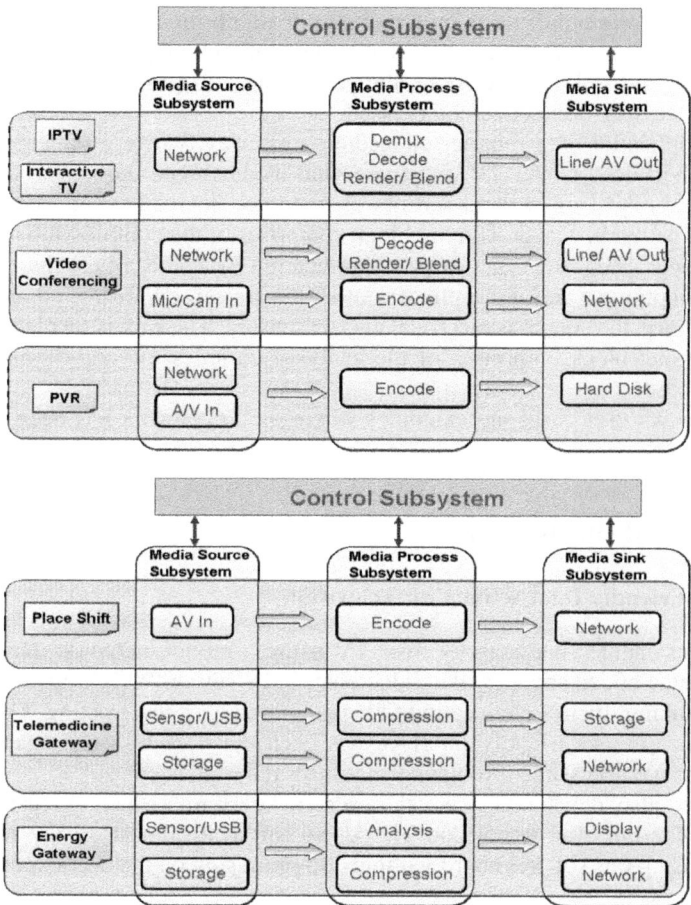

Fig. 3. Solution framework representations

In IPTV applications, the source is a network multi-cast RTP and the sink is display. The processing may involve de-multiplexing and decoding of the audio and video signals.

In Interactive TV applications, the source is taken from normal audio/video line-in, the processing block would ensure the proper blending and rendering of TV content with application GUI and the sink would be the TV display interfaces.

Video Conferencing being a peer-to-peer case has symmetric source and sink. For each pair the source is auxiliary audio/video (camera and headphone), in the processing block it is encoding and compression and the sink is network. Again for peer data the source is network, the processing is decoding/decompression and the sink is display and audio out.

Programmable Video Recording (PVR) can be identified as a use case where the source subsystem is configured as audio/video line in and the sink as storage. The processing block is encoding/compression and multiplexing (optional).

The case of place-shifting is pretty simple in which the source is audio/video line in and the sink is a composite sink that means the output goes both to display and network. For the sink to be display, the processing is bypassed and for the network case the processing is encoded/compressed.

If the application is a remote telemedicine gateway, where a patient can consult with an expert doctor over TV and share vital medical data during the consultation, the source is a host of medical sensors or a storage device having medical records. The sink is network. The processing block comprises of the compression algorithms.

For an Energy Information Gateway Application for home, where the electrical energy consumption of various appliances at Home are sensed, displayed and/or sent to utility provider, the source is electrical energy sensors. The sink is display or network. The processing block comprises of the analysis/ compression algorithms depending on the use case.

The last two uses cases are examples where the Framework has been extended to sensor systems.

5 Novelty of the Solution

5.1 User-Friendly Interactivity on Television

The product enables interactivity over TV using a mobile network. This opens the scope of value added services like video chat, SMS voting, Web browsing, Webmail, Internet banking, distance education, TV commerce over the existing TV set among many others. A user-friendly interface has been developed so that majority of the applications are accessible through normal Infra-red remote control.

We have also developed a novel onscreen keyboard, which is customized and optimized for Infra-red remote on TV. Users can avail almost all the features of a keyboard using this soft keyboard without compromising on the user experience [2].

5.2 Robust and Adaptive Design for Quality-of-Service

The overall design and implementation of an extremely bandwidth-efficient video chat system which automatically adapts to fluctuating wireless network conditions also adds to the novelty the proposed system [3]. This is an important feature for deployment in all developing countries, where the bandwidth availability and QoS is still a big issue (especially for wireless).

5.3 Blending of TV for Interactivity

The solution supports the unique aspect of blending TV content with connected network thereby enabling novel services like SMS voting, with a remote, for a TV show even as you watch it.

5.4 Over-the-Air Upgrade

The framework also allows robust over-the-air software upgrades for the system. The upgrade is designed for robustness to take care of various failure scenarios like power failure, network failure etc.

5.5 Aggressive Pricing

HIP is in the sub-$100 price range, while still supporting the use of common computer peripherals such as the keyboard, mouse and webcams.

To keep the cost minimal, it employs an open source based approach for all supported applications and related software components.

Also, by keeping the hardware same and changing the software, it is possible to build newer applications. This way one can take advantage of the volume based low cost pricing of the hardware.

5.6 Competition Analysis

Existing products in this space either lack the interactive element (as compared to traditional Set top Boxes), or use only high-end connectivity like ADSL only (which is not available to majority of the users), or are too complicated to use (thereby decreasing the mass adoption), which differentiates Home Infotainment Platform as an innovative solution.

For instance, DTH set-top boxes only offer a downlink connectivity by which the subscriber can download only stored information from the service provider's Web repository. The lack of uplink connectivity prevents the TV, which is a very powerful medium, from becoming truly interactive.

Thin clients also try to provide similar kind of features. However they normally depend on high-speed ADSL connections, which are not available in many parts of the country, especially in rural areas. The output display is not customized for TV and they do not provide truly interactive mass applications like SMS on TV and blending of Internet content with TV programs.

6 Benefits

The following section illustrates how HIP contributes to the society at large.

6.1 Improving Healthcare

The Home Infotainment Platform supports remote medical consultation for rural people by connecting with medical specialists in super specialty hospitals. This product acts as a portable telemedicine console connected to the Internet via any mobile or broadband network. It is integrated with diagnostic device interfaces at the remote end and a laptop or desktop at the specialist doctor's end. Doctors can have live chat sessions with the patient and also see live diagnostic data. This is particularly beneficial for patients in rural areas as they find it difficult, expensive and time consuming to reach hospitals in big towns/cities.

6.2 Improving Education

HIP can be used as a platform for distance education for students in rural areas. Lack of sophisticated educational facilities in remote villages and towns is a problem in most developing countries. Distance education via an existing TV at home can tremendously benefit rural students. This platform will enable direct interaction with faculty via Video chat. Users can send and receive study materials through webmail and channel broadcasts.

6.3 Improving Social Networking

HIP enables video chat with family/friends that are geographically apart like aged parents and working progeny. Web mailing also connects people for both professional and personal networking. It enables people to share their thoughts through standard Web 2.0 technologies like community blogging (Face book etc.).

6.4 Improving Information Penetration

Information through HIP Web access supports entertainment options like audio/video downloads information on career development, consumer products, agriculture-related information such as weather alerts, fertilizers, seed prices and railways information and booking.

6.5 Improving Financial Inclusion

TV based Internet banking can be offered through HIP. It can be used to improve awareness on investment options and to cultivate a savings/banking culture among low income groups. This platform may also be used as a promotional gateway for financial products and insurance products.

6.6 Improving the Environment

This platform can be used as an energy gateway for home owners to optimize power usage. HIP can be connected to a smart meter using Zigbee connectivity to get a continuous update on the energy consumption of all devices and appliances in a household along with the local energy prices. This will enable users to tailor their power consumption accordingly. It can also provide users with direct feedback on costs and environmental impact of their consumption.

7 Conclusion

In summary, with reference to the 3 P's, People, Profit & Planet, the proposed solution has the following to offer:

People: Information is power. Connectivity empowers people. Apart from providing simple internet and email connectivity, HIP can act as a platform for two services of key importance to rural populations – Health and Education.

HIP can act as a low cost Telemedicine portal. The advantages are that it connects to the Internet via any mobile or broadband network and provides video even over low bandwidth and uses the TV for display.

HIP also supports distance education for students in rural areas. Distance education on a low cost infrastructure such as an existing TV at home can tremendously benefit such students.

Profit: In spite of having tremendous social impact, no solution offering can be made scalable in mass-scale unless it is backed by a viable business model. HIP enables Telecom service providers to increase their ARPU in the mass market by allowing them to provide data services.

Planet: From the environmental perspective, Smart Grid and Smart metering are significant contributors. HIP can be a very good solution enabler in this space for the utility sector. HIP can act as a gateway for exchanging metering information over the home television. Customers would have the choice of monitoring and customizing their daily electricity/ gas and water consumption patterns sitting in the comfort of their homes. HIP can also serve as a gateway which would allow users to control their electronic equipments at home using Zigbee controlled switches. The devices can be controlled over the web from the remotest corner.

All these have been achieved through building a reusable and flexible framework that uses a lot of open-source components and creation of technology that can take care of the two main issues of developing countries –

1) Unreliable QoS of the available network
   and
2) Unwillingness of the end-users to use computer-like interfaces.

References

1. CIA Fact book 2008 and World Bank WMDS 2008 (2008)
2. Pal, A., Bhaumik, C., Kar, D., Ghoshdastidar, S., Shukla, J.: A Novel On-Screen Keyboard for Hierarchical Navigation with Reduced Number of Key Strokes. In: IEEE International Conference on Systems, Man, and Cybernetics (SMC), San Antonio, Texas (2009)
3. Chattopadhyay, D., Sinha, A., Chattopadhyay, T., Pal, A.: Adaptive Rate Control for H.264 Based Video Conferencing Over a Low Bandwidth Wired and Wireless Channel. In: IEEE International Symposium on Broadband Multimedia Systems and Broadcasting, Bilbao, Spain (May 2009)

A New Experiment on Bengali Character Recognition

Sumana Barman[1], Debnath Bhattacharyya[2], Seung-whan Jeon[2],
Tai-hoon Kim[2,*], and Haeng-Kon Kim[3]

[1] Computer Science and Engineering Department
Heritage Institute of Technology
Kolkata-700107, India
sumanabarman@gmail.com
[2] Multimedia Department, Hannam University,
Daejeon, Republic of Korea
[3] Dept. of Computer Engineering, Catholic University of Daegu,
Daegu, Republic of Korea
debnathb@gmail.com, jeoninoldenburg@hanmail.net,
taihoonn@empal.com, hangkon@cu.ac.kr

Abstract. This paper presents a method to use View based approach in Bangla Optical Character Recognition (OCR) system providing reduced data set to the ANN classification engine rather than the traditional OCR methods. It describes how Bangla characters are processed, trained and then recognized with the use of a Backpropagation Artificial neural network. This is the first published account of using a segmentation-free optical character recognition system for Bangla using a view based approach. The methodology presented here assumes that the OCR pre-processor has presented the input images to the classification engine described here. The size and the font face used to render the characters are also significant in both training and classification. The images are first converted into greyscale and then to binary images; these images are then scaled to a fit a pre-determined area with a fixed but significant number of pixels. The feature vectors are then formed extracting the characteristics points, which in this case is simply a series of 0s and 1s of fixed length. Finally, an artificial neural network is chosen for the training and classification process.

1 Introduction

Pattern recognition in image processing encompasses several areas of research, viz., face recognition, signature recognition, text recognition, and fingerprint recognition. High accuracy text recognition or optical character recognition (OCR) is a challenging task for scripts of languages. The OCR research for the English script has matured. Commercial software is available for reading printed English text. However, for the majority of other scripts such as Arabic and Indian, OCR is still an active domain of research. For English and Kanji scripts, good progress has been made towards

---

* Corresponding author.

G.S. Tomar et al. (Eds.): UCMA 2010, CCIS 75, pp. 20–28, 2010.

the recognition of printed scripts, and the focus nowadays is on the recognition of handwritten characters. OCR research for different Indian languages is still at a nascent stage. There has been limited research on recognition of Oriya, Tamil, Devanagari and Bengali.

Many techniques are available for offline recognition of English, Arabic, Japanese and Chinese characters but there are only a few pieces of work available towards Indian characters although India is a multi-lingual and multi-script country. Also for offline printed word recognition very few works are there in Indian languages. For e.g. in Tamil language some works are there. Some works are available in English, Japanese and in Chinese.

The goal of this paper is to develop a new system for view based approach for recognition of offline printed Bengali character. First the approach I had used for recognition is without segmentation. Some morphological operations like thinning and thickening is needless here.

There are twelve scripts in India and in most of these scripts the number of alphabets (basic and compound characters) is more than 250, which makes keyboard design and subsequent data entry a difficult job. Hence, offline recognition of such scripts has a commercial demand.

2   Previous Works

Various strategies have been proposed by different authors. Multi font character recognition scheme suggested by Kahan and Pavlidis [1]. Roy and, Chatterjee [7] presented a nearest neighbour classifier for Bengali characters cniploying features extracted by a string connectivity criterion. Abhijit Datta and Santanu Chaudhuri [3] suggested a curvature based feature extraction strategy for both printed and handwritten Bengali characters.

B.B. Chaudhuri and U.Pal [4] combined primitive analysis with template matching to detect compound Bcngali characters. Most of the works on Bengali character are recognition of isolated characters. A very few deal with a complete OCR for printed document in Bengali.

Mahmud,Rihan and Rahman [5] have used the chain code method of image representation. Thinning of the character image is needless when chain code representation is used. Angshul Majumdar [6] has used 'a novel feature extraction scheme based on the digital curvelet transform'. The curvelet transform has been heavily utilized in various areas of image processing. The curvelet coefficients of an original image as well as its morphologically altered versions are used to train separate k–nearest neighbour classifiers. Segmentation in Bangla text is very common and there has been particular interest over the last decade. Segmentation of Bangla text is itself a challenging problem since there is a variation of the same character due to change of fonts or introduction of noise. Segmentation of Bangla character is a subject of special interest for us and many works have been done in this area. Various strategies have been proposed by different authors. A two phase approach is applied by Mahmud et. al. [2] in order to overcome the common problems related to the segmentation of printed Bangla characters. Their approach contains the text digitization and noise cleaning and skew detection and correction.

Md. Abdul Hasnat[8] represent the training and recognition mechanism of a Hidden Markov Model(HMM) based multi-font Optical Character Recognition (OCR) system for Bengali character. In our approach, the central idea is to separate the HMM model for each segmented character or word. The system uses HTK toolkit for data preparation, model training and recognition. The Features of each trained character are calculated by applying the Discrete Cosine Transform (DCT) to each pixel value of the character image where the image is divided into several frames according to its size. The extracted features of each frame are used as discrete probability distributions which will be given as input parameters to each HMM model. In the case of recognition, a model for each separated character or word is built up using the same approach. This model is given to the HTK toolkit to perform the recognition using the Viterbi Decoding method. The experimental results show significant performance over models using neural network based training and recognition systems.

3   Properties of Different Bangla Scripts

Bangla scripts are moderately complex patterns. Unlike simple juxtaposition in Roman scripts, each word in Bangla scripts is composed of several characters joined by a horizontal line (called 'Maatra' or head-line) at the top. Of-ten there may be different composite characters and vowel and consonant signs ('Kaar' and 'Falaa' symbols). This makes the development of an OCR for Bangla printed scripts a highly challenging task. There are some basic features or properties of any Bangla printed script.

a.   Writing style of Bangla is from left to right.
b.   The concept of upper and lower case (as in English) is absent here.
c.   Among the characters, the vowels often take modified shapes in a word. Such characters are called modifiers (in Bangla 'Kaar').

Consonant modifiers are possible (called 'Falaa'). These are shown respectively in Table 1a and Table 1b.

Table 1a. Bangla vowels and their modifier forms

Vowel	Corresponding Vowel Modifier
আ	া
ই	ি
ঈ	ী
উ	ু
ঊ	ূ
ঋ	ৃ
এ	ে
ঐ	ৈ
ও	ো
ঔ	ৌ

Table 1b. Bangla consonants and their modifier forms

Consonant	Corresponding Consonant Modifier
ন	ৗ
র	৾
র	৾
হ	ট

d. In a single syllable of a word, several consonant characters may combine to form a compound character that partly retains the shape of the constituent characters (e.g. Na + Da, Ka + Ta, Va + Ra-falaa, Na + Daa + Ra-falaa shown in Table 2).

Table 2. Bangla consonants and their modifier forms

Compound Character	Formation of the Character
ন্ড	ন + ড
ক্ট	ক + ট
ব্র	ব + ্র
ন্দ্র	ন + দ + ্র

e. Except very few characters and symbols(e.g. Ae, Oy, O, Ow, Kha, Ga, Ungo, Nio etc), almost all Bangla alphabets and symbols have a horizontal line at the upper part called 'maatra'. Some are shown in Fig.1a.

f. In a word, the characters with 'maatra' remain connected together through their maatra' and other characters and symbols (e.g. Khondota, Bishorgo, Ungo, Ae, Oy etc) remain isolated in the word. Some are shown in Fig.1b.

Fig. 1a. Some alphabets with 'maatra' or headline

Fig. 1b. Some alphabets without 'maatra'

g.   Each syllable in a Bangla word can be divided into three horizontal layers (shown in Fig. 2). These are:

   i.   Upper Layer containing the upper-extended potion of some alphabets and symbols (e.g. Oy, Uu, Ta, Tha, Chandra-Bindu etc). It starts from the top most abstract line of the syllable and runs till the 'maatra'. It covers about upper 20% of the whole syllable.
   ii. Middle Layer containing the major part of the alphabet or symbol. It begins from just below the 'maatra' and ends to an abstract base line. It covers almost 80% of the whole syllable.
   iii. Lower Layer containing the lower extended portion of some alphabets and symbols (e.g. Ra,Uuu, Uu-Kar, Ree-Kar, Hashanta etc). It is situated between the base line of the middle layer and the bottom most abstract line of the syllable. It also covers approximately lower 20% of the whole syllable.

Fig. 2. Three layers of Bangla scripts

h.   Several characters including some vowel and consonant modifiers, punctuations etc have vertical stokes, too [9].
i.   All the basic alphabets, compound characters and numerals have almost same width. Whereas, the modifiers and punctuations vary in their width and height.

4   Our Work

4.1   Pre-processing

To overcome some problems, we use pre-processing, which involves matra removal, scaling and binarization, and/or extraction of the data. Pre-processing eliminates noise, reduces the amount of redundant information and facilitates encoding of raw data into feature vectors. (I) Noise and Data reduction (II) Matra Removal (III) Scaling (IV) Binarization.

4.2   Design Methodology

Here we have proposed a new system for character recognition. The system is based on the view-based approach. The system does not need thinning of analyzed character. The characteristic vectors taken from both top and bottom views. Here we are considering only two views that is top and bottom among four. The obtained characteristics vectors are used for classification with Artificial Neural Networks. The input of the experiment is a set of common bangla characters.

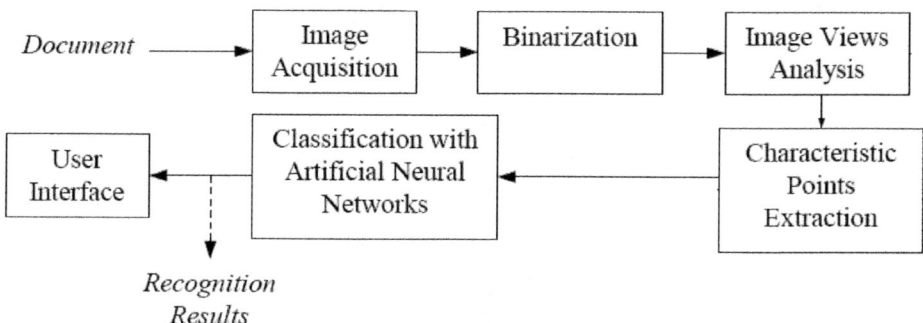

Fig. 3. Block diagram

The main idea in this method is based on the view-based algorithm. The essential ideas of the view-based recognition system were presented in [10-11]. In case of characters only two of four views are analyzed, the upper and lower views. The most significant characteristic points are extracted from each image to form the feature vector describing the tested word or character. The features vectors are obtained from these images are the basis for further classification. Fig. 3 shows the block diagram of bangle character recognition.

At first it was used for recognition of single characters. Then we will apply it to recognize whole words. This method is based on the fact, that for correct image recognition we usually need only partial information about its shape – its silhouette or contour.

Two "views" of each character are examined to extract from them a characteristic vector, which describes the given character. The view is a set of points that plot one of two projections of the object (top or bottom) – it consists of pixels belonging to the contour of a character and having extreme values of y coordinate – maximal for top, and minimal for bottom view (Fig. 4).

Fig. 4. Two views of sample characters

Both of the essential conventional stages of segmentation and thinning in the image processing techniques are unnecessary here. Only the shape of the character is analyzed.

Next, characteristic points are marked out on the surface of each view to describe the shape of that view. The method of selecting these points and their amount may vary. In our experiments 3 points are taken for each view of a character.

To find the characteristic points, one needs to divide the image vertically into a number of identical segments equal to the number of points we want to obtain. Next, we find the position of the highest and the lowest pixel in each segment – these are the points of top and bottom views (Fig. 5).

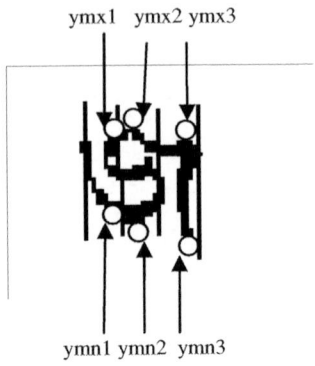

Fig. 5. Characteristic points

The next step is the calculation of y coordinates for the selected points. Thus we obtain two 3-element characteristic vectors describing the given character. Next, these two vectors together with their two values describing the aspect ratio of the picture (width by height) are transformed into a one 8-element vector, which describes the given character to be the base for further analysis. It is also possible to directly use this vector in the classification process.

5   Result and Discussion

The experimental evaluation of the above technique was carried out using isolated bangla characters. The data was collected from different Bengali fonts like Avro keyboard, Tanmatra etc. We have collected five data samples of all bangla characters. Among these five samples three data samples have been used for training purpose and two data samples have been used for testing dataset. From the experiment it was found that the overall accuracy of the proposed scheme was around **74.166%**. Some problems occur due to invariant size of bangla characters. We have checked that **accuracy** of **recognition** is around **75%**, not very high due to less number of training data set in Artificial Neural Network (i.e only 3 samples), shown in Table 3.

Table 3. Recognition results on Bangla Character

Data	Correct Recognition rate	Error rate
120 Characters	74.166%	25.834%

Our goal is to test how our system performs in noticeably different conditions than the typical character recognition system deals with. Many other methods concentrate on finding a large number of characteristic data and a large number of examples for each class. Another way is followed in order to limit unnecessary growth of data and to show how our system performs with the reduced data set dimension. Because we are handling with the characteristics vector rather than the whole image matrix which will take a lot of space and therefore execution time will be more. Once we get the characteristics vector the image is of no more use. From then we will handle with only the characteristics vectors. The size of this vector is so small with compared to the original image matrix. And the execution time will be less while we are working with the characteristics vectors. If we work with an image of a piece of printed paper that will be a very large image. In that case if we work with the whole image no memory will be able to execute this program within a reasonable time. And also no cache memory will be there to provide such large space.

6 Future Scope

Our goal is to develop such system to improve the system efficiency. Till now we have seen that almost all methods handle with the whole image. Here we will use only characteristics vector instead of the whole image. View based approach has not been used for Bengali Character Recognition. First time we are going to use this approach for Bangla Character recognition.

7 Conclusion

The advantage of the proposed system is its efficiency. Because we do not need the whole image for execution; characteristics vectors would be executed. We can handle with a large image i.e. a large scanned document. Here thinning is not required. We will apply this method to a word without segmentation. Disadvantage of this proposed system is that it is size dependent. We need matra removal. We have considered only basic characters not the compound characters. But we have future goals to apply this classification to recognize compound characters.

References

1. Kahan, S., Pavlidis, T.: Recognition of printed characters of any font and size. IEEE Trans. Pattern Anal. Arid Mach. InteN. 9, 274–288 (1987)
2. Milky Mahmud, S.M., Shahrier, N., Delowar Hossain, A.S.M., Tareque Mohmud Chowdhury, M., Abdus Sattar, M.: An Efficient Segmentation Scheme for the Recognition of Printed Bangla characters. In: Proceedings of ICCIT 2003, pp. 283–286 (2003)
3. Dutta, A., Chaudhury, S.: Bengali Alpha- Numeric Character Recognition Using Curvature Features. Pattern Recognition 26, 1707–1720 (1993)
4. Chaudhuri, B.B., Pal, U.: A Complete Printed Bangla OCR System. Pattern Recognition 31, 531–549 (1997); Graphics and Image Processing, NCCIS (1997)
5. Mahmud, J.U., Raihan, M.F., Rahman, C.M.: A Complete OCR System for continuous Bengali Character. In: TENCON 2003, Conference on Convergent Technologies for Asia-Pacific Region, October 15-17 (2003)
6. Majumdar, A.: Bangla Basic Character Recognition using Digital Curvlet Transform. Journal of Pattern Recognition Research 1, 17–26 (2007)

7. Roy, A.K., Chatterjee, B.: Design of nearest neighbour classifier for Bengali character recognition. J.IEEE 30 (1984)
8. Abul Hasnat, M.: Research Report on Bangla OCR Training and Testing Methods, Working Papers (2004-2007)
9. Garain, U., Chaudhuri, B.B.: Segmentation of Touching Characters in Printed Devnagari and Bangla Scripts Using Fuzzy Multifactorial Analysis. IEEE Transactions on Systems, MAN, and Cybernetics—Part C: Applications and Reviews 32(4) (November 2002)
10. Rybnik, M., Chebira, A., Madani, K., Saeed, K., Tabedzki, M., Adamski, M.: A Hybrid Neural-Based Information-Processing Approach Combining a View-Based Feature Extractor and a Treelike Intelligent Classifier. In: CISIM – Compute Information Systems and Industrial Management Applications, pp. 66–73. WSFiZ Press, Bialystok (2003)
11. Saeed, K., Tabedzki, M.: A New Hybrid System for Recognition of Handwritten-Script. COMPUTING – International Scientific Journal of Computing 3(1), 50–57 (2004); 332 Advances in Information Processing and Protection
12. Saeed, K., Tabedzki, M.: New Experiments on Word Recognition Without Segmentation. In: Conference Proceedings of ACS-CISIM 2007 under the title, A Hybrid Word-Recognition System (2007)

Human Inspired Self-developmental Model of Neural Network (HIM): Introducing Content/Form Computing

Jiří Krajíček

Brno University of Technology, Faculty of Information Technology, Department of
Information Systems, Božetěchova 2, Brno 612 66, Czech Republic
ikrajice@fit.vutbr.cz

Abstract. This paper presents cross-disciplinary research between medical/psychological evidence on human abilities and informatics needs to update current models in computer science to support alternative methods for computation and communication. In [10] we have already proposed hypothesis introducing concept of human information model (HIM) as cooperative system. Here we continue on HIM design in detail. In our design, first we introduce Content/Form computing system which is new principle of present methods in evolutionary computing (genetic algorithms, genetic programming). Then we apply this system on HIM (type of artificial neural network) model as basic network self-developmental paradigm. Main inspiration of our natural/human design comes from well known concept of artificial neural networks, medical/psychological evidence and Sheldrake theory of *"Nature as Alive"* [22].

Keywords: informatics walls, human information model (HIM), neural networks, morphic fields, morphic computing, content/form computing.

1 Introduction

The computing industry has passed parallel hardware revolution and beside proposed parallel challenge in hardware and software design, even toady we can observe certain limitations, walls we are facing [1]. These walls are mostly consequences of physical limitations of silicon chip design (concerning size, overheating, unsustainable power consumption), theoretical limitations (non-algorithmable tasks, NP-hard or NP-complete problems) restricted by model of Turing machine [14] and open human-computer interaction (HCI) issues that implicate from differences, gulfs between classical computer design and human cognition ability [13].These limitations are also main motivation for alternative approaches, efforts (compute and communicate) in computer science. Well known representatives of alternative approaches are quantum and DNA computation but due to its "own" restrictions it cannot be widely used in practice [18].

In compare to present alternative approaches adopted from nature/human to artificial intelligence - computer science subfield (e.g. iterative evolutionary approach, artificial neural networks, fuzzy logic), these approaches are commonly studied separately or oversimplified (e.g. artificial neural networks) in contrast to real world evidence. Some of these models are old-fashioned today and do not reflect latest

G.S. Tomar et al. (Eds.): UCMA 2010, CCIS 75, pp. 29–43, 2010.

observations from physics, medical science and psychology. Thus we are losing some possibilities that nature or human can operate with. By looking at the present scientific medical/psychological publications we can observe new knowledge which is worth to include to current informatics models. For example, in case of an artificial neural network it is unsustainable to consider each neuron as just simple switch. In spite of the present progress in artificial neural networks, there exist many properties of biological neural systems that are largely ignored in classical models and as Miller [12] noted these properties can be essential, significant for power and efficiency issues (walls) that computer science is trying to deal with.

In our research we also consider human information potential as another alternative approach how to make computation and communication. In previous work [10] we have already proposed information hypothesis that assumes information processing (computation and communication) human inspired model (HIM) based on neural networks concept as cooperative system, research synthesis rather than stand alone approach (to be closer to real human) consisting of multi-levels. Thus we have forwarded a research question: *How we can benefit from these human abilities in computer/information science?* In another paper [11] we have designed several experiments to investigate the possibility of classically unexplainable human information capabilities and its possible impact for information science. Implementation, testing and evaluation of these experiments can be useful for proposed model (HIM) correction as feedback but due its long term estimation is left as a future work.

Considering first HIM concept in [10], it was introduced as sketch, therefore here we continue on HIM design in more detail and therefore we also propose new type of evolutionary computation - content/form computing which is essential in HIM information developmental process.

In the following chapter we introduce main inspiration by medical/psychological evidence on human abilities and its possible theoretical explanations which stand for the theoretical background, foundation in our design. Chapter three discusses areas of present related work. Further chapter three describes *Content/Form* computing as new developmental process and subsequently in chapter four we apply *Content/Form* computing on our model of artificial neural network – HIM. Finally, chapter five discusses future and on-going work.

2 Related Work and Critical Review

In the introduction chapter we have briefly described motivation for alternative approaches in information science and noted our research interest in alternative approach inspired by human information abilities (for purpose of informatics information model design).

2.1 Natural/Human Motivation

In effort to show relevant scientific contributions and publications (describing nature/human possible theoretical potential), we can highlight Lucas and Penrose contributions, for example. Lucas, in his paper "Minds, machines and Gödel" [6], is arguing that the human mathematician cannot be represented by any machines and

Penrose [15] has suggested that the human mind might be the consequence of quantum-mechanically enhanced, "non-algorithmic" computation. Penrose uses variation of the "halting problem" to show that mind cannot be an algorithmic process [14]. Rosen has proposed that computation is an inaccurate representation of natural causes that are in place in nature [20]. Moreover Kampis [7] assumes that information content of an algorithmic process is fixed and no "*new*" information is brought forward. These contributions stand for inspiration and further motivation when re-thinking about nature/human concepts as inspirations for informatics problems.

2.2 Biological Aspects of Neural Networks

Generally, in artificial intelligence there exist many models, systems inspired by nature/human (neural networks, fuzzy systems, evolutionary design, genetic programming). But these approaches are commonly studied separately in contrast to real world evidence and some of these models are old-fashioned today and do not reflect observations from physics, medical science, psychology. By looking at present scientific medical/psychology publications we can observe knowledge which is worth to include to current informatics models. Some researchers are aware of this situation, for example Penrose and Hameroff [3] had introduced the neural model with quantum properties – Orch-OR model and assume its behavior essential for ability of being consciousness. Further Miller extends model of neural networks by the developmental (evolutionary) system with "seven programs" reflecting liveness neural properties. To describe a huge gap between medical/biological knowledge and classical informatics assumption let us cite from recent Miller's paper [12]:

"In spite of the success of Artificial Neural Networks (ANNs), there are many aspects of biological neural systems that have been largely ignored. Marcus argues convincingly about the importance of development in the understanding of the brain; mechanisms that build brains are just extensions of those that build the body. Despite this, there are virtually no evolved artificial developmental neural approaches in the research literature. There is now abundant evidence that sub-processes of neurons are highly time-dependent so that many structures are in a constant state of being rebuilt and changed. In addition, memory is not a static process and the location and mechanisms responsible for remembered information is in constant (though, largely gradual) change."

As we can see, there is still enough motivation and inspiration for extending classical models of neural networks. In case of detail Miller's model [12] (Developmental Model of Neural Computation), the neural network is consisted of 2D grid of neurons, each neuron has its genotype representing the genetic code of the neurons. Further each genotype includes seven chromosomes representing small procedures/programs where each encodes specific neural functionality. Thus chromosomes are directly linked to the functionality of neuronal parts. By using specific evolutionary approach (Cartesian genetic programming) genetic code is changed/developed during the computable process based on evolutionary strategy. The chromosomes are subjected to evolution until requested behavior is not reached. In other words, the living properties handled by chromosome programs are changed too and thus specific biological aspects of real/live neurons are reflected.

In compare to other neural network models Miller has observed that different Wumpus (game) worlds were able to preserve network properties like sustainability and prevention of pits. It was not possible (at that time) to compare its effectiveness with any other artificial neural networks.

Although noted Miller's model is contributive and highlights hidden potential of biological neural networks, this model **still assumes that main changes in neural networks (e.g. structure, weights and health) are handled by evolution through genetic code changes**. In real biological neural networks there are many changes but only a few are caused by change in genetic code (long time estimation) and real changes in biological neural structure, metabolic brain activity are much faster (short time estimation) than changes in DNA. Moreover in this model, behavior of neurons (procedure/programs) is assumed to develop using **predefined evolutionary operators** (excluded from evolutionary process, classical Darwinian assumption) which is also in contrast with our Content/Form computation applied on HIM neural network design, see chapter 3 below.

However the evolutionary gene extension, biological growth and die aspects in neurons seem to be essential for natural ability approximation, simulation, there are still many hidden aspects. For example there is a huge evidence of human abilities which cannot be explained on basis of established physical concepts and statistical theory. It is assumed that such activity is executed beyond any physical part of human body (brain) [23, 21, 8]. Although the explanation of such scientific evidence [21], near death experiences [5] is still matter of discussion and open questions, we should at least consider such evidence as part of human information capabilities.

2.3 Evidence on Unexplainable Human Abilities and Theoretical Explanation

From point of psychology C. G. Jung was one of the first who was scientifically interested in human unexplainable phenomena. To describe some interesting observables he defined term *synchronicities as events that can be non-causally correlated if they belong together in the sense of expressing a common underlying archetype* [9]. Later with increased theoretical background of quantum mechanics he was positively surprised how his intuitive macroscopic definition of synchronicity is analogous to microscopic definition of *quantum entanglement.*

Scientific focus on medical and psychological evidence supporting unexplainable phenomena had arisen mostly at the end of 70s. Biologist Sheldrake was one of the first initiators who proposed the *hypothesis of formative causation and theory morphic fields/resonance* that led to re-thinking of Darwinian theory of evolution, morphogenesis and further to explanation of classically *unexplainable* phenomena in nature. This also led to increasing demands of psychological experimental testing. For example, in recent biological studies, Sheldrake [24] has conducted experiments with animals and human subjects and has found statistically significant results that support unexplainable human abilities (e.g. telepathy). In consequence also psychological experiments were conducted to investigate such phenomena and some of them were replicated several times [4]. Moreover recent medical studies based on near-death experiences (NDE) [5] pointed out the critical review of classical medical paradigm: *observing metabolic brain activity in response to specific thinking process does not necessarily implies the role of brain neurons as origin of thinking process and can be consequence (mediator) of unexplainable non-neuronal activity.* Described studies have evoked broad discussions in biological, medical and psychological publications [7] and turned research focus more into inner human scope.

As far as we know, Sheldrake morphic fields/resonance explanation is applicable to the most cases of classically unexplainable phenomena (including human abilities, near death experiences) and moreover it is scientifically testable too. This theory has large impact for psychological findings, evolution of nature forms/ morphogenesis. It rebuilds classical paradigm of science and think of all Nature as being alive with inherent memory. Although the hypothesis of a memory inherent in Nature is very radical, controversial, and unconventional some recent finding (experimental verification) conducted independently by Sheldrake [23, 24] and others [17, 21] led to statistical significant results supporting this theoretical assumption.

In more detail Sheldrake theory [22] assumes that nature is capable to operate with inherent memory, and what science classically thinks about the laws of nature, he suggests habits instead. Base of memory processing is morphic resonance that is influenced across space or time. Memory is described by existence of morphogenetic fields. Members of a species are united by the ability to access and transmit information to and from these fields right through morphic resonance. These morphic fields are organized and inherited in hierarchy according to similarity between members of species. Organisms then evolve by inheriting the habits of previous members of their species through this process. Thus from point of evolution, Sheldrake assumes that evolution is not static, but it evolves itself. Main implication is that behavior/reactions depends not only on the chemical genes coded in DNA but are also influenced by morphic resonance from past members of the species. In this way not only the form is evolved but also the laws of nature (not static) and are changed dynamically depending on past members. In case of individual memory application, it is mostly depended on self-resonance morphic field, not directly stored in the brain and on the existence of a collective memory (field of memories), to which we all contribute. Sheldrake proposes that brain it is more like a tuning system, like a radio receiver, to pick up memory inherent in the morphic fields. Basically morphic fields are described similarly as the gravitational or electro-magnetic fields (field is expanded beyond the form of its source). Meanwhile these two kinds of fields are material fields, although they are not material themselves, but are created by and maintained by physical mass, Sheldrake morphic fields are assumed as immaterial fields, because are not restricted only to sources of material forms (e.g. single word, symbol or piece of SW can has its own morphic field too).

From point of related theories, it is interesting, that Sheldrake theory converges and follows C.G. Jung findings on *collective unconsciousness*. There is also correlation with interpretation of quantum mechanics - his theory was merged with quantum physician Bohm holonomic interpretation of quantum physics [2], in later years Bohm suggested that Sheldrake's hypothesis is in keeping with his own ideas on what he terms *"implicate"* and *"explicate"* order [22, 2]. Furthermore there is direct relation to K.H. Pribram holomic brain model, which assumes memory spread over physical brain instead of specific location at certain part [16].

2.4 Morphic Computation

In recent years (2008), Resconi [19] has introduced general concept of morphic computation which is also inspired by Sheldrake hypothesis of morphic fields. His computation is expressed through changes in morphic field which is mathematically substituted by deformation in space whose geometry in general is non-Euclidean. Further Resconi claimed [19] that Morphic Computing is a natural extension of Holographic Computation, Quantum Computation, Soft Computing, and DNA Computing and all natural computations bonded by the Turing Machine can be formalized and extended by his new type of computation model – Morphic Computing. These findings have fundamental implication for computer science and represent its theoretical background as well. In compare to Resconi's concept of morphic computation, here presented Content/Form computation is simple abstraction (operating with two terms only – *Content, Form*) of Sheldrake theory, which can be easily applied on different models/problems and implemented using exist HW/SW resources, see chapter 3 below.

3 Introducing Content/Form Computing

As we can see above, in nature/human design there are still many hidden aspects which are worth to include in current informatics models. For example as discussed on Miller's model, one can observe inspiration to design developmental model not restricted only to "*naturally long-term*" genetic code evolution or to consider Sheldrake theory assuming evolution as dynamic living process itself.

In this chapter first we introduce Content/Form computing architecture which is new generalized principle of present methods used in evolvable computing, design (genetic algorithms, genetic programming) based on simple abstractions inspired by Sheldrake's theory of Morphic Fields/Resonance.

3.1 Premise on Content and Form

Before applying new type of computation – Content/Form computation on neural network model HIM model, let us first define basic terms of Content and Form and explain how this computing methodology can be used. As we can see below these terms are simple abstractions analogous to Sheldrake's theory of Morphic Fields/Resonance (defined for purposes of informatics). Once this principle is adopted, the rest about application on computing can be easily understood as well.

***Def. 3.1.* (On Content/Form Terms):** *Content is denoted by non-physical, abstract "empty term" that exists without boundary on Form.*

If there is a Form then it is filled (spread over) by Content depending on type of the Form. Thus without any Forms empty Content still persists. Form can be represented by any physical mass or by non-physical abstract terms too (except for empty term - Content). Form itself cannot exist without boundary to the Content.

There is a hierarchy of Contents according to its type of similarity (reflecting the hierarchy of Forms too). Thus higher Contents encapsulate inherited Contents. The top most Content is denoted as the Root.

Example 3.1: It is generally known that inheritance properties in nature like growth depends on Form of DNA, thus we could be thinking that DNA drives the behavior of growth itself. But by reflecting Sheldrake theory and considering the definition 3.1, since DNA is also a Form it is subjected to DNA Content, which drives growth indirectly through DNA Form (see figure 2 for Form dynamics illustration). Furthermore DNA Content is encapsulated according to hierarchy in Root which propagates its goals to lower, inherited Contents. Since all types of Contents are encapsulated in Root, its separation is only illustrative/virtual and is closer to holomic interpretation.

Def. 3.2. **(On Form Behavior, Transformation):** *According to definition 3.1 any physical mass or non-physical abstract term too (except for empty term – Content, that exist without boundary of the Form) is type of the Form. Then any natural form (species) is type of the Form too, including laws of nature.*

Form behavior (e.g. laws of nature, methods) is driven directly by its Content which encapsulates past states (memory) of the Form. Higher Forms – e.g. laws of nature changes lower Forms – lower e.g. species. This process of self-development is denoted as Transformation. This process continuous for each type of Form, until requested behavior specified by Content is not satisfied.

Example 3.2: Referring to previous example 3.1, it is generally known that in natural evolution processes of mutation, crossover or reproduction are natural operators that leads to gene code changes in population evolution. But by considering Sheldrake theory and reflecting the definition 3.2 too, we can observe that since natural operators (laws) like mutation or crossover are also types of *Form* it is subjected to *Transformation* process too and thus its behavior is not static - evolutionary operators are developed itself (according to past memory and objectives in *Content*). See figure 1 for illustration.

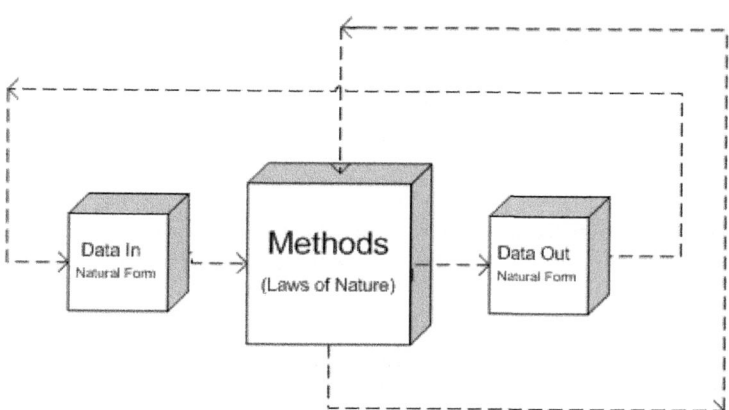

Fig. 1. Form dynamics (without Content interaction), data and methods are both type of Form, thus each of them is dynamic. Input is driven by methods and output; meanwhile methods are driven by past applications on input.

3.2   Content and Form Computing

Here we discuss consequence of Content/Form architecture on computing. As described in introduction and related work chapters, the classical scientific paradigm assumes that natural forms are driven by laws of nature (evolution, morphogenesis), see chapter Comparison of Related Forms in [16] for detail. Meanwhile the forms are not static (are morphed), laws are assumed as static and not changing [22].

In computer science, computation also generally assume that data (basic forms) as not static meanwhile methods/functions (laws) mostly expected as static (except for a few programming languages like Python or C#).

3.2.1   Form: Data (Members) and Methods

Analogically to natural evolution where morphogenesis is represented by *basic forms* and *laws of nature*, in computer science we can be thinking about morphogenesis - *transformation* represented by *Data* as basic forms and by *Methods* as laws of nature.

But since laws of nature and basic forms are both types of Form, in computer science Data and Methods are Forms too (see figure 2 and chapter 3.1 above).

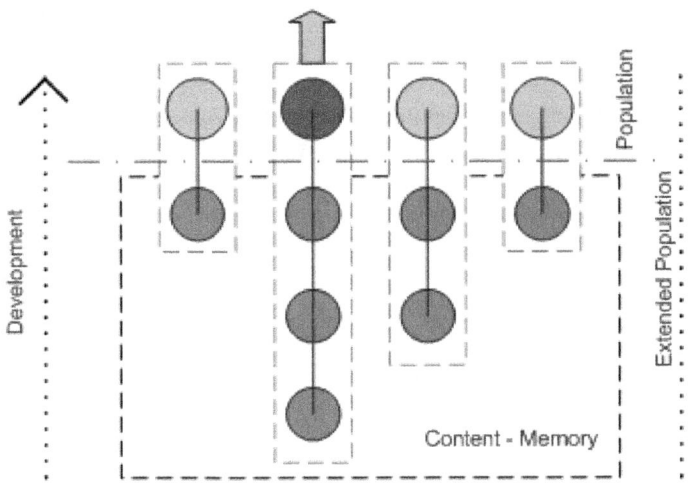

Fig. 2. Example of extended population, where memory of member past states is stored in *member-Content* meanwhile all past states are stored in *population-Content*

From this perspective there is no longer separation between operations with Data and Methods, since both Data and Methods become Form, thus Data and Methods are treaded (operated) in similar way. In other words, we can say that Methods are assumed as Data too and operated by Content based on its goals and past states of its Form.

Here we distinguish two types of methods:

• methods for *Data* (basic form) development
• methods for *Method* (higher form) itself development

3.2.2 Content: Goals and Memory

Same types of *Form* are grouped together – form population, where each type has its own *Content* plus *population Content* which encapsulate new type of *Form* – population. Current population and past states of each type forms *extended population*. Even without direct links - connections among forms of the same type, each type is implicitly connected with others via its own *Content* through *population Content*. Each *Content* has the memory which holds past states of specific type of *Form*. Moreover Content includes Goals (set of statements – required scores for each goal) that whole system is trying to satisfy during the computing process.

3.2.3 Content/Form: Computing Process

Here we describe general methodology of Content/Form computing process. To describe how *Methods* are applied on *Data* and *Methods* respectively - *Form* dynamics, we start by describing the comparison process on extended population. In first computing step, methods are applied randomly with random setting.

In each next computing step, state of actual member of population is compared with its past states and with goals in *population-Content*. According to this comparison specific methods are selected (from set of methods for *Data development*) to be probabilistically corrected and applied - locally (meaning in range of actual member). Where the probability of method correction – development depends on frequency of its past application at specific configuration (as more often is method at specific setting applied, as more probable is next application without method correction - development). Please note that method correction - development is controlled by methods from set of methods for *Method* - itself development.

For simplicity we assume that these methods are fixed for now, but generally could be also developed by itself or higher-level methods.

3.3 On Comparison with Present Methods in Evolutionary Computing

In compare with present techniques in evolutionary computing (genetic algorithms, genetic programming) we assume that Content/Form development process is similar but different developmental process. This is due to the fact that the most of present evolutionary strategies are still based on generally accepted Darwinian paradigm of natural selection, meanwhile in our design we are taking inspiration from Sheldrake's theory instead.

At first Content/Form system is not restricted by member (individual) selection – methods are applied on each member of population. Further main distinction is done by extension of population by past states (memory) plus dynamic methods (operators) development.

In contrast with genetic programming we also assume hierarchy of dynamic methods (operators), so meanwhile operators change methods in genetic programming, here these operators are not static and can change/develop too. Thus methods (operators) are not excluded from evolutionary process, but are evolved too.

Finally, fundamental difference is that the state of member is not expressed with genetic code (development of genetic code), but as actual configuration *Form* – state plus *Content* - memory in development process, where each state of the *Form* is manifestation of the *Content*. This reflects the phenomenon, that there are many changes in natural development that are much faster than change of genetic code and Sheldrake assumption that genetic code is not primary cause in evolution process.

4   Design of HIM with Application of Content/Form Computing

Now let us consider the application of definition 3.1 according to Sheldrake theory and apply principle of Content/Form computing on HIM concept.

This chapter subsequently describes whole design of HIM as computing model. First in 4.1, we briefly recall abbreviation of our information hypothesis and multi-level reference model as proposed in [10].

Note: Here, meaning clearly from point of information science/informatics it is not strictly important whether the biological/psychological theoretical explanation on human abilities (we are taking inspiration from) is necessarily the most accurate one or whether there is already enough evidence to support it in present. If there is significant effect for solving problems in informatics then the theory is welcome to be adopted as well.

4.1   Multi-layered View on HIM, Working Hypothesis

In classical computer science there exist many human/natural based approaches (e.g. iterative evolutionary approach). These approaches are commonly studied separately in contrast to real world evidence. We have already presented information hypothesis which assumes human inspired information model (HIM) as cooperative system operating on multiple levels including non-physical level (see figure 3). The proposed information hypothesis (see H_1 4.1, H_1 4.2) and related reference model were introduced just as theoretical sketch.

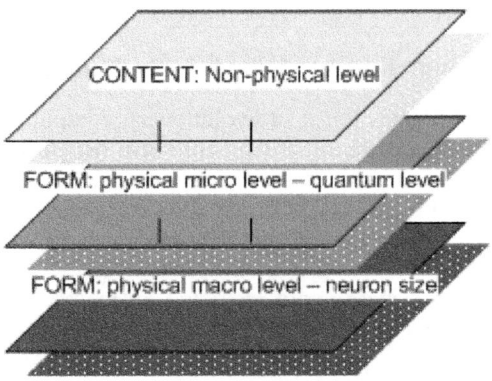

Fig. 3. general multi-level model of human information capabilities, each level is linked with others as cooperative system. This is a reference model, see below Content/Form architecture.

H_1 **4.1:** *Rather than describing human information capability like independent neural network, iterative evolutionary computation or fuzzy system, etc, we are assuming the synthesis of these approaches as cooperative information (computing and communicating) system based on neural networks, molecular neurobiology, evolutionary approach and phenomena related to quantum mechanics at least (as proposed on reference information human model, see figure 1).*

H_1 **4.2:** *By considering and supporting all phenomena in cooperative information system as stated in H1 information processing (in such designed information model) is positively changed in terms of complexity/efficiency, in contrast with considering each phenomenon as independent model, stand alone information processing approach.*

4.2 Form of HIM

According to proposed reference model (see figure 3), HIM model is based on concept of artificial neural networks. Hence here Form is consisted from neural structure (set of interconnected neurons), set of default methods (stands for natural laws) and input data.

4.2.1 Neurons and Data

The key element of neural artificial paradigm is neuron itself. Here the form of neuron is represented by classical model of artificial neuron (including inputs, weights, threshold, transfer function and output). At each step of computation each neuron has its state that indicates its current configuration. Input data indicates proper inputs for neuronal propagation and goals (instructions) for Content (see below).

4.2.2 Neuronal Structure

Although the structure of neural network influences its efficiency and complexity, in case of HIM model, the default interconnection, number of hidden layers, proper structure representation and type of propagation is not the key factor here. Thus for instance we can assume Hopfield recurrent network structure as its Form.

4.2.3 Methods – Laws of Nature

Similarly to Miller's abstraction [12] of biological – natural laws in real neuron, here we also assume several basic methods reflecting livness properties of neurons. Biological neurons have number of input dendrites and a single axon as output. Each dendrite can split in branches like tree-growth and axons can too. According to standard neuron livness behavior we assume following default methods:

Branch-Growth: creation, destruction, growth of new branches on dendrites and axons.

- Axon-Reconnection: axon can reconnect to another dendrite of neighbor neurons.
- Signal-Process: process input signals in neuron's body – soma.
- Neuron-Growth: creation, destruction of neurons.
- From Axon to Dendrite Propagation: pass output of potential through axon to the dendrite branches.
- Weight-Update: update neuron's weights.

Since methods are Form it can be locally changed, removed or new methods can be added. Methods are updated locally for each neuron processing according to current neuron's Content and its present state. Since methods are Form that can be changed in runtime, it is also necessary to distinguish methods configurations (states).

4.3 Content of HIM

In proper design reflecting the definition 3.1 we should define each Content for each type of Form (or group of related/similar Forms), thus we should distinguish Neural-Structure-Content, Neurons-Content and Methods-Content plus Root-Content. But in case of our design we make simplification and distinguish only Network-Content as Root and Neuron-Content as encapsulated lower, inherited Content.

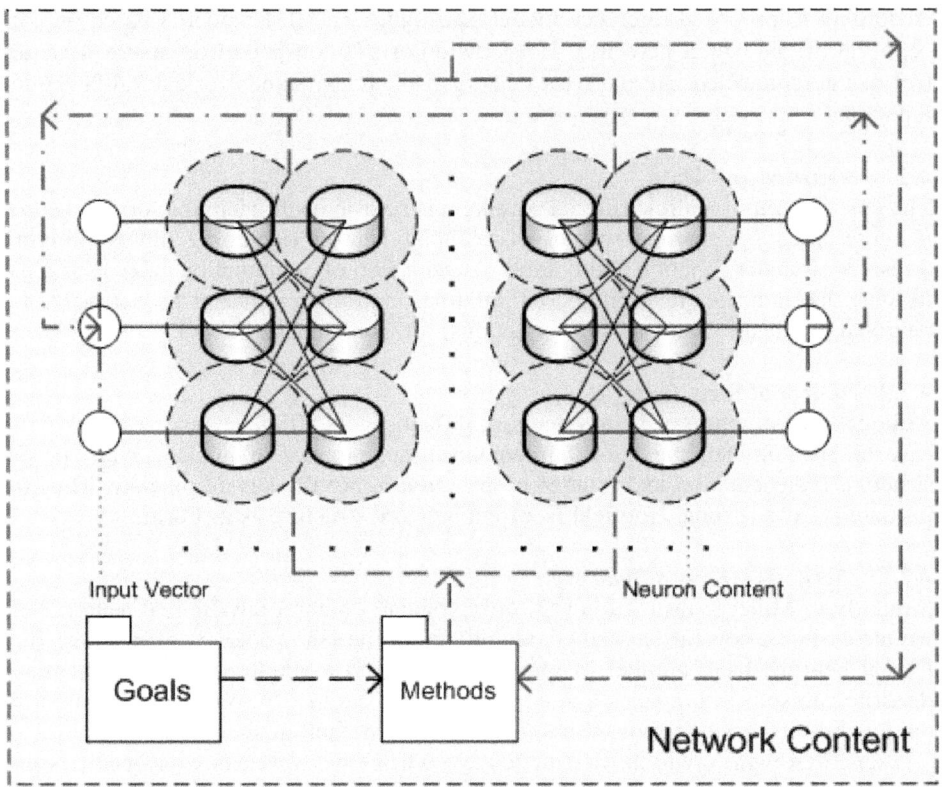

Fig. 4. Schematic diagram of HIM computing model with Content/Form architecture. All Neuron-Contents are part of Network-Content, thus neurons can indirectly interact through its Contents too. Network Content objectives (goals) are represented as fuzzy logic statements which are satisfied by Form transformations (computation in network).

4.3.1 Neuron Content

In our simplification Neuron-Content is memory of past states of each neuron Form. It is updated after each neuron input processing. It also encapsulates states of all methods applied at each neuron input processing. Before each neuron processing, current neuron state (configuration) is compared with its all past states (as evolution review) and objectives in Network-Content to decide how methods should be applied and modified.

4.4 Network Content

Network-Content drives the processing in whole network through its goals (passed through inputs) and memory - past states of Neuron-Content. Thus it encapsulates all previous states of each neuron including methods locally applied (see Neuron-Content below). Goals are represented by set of objectives that Content is going to achieve via Form transformation. As all Neuron-Contents are part of Network-Content, neurons can indirectly interact through its Contents too (beside main interactions through interconnections in network Form). For detail description of Network-Content processing see figure 4 and section 3.6.

4.5 Information Processing in the Network

At the beginning of computation, network contains default grid size – amount of interconnected neurons (set to initial states), default set of methods (see above) and input (including proper input data and Content objectives). In first preparation step, objectives from input are passed to Network-Content. In network information processing we distinguish two types of computational steps: neuron step (processing of information by neuron) and network step (processing of information by all neurons in network).

At first network step, input is processed through first neurons in input layer that propagates it to other neurons until all neuron steps are completed. Here, type of propagation depends on neuronal structure assumption (e.g. Hopfield recurrent network), as noted above. Before each neuron step its state is compared with its Neuron-Content (memory – including all states of neuron and states of methods that were previously, locally applied on this neuron) and with objectives in Network-Content. According to this comparison methods are locally (meaning in range of specific neuron) probabilistically corrected and then applied. Note that generally here holds the same computing methodology as stated in chapter 3.2.3 of Content/Form computing process. For illustrative description of Network processing see figure 4.

Until the objectives in Content are satisfied (fitness factor reached) network steps are repeated. Proper Content objectives are not defined as precise logical formulas but as fuzzy logic statements.

4.6 Implementation

We have proposed model of computation (HIM), using introduced Content/Form architecture. Model is based on well known concept of artificial neural networks and mostly inspired by Sheldrake theory of *"Nature as Alive"* [22]. Although this theory is very radical, it has deep impact to classical scientific paradigm and although it operates with non-physical terms like morphic fields/resonance (that is hard to represent by existing technology), our simplified Content/Form abstractions applied in HIM model can be easily SW implemented, simulated on existing HW.

Simulation can done on generic HW or using specific HW as accelerator with dozens of small computational units as neurons with direct access to shared memory substituting for non-physical Content (e.g. using inexpensive graphic processing units as accelerators).

Regarding SW resources, since existing object oriented programming (OOP) languages operate with terms like hierarchy, inheritance or encapsulation Content/Form architecture including dependency hierarchy can be lightly represented.

5   Conclusion and On-going Work

In this contribution we have presented cross-disciplinary research between psychological evidence on human abilities and informatics demands to update current models in computer science. Main aim was to reassume information hypothesis on nature inspired cooperative developmental system (see [10]) by:

- Introducing new Content/Form computing paradigm.
- Application this paradigm on HIM – neural network concept.

Natural/human inspiration on HIM concept was reflected by understanding HIM as cooperative system instead of stand-alone approach. Whole inspiration mostly comprises evolutionary theory, neural networks concept, neuron's biological-living aspects, fuzzy logic and Sheldrake theory of *"Nature as Alive"*.

5.1   Implication and Further Investigation

Introduced methodology of Content/Form computation can be applied on different existing models, problems as main developmental paradigm. In our application on neural network – HIM model can be used for:

- Problem solving (games) by using specific HIM – neural network configuration.
- As heuristic method to discover new configuration of specific neural network in solving problem approximation.

In future work we are going to focus on implementation and on investigation of designed HIM model properties on different tasks (e.g. game solving) on various HW configurations. In conclusion of this research we would like to observe results to be able to compare/highlight advantages/disadvantages of designed model with other existing models of artificial neural networks.

References

1. Asanovic, K., et al.: The Landscape of Parallel Computing Research: A View from Berkeley, white paper (2006)
2. Bohm, D.: Wholeness and the Implicate Order. Routledge, London (1983)
3. Hameroff, S.: The Brain Is Both Neurocomputer and Quantum Computer. Cognitive Science Society 31 (2007)
4. Lobach, E., et al.: Who's calling at this hour? Local sidereal time and telephone telepathy. In: Proceedings of the Parapsychological Association, 47th Annual Convention, pp. 91–98 (2004)
5. Lommel, P., et al.: Near-death experience in survivors of cardiac arrest: a prospective study in the Netherlands. The Lancet (2001)

6. Lucas, J.R.: Minds, machines and Gödel. In: Anderson, A.R. (ed.) Minds and Machines. Prentice-Hall, Englewood Cliffs (1954)
7. Kampis, G.: Self-Modifying systems in biology and cognitive science. Pergamon Press, New York (1991)
8. Jung, C.G.: Psychic conflicts in a child. Collected Works of C. G. Jung, vol. 17. Princeton University Press, Princeton (1970)
9. Jung, C.G.: Synchronicity: An Acausal Connecting Principle. Princeton University Press, Princeton (1973)
10. Krajíček, J.: Information Hypothesis: On Human Information Capability Study. In: Zhong, N., Li, K., Lu, S., Chen, L. (eds.) BI 2009. LNCS, vol. 5819, pp. 25–35. Springer, Heidelberg (2009)
11. Krajíček, J.: The Design of Experiments for Hypothesis Testing: ESP as Informatics Model Extension. In: The 2010 International Conference on Behavioral, Cognitive and Psychological Sciences, Singapore (2010)
12. Miller, J., et al.: An Evolutionary System using Development and Artificial Genetic Regulatory Networks. In: 9th IEEE Congress on Evolutionary Computation (CEC 2008), pp. 815–822 (2008)
13. Norman, D.A.: The Design of Everyday Things. Basic Books (2002)
14. Penrose, R.: Shadows of the Mind: A search for the missing science of consciousness. Oxford University Press, Oxford (1994)
15. Penrose, R.: The Emperor's New Mind: Concerning Computers, Minds, and The Laws of Physics. Oxford University Press, Oxford (1989)
16. Pribram, K.H.: Rethinking Neural networks: Quantum Fields and Bio-logical Data. In: Proceedings of the first Appalachian Conference on Behavioral Neurodynamics. Lawrence Erlbaum Associates Publishers, Hillsdale (1993)
17. Radin, D.I.: The Conscious Universe. In: The Scientific Truth of Psychic Phenomena. HarperCollins, New York (1997)
18. Reif, J.H.: Alternative computational models: A comparison of biomolecular and quantum computation. In: Arvind, V., Sarukkai, S. (eds.) FST TCS 1998. LNCS, vol. 1530, pp. 102–121. Springer, Heidelberg (1998)
19. Resconi, G., et al.: Morphic Computing. Journal of Applied Soft Computing (2007)
20. Rosen, R.: Life Itself: A comprehensive Inquiry into the nature, origin, and fabrication of life. Columbia University Press, New York (1991)
21. Schmidt, S., Walach, S.: Distant intentionality and the feeling of being stared at: two meta-analyses. British Journal of Psychology (2004)
22. Sheldrake, R.: A New Science of Life: the hypothesis of formative causation, 2nd edn. J.P. Tarcher, Los Angeles (1981); (2nd edn., 1985), ISBN 0874774594
23. Sheldrake, R.: An experimental test of the hypothesis of formative causation. Rivista di Biologia – Biology Forum 86, 431–444 (1992)
24. Sheldrake, R.: Videotaped experiments on telephone telepathy: Reply. Journal of Parapsychology 67(2) (2003)
25. Stevanovic, R., et al.: Quantum Random Bit Generator Service for Monte Carlo and Other Stochastic Simulations. In: Lirkov, I., Margenov, S., Waśniewski, J. (eds.) LSSC 2007. LNCS, vol. 4818, pp. 508–515. Springer, Heidelberg (2008)
26. Thompson, D.W.: On Growth and Form. Dover reprint 2nd edn. (1st ed., 1917) (1992), ISBN 0-486-67135-6

Ubiquitous Computing in Creation of Cognitive Systems for Medical Images Interpretation

Lidia Ogiela[1], Marek R. Ogiela[2], and Ryszard Tadeusiewicz[2]

[1] Faculty of Management [2] Institute of Automatics
AGH University of Science and Technology
Al. Mickiewicza 30, PL-30-059 Krakow, Poland
{logiela,mogiela,rtad}@agh.edu.pl

Abstract. This publication discusses intelligent systems for cognitive data cate-gorisation with a particular emphasis on image analysis systems used to analyse medical images. This type of systems used to interpret, analyse and reason work following the operating principles of cognitive information system. Cognitive systems interpret complex data by extracting semantic levels from it, which they use to determine the meaning of the data analysed, to cognitively under-stand it, as well as to reason and forecast changes in the area of the phenomena researched. Thus the course of human processes of leaning about the described phenomenon becomes the foundation for developing automatic cognitive sys-tems which are called cognitive data analysis systems.

Keywords: Cognitive processes, cognitive information systems, cognitive in-formatics, graph image analysis, pattern recognition, UBIAS systems (*Under-standing Based Image Analysis Systems*).

1 Introduction

Cognitive systems are currently developed very rapidly, and the operating algorithms applied in such systems and illustrating their processes of data analysis and interpreta-tion increasingly frequently use the semantic layers contained in data/information sets as well as techniques of linguistic data description. Until recently, processes of this type were based on classical cognitive analysis processes, but today they are being replaced by methods of the extended cognitive analysis, which not only unanimously identifies the relationships between cognitive resonance and the data understanding process, but also shows that the system is capable of learning based on the results of the completed data analysis in order to optimise analysis processes. This situation is presented in Figure 1.

In the cognitive data analysis process, the process whereby the system learns new solutions which may impact the decision-making solution obtained is of key impor-tance. So far, in the cognitive categorisation processes, the understanding of analysed data was based on the classical cognitive analysis process, whereby **connections** were indentified **between pairs of consistent expectations** of the system acquired from expert knowledge bases **and** characteristic **features** extracted from analysed datasets,

G.S. Tomar et al. (Eds.): UCMA 2010, CCIS 75, pp. 44–50, 2010.

and this led to cognitive resonance during which the above connections were determined as consistent or inconsistent. Only pairs that were completely consistent were selected for further analysis and a group of solutions could be defined which included the identified consistent pairs. This definition of the group made it possible not only to recognise the analysed data by naming it correctly, but also made the understanding of data complete, which lead to determining semantic features of the analysed data.

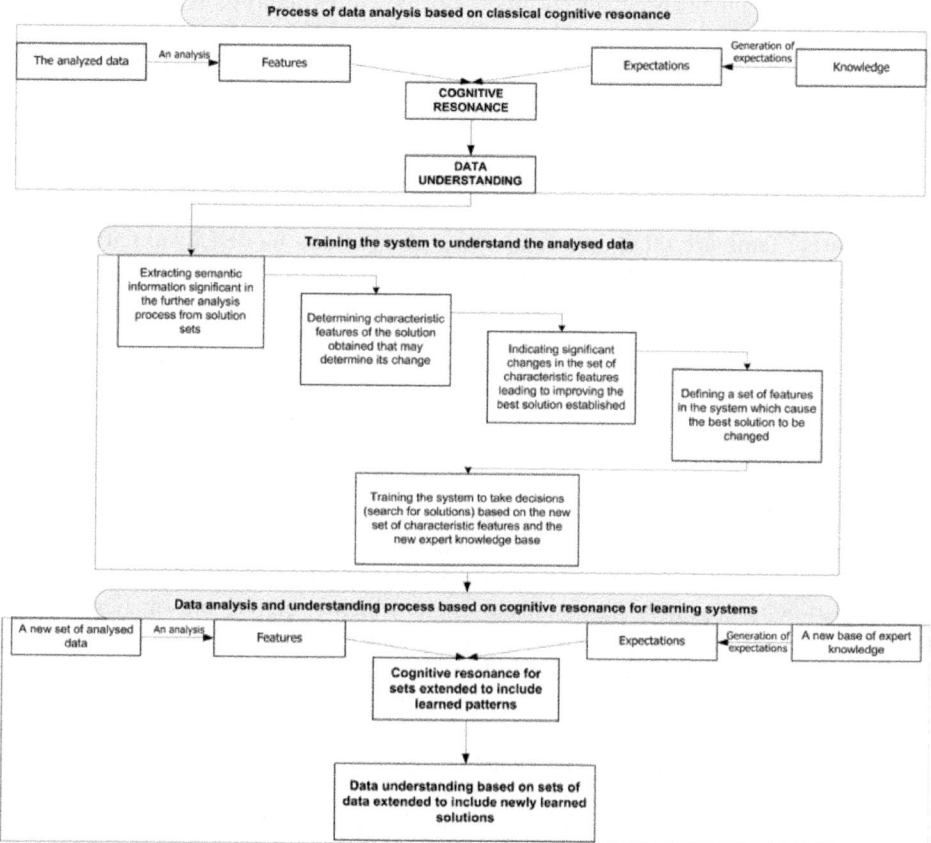

Fig. 1. Cognitive resonance in the process of data analysis and understanding enhanced with the process of training the system in new solutions

Research has shown that in this solution, pairs of characteristic features of the analysed data and expectations generated based on the expert knowledge base collected in the system which were not consistent were omitted at further analysis stages. This made it possible to envisage a situation in which the system encounters a solution it does not know and which is not defined at all in its bases. The question is, is it possible to recognise this type of a situation? Yes, the solution proposed in this publication shows that it is possible to introduce a stage at which the system is trained in solutions new to the system. This process is possible only when the set of solutions obtained (both optimum ones and those eliminated from further analysis) is used to create a set of features of analysed data and a set of new expectations not defined in the original bases of the system. The new features and expectations are input into the system base in which data is re-analysed, this time using the much broader expert knowledge set containing new patterns learned by the system. Such patterns constitute an extended expert knowledge base which the system uses to generate a set of expectations, and these are compared to the set of characteristic features of the analysed data. This process thus becomes an enhanced process of cognitive analysis based on cognitive resonance for learning systems. A system can be trained in any situation and this training can be multiplied depending on the needs and the necessity of extending the knowledge bases built into the system.

2   Cognitive Systems and Cognitive Informatics

Cognitive systems are those in which types of solutions modelled on data analysis processes taking place in the human brain have been applied to analyse complex data using layers of the semantic essence of data contained in every analysed set.

Processes of data analysis executed in cognitive systems based on cognitive resonance are very often equated with processes which form the cornerstone of cognitive informatics. However, we have to clearly distinguish between these two concepts associated with cognitive science and used in similar fields.

Cognitive informatics is a science dealing with the combination (one is tempted to say) of the traditional hardware informatics and cognitive science, that is the sciences concerned with learning, namely psychology, neurobiology, philosophy etc. Such combinations are possible if common ground or overlapping fields joining different scientific disciplines are found. Detailed solutions in the area of cognitive science, and in particular cognitive machine science, to which cognitive informatics belongs, make it necessary to look for specific applications. Such applications are created as system solutions combining the use of IT and cognitive tools. It is those combinations which lead to designing new classes of IT systems – cognitive systems.

This paper presents new solutions proposed for cognitive data analysis systems, showing how learning systems can enhance the image analysis processes executed by UBIAS (*Understanding Based Image Analysis Systems*). UBIAS systems have been described by the authors previously, and are detailed in the following publications [4-9].

3   UBIAS as an Example of Learning Cognitive Systems

This section discusses UBIAS systems enhanced with a stage for learning new solutions. This example will be illustrated by reference to cognitive data analysis systems, described in [6], used for analysing lesions occurring within foot bones. It should be noted that in such systems, formalisms of linguistic data analysis have been defined in the form of the following formal grammar [6]:

$$G_{dp_2} = (N, \Sigma, \Gamma, ST, P)$$

where:
The set of non-terminal labels of apexes:

N={ST, TALUS, CUBOIDEUM, NAVICULARE, LATERALE, MEDIALE, IN-TERMEDIUM, SES1, SES2, TM1, TM2, TM3, TM4, TM5, MP1, MP2, MP3, MP4, MP5, PIP1, PIP2, PIP3, PIP4, PIP5, DIP2, DIP3, DIP4, DIP5, TPH1, TPH2, TPH3, TPH4, TPH5, ADD1, ADD2, ADD3, ADD4, ADD5, ADD6, ADD7, ADD8, ADD9, ADD10, ADD11, ADD12, ADD13, ADD14}

The set of terminal labels of apexes:
$\sum$={c, t, cu, n, cl, cm, ci, s1, s2, tm1, tm2, tm3, tm4, tm5, mp1, mp2, mp3, mp4, mp5, pip1, pip2, pip3, pip4, pip5, dip2, dip3, dip4, dip5, tph1, tph2, tph3, tph4, tph5, add1, add2, add3, add4, add5, add6, add7, add8, add9, add10, add11, add12, add13, add14}

Γ–{p, q, r, s, t, u, v, w, x, y, z} – the graph shown in Fig.2

ST–The start symbol

P–set of productions.

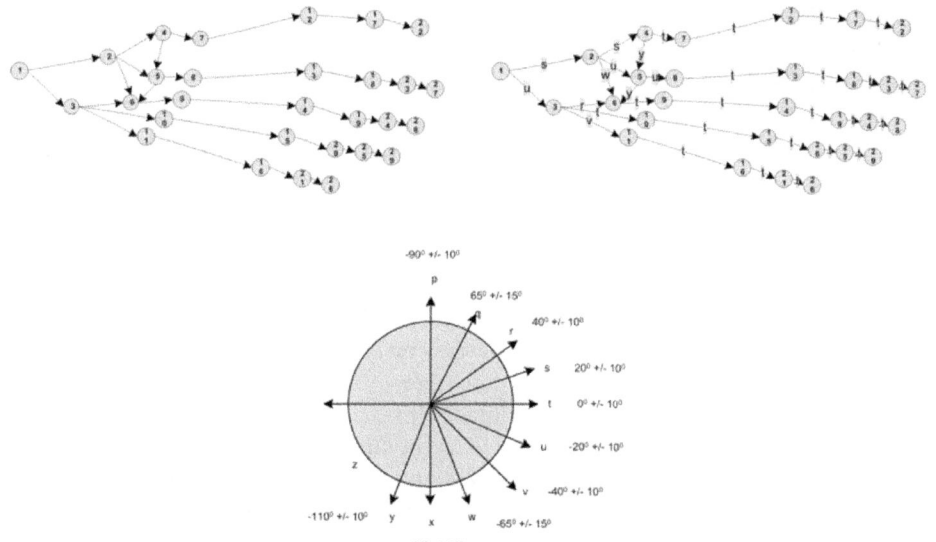

Fig. 2. The definition of an EDG graph describing the foot bone skeleton in the proper dorso-planar projection, a graph of spatial relationships, a graph with numbers of adjacent bones marked based on the graph of spatial relationships. Source: [6].

The new graph representation showing numbers consistent with the neighbourhood relationships of these structures and a graph of special topological relationships between particular elements of the graph was defined. A graph of spatial relationships is show in Fig. 2. with a graph of spatial relationships to build a graph containing the numbers of adjacent foot bones for an dorsoplanar projection.

An analysis has shown that the expert knowledge bases defined in the system were complex enough to correctly analyse selected images of foot bone lesions.

Defining such proper elements of the grammar showing the correct structure of foot bones in dorsoplanar projection. It should be kept in mind that this is a different set of grammatical rules for every projection. Figure 3 shows a set of graphs defining the correct structure of foot bones visible in the dorsoplanar projection. Determining the correct relationships and the correct structure of foot bones enables UBIAS systems to conduct a meaning analysis. For such projections of foot images, these analyses can generate results of reasoning about and interpreting selected types of fractures and pathological situations whose examples are shown in Fig. 3.

Examples of automatic data understanding presented in Figure 3 have been fully successful, meaning that selected foot bone lesion images have been fully understood and analysed.

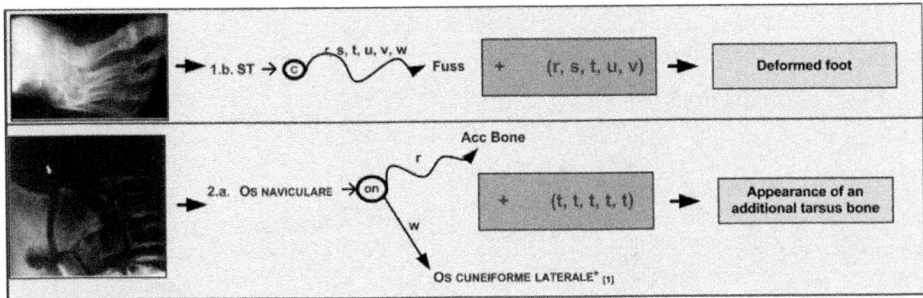

Fig. 3. The automatic understanding of foot bone lesions detected by the UBIAS system. Source: [6].

By introducing new learning solutions to the system, it becomes possible to understand images which have not been correctly classified for various reasons during the original attempt at data analysis. Let us remember that such incorrect classification can result from the system lacking knowledge of the analysed phenomenon, but it might as well be due to the incorrect quality of the image analysed. The authors of this publication are particularly interested in the first reason for the failure of correct classification, and it became the reason for optimising the operation of UBIAS systems by adding stages at which systems are trained in new solutions. The results of activities taken are shown in Figure 4.

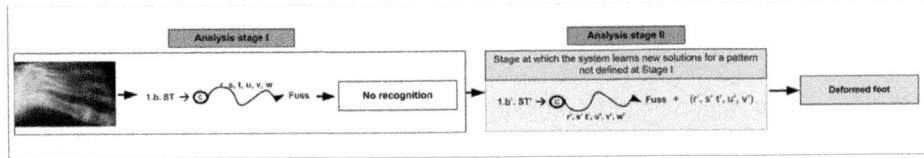

Fig. 4. Automatic data understanding in a UBIAS learning system

As a result of the analysis conducted, the UBIAS system has received an example for which there was no correctly defined pattern, so the system, without having a proper reference, compared the characteristic features of the analysed image with expectations of the image meaning using algorithms of semantic analysis of data defined in the form of a formal grammar, but did not complete the correct analysis. Consequently, it was necessary to input new definitions of patterns into the system and to extend the set of characteristic features to include those perceived in the analysed case. As a result of this action, new classes of features characteristic for the analysed images were obtained and the expert base has been supplemented with new characteristic patterns, and this has led to the correct analysis of data ending in the recognition and the semantic understanding of data.

4 Conclusion

Cognitive analysis systems, also referred to as cognitive systems, are constantly developing. Increasingly frequently attempts at their improvement bring about successive improvements of the effectiveness of the analysis conducted and the increased utility of these systems.

UBIAS cognitive systems have been extended to include new solutions aimed at improving not just the effectiveness of the analysis process, but mainly the reliability of the semantic reasoning and forecasting processes. This last stage of analysis, aimed at correctly forecasting changes in the analysed data, is significant in that during a failed attempt to understand data this stage is omitted altogether. Implementing the capacity of learning new solutions in the system leads to a successful determination during subsequent attempts of the analysis undertaken, then to data understanding, and once that is successful, it supports making further forecasts.

Learning systems are therefore becoming a new class of cognitive data analysis systems and they now seem to have a bright future.

Acknowledgement. This work has been supported by the Ministry of Science and Higher Education, Republic of Poland, under project number N N516 196537.

References

1. Burgener, F.A., Meyers, S.P., Tan, R.K., Zaunbauer, W.: Differential Diagnosis in Magnetic Resonance Imaging. Thieme (2002)
2. Liu, H.: A Fuzzy Qualitative Framework for Connecting Robot Qualitative and Quantitative Representations. IEEE Trans. on Fuzzy Systems 16(6), 1522–1530 (2008)
3. Meystel, A.M., Albus, J.S.: Intelligent Systems – Architecture, Design, and Control. John Wiley & Sons, Inc., Chichester (2002)
4. Ogiela, L.: UBIAS Systems for Cognitive Interpretation and Analysis of Medical Images. Opto-Electronics Review 17(2), 166–179 (2009)
5. Ogiela, L., Ogiela, M.R., Tadeusiewicz, R.: Mathematical Linguistic in Cognitive Medical Image Interpretation Systems. Journal of Mathematical Imaging and Vision 34, 328–340 (2009)

6. Ogiela, L., Ogiela, M.R., Tadeusiewicz, R.: UBIAS – type cognitive systems for medical pattern interpretation. In: Velásquez, J.D., Ríos, S.A., Howlett, R.J., Jain, L.C., et al. (eds.) Knowledge-Based and Intelligent Information and Engineering Systems. LNCS, vol. 5711, pp. 177–183. Springer, Heidelberg (2009)
7. Ogiela, L., Ogiela, M.R.: Cognitive Techniques in Visual Data Interpretation. Studies in Computational Intelligence, vol. 228. Springer, Heidelberg (2009)
8. Ogiela, M.R., Tadeusiewicz, R.: Modern Computational Intelligence Methods for the Interpretation of Medical Images. Springer, Heidelberg (2008)
9. Tadeusiewicz, R., Ogiela, M.R.: Medical Image Understanding Technology. Springer, Heidelberg (2004)
10. Wang, Y.: The Theoretical Framework and Cognitive Process of Learning. In: Proc. 6th International Conference on Cognitive Informatics (ICCI 2007), pp. 470–479. IEEE CS Press, Lake Tahoe (2008)

A BitTorrent-Based Dynamic Bandwidth Adaptation Algorithm for Video Streaming

Tz-Heng Hsu[1], You-Sheng Liang[1], and Meng-Shu Chiang[2]

[1] Department of Computer Science and Information Engineering,
Southern Taiwan University, Tainan, Taiwan, R.O.C.
[2] Department of Computer Science and Information Engineering,
Far East University, Tainan, Taiwan, R.O.C.
hsuth@mail.stut.edu.tw

Abstract. In this paper, we propose a BitTorrent-based dynamic bandwidth adaptation algorithm for video streaming. Two mechanisms to improve the original BitTorrent protocol are proposed: (1) the decoding order frame first (DOFF) frame selection algorithm and (2) the rarest I frame first (RIFF) frame selection algorithm. With the proposed algorithms, a peer can periodically check the number of downloaded frames in the buffer and then allocate the available bandwidth adaptively for video streaming. As a result, users can have smooth video playout experience with the proposed algorithms.

Keywords: Peer-to-Peer network, BitTorrent, Streaming, Rarest first algorithm.

1 Introduction

Multimedia streaming services have become extremely popular and its use grows exponentially in recent years. For applications, such as Youtube and IP-TV, overload the media transmission over Internet. To alleviate the congestion problem, Content Delivery Networks (CDNs) are often deployed in networks to support large numbers of users. However, this may require the deployment of special infrastructure and cost a lot of money. As an alternative, peer-to-peer (P2P) networks are introduced to solve the aforementioned problems. With the popularity of the Internet and the increase of computing processing power, peer-to-peer network has become a popular distributed computing model. Peer-to-peer networks make resources, e.g., storages, CPU cycles, and media contents, available at the edges of the Internet.

Peer-to-peer networks have recently been realized through file sharing applications. However, there are still a lot of problems for supporting multimedia streaming over peer-to-peer networks. BitTorrent is a P2P file-sharing technology, which is one of the most popular application softwares in Internet. In BitTorrent, a file is partitioned into multiple fixed-size chunks called pieces [5][7]. Peers exchange piece information while downloading, which let peers know the status of sharing pieces among each other. In order to share a file with peers as fast

G.S. Tomar et al. (Eds.): UCMA 2010, CCIS 75, pp. 51–62, 2010.
© Springer-Verlag Berlin Heidelberg 2010

as possible, BitTorrent peers employ a rarest-first piece selection algorithm to ensure that rare pieces are replicated sufficiently. The goals of rarest-first piece selection algorithm are (1) to ensure file integrity and (2) to achieve resource abundance. In order to ensure file integrity, the rarest-first piece selection algorithm selects rarest pieces of a file and downloads these pieces first. To avoid the lack of pieces and achieve resource abundance, BitTorrent adopts the rarest-first strategy for piece selection to speed up the distribution of files[6][12][1][4].

Since BitTorrent was designed for sharing large files, its piece selection algorithm is not suitable for streaming media. BitTorrent broke streaming capabilities because it transfers file pieces non-sequentially. To satisfy the requirements of continuous media, e.g., video and audio, BitTorrent needs to consider following design concerns of multimedia streaming. First, pieces must be downloaded in sequence to meet the sequential-order requirements of the streaming media. Second, the download pieces must be able to arrive at a peer before its scheduled playout time. If a piece arrives too late for its playout time, the piece is useless and can be treated as effectively lost. Third, the BitTorrent's tit-for-tat policy must be changed to fit the needs of retrieving streaming media [8][10][13][14].

In this paper, we propose a BitTorrent-based dynamic bandwidth adaptation algorithm for video streaming. In order to support the video streaming for BitTorrent-based systems, the BitTorrent's original data piece selection algorithms are modified to fit the nature of continues media, i.e., video frames should be downloaded sequentially. We proposed frame selection algorithms named (1) decoding order frame first (DOFF) and (2) rarest I frame first (RIFF). Decoding order frame first (DOFF) frame selection algorithm selects downloading frames according to video frame decoding order, which makes a peer can successfully play out video frames in sequence when frames are steadily and continuously downloaded. Rarest I frame first (RIFF) frame selection algorithm selects downloading frames according to frame's importance, e.g., I, P, and B picture frame. For MPEG-4 video streams, I picture frames are downloaded first in RIFF frame selection algorithm, followed by the P picture frame, and finally the B picture frame. A dynamic bandwidth adaptation algorithm periodically checks the streaming buffer to have knowledge of downloaded frames, and then allocates the available bandwidth for adapting frame downloading jobs with DOFF and RIFF frame selection algorithms. In order to evaluate the performance of the proposed algorithms, comparisons of the proposed mechanisms with traditional BitTorrent data piece selection algorithm are performed in the paper.

The rest of this paper is organized as follows: Section 2 introduces related works. Section 3 depicts the proposed frame selection and dynamic bandwidth adaptation algorithms for supporting video streaming in BitTorrent-based systems. Section 4 shows the experimental results. Section 5 concludes the proposed algorithms.

2   Related Works

Since many video files in BitTorrent using MPEG-4 file format, a brief introduction of MPEG-4 frame coding scheme is introduced in this Section.

2.1   MPEG-4 Frame Coding Scheme

MPEG-4 is an ISO/IEC standard for compressing and representing multimedia content developed by the Moving Picture Experts Group (MPEG), where its format designation is in ISO/IEC 14496. In MPEG-4, visual information is organized on the basis of the video object (VO) concept, which represents a time-varying visual entity with arbitrary shape. The information associated to a VO is represented as a set of video object layers (VOLs). Each VOL is considered as a sequence of video object planes (VOPs). A Video Object Plane (VOP) can have any shape. A traditional video frame is represented by a VOP with a rectangular shape. In MPEG-4, each VOP can be coded (as in previous MPEG standards) as an I-VOP (without temporal prediction), as a P-VOP (with prediction from the previous VOP), or as a B-VOP (with predictions from a previous and a future VOP). In this paper, we use the term frame and VOP equivalently [9][2].

A MPEG-4 video stream can be regarded as a sequence of video frames. A MPEG-4 video stream consists of three types of frames: intra (I), predictive (P), and bidirectional predictive (B). I frame is an intra frame, which means that it is coded by itself without any motion compensation. P frame is a predictive frame which means that it is coded with motion compensation from a previous anchor frame. B frame is an interpolative frame which is coded with motion compensation both from a previous anchor frame and from a future anchor frame. MPEG-4 encodes P and B frames using motion estimation and interpolation techniques that let them be substantially smaller than I frames. MPEG-4 uses preceding P or I frames to estimate the motion of P frames. It uses either or both preceding and successive P or I frames to estimate the motion of B frames.

Usually a MPEG-4 encoder defines frame types using a predefined repeating sequence of I, P, B frames, like IBBPBBP or IPPBIP. From the decoding dependency view, I frame is the most important frame. Without I frame, the dependent P and B frames cannot be decoded. P frame is the second most important frame; loss of P frame results inability to decode the subsequent frames. B frame has minimal effect on decoding. Figure 1 shows the relations between display order and decode order of a video stream. In Figure 1, it shows that a video's display order is not the same as the decode order. Frame P1 references the preceding frame I1, frame B1 references the preceding frame I1 and successive frame P1. In order to decode the frame B1, a peer needs to download frames

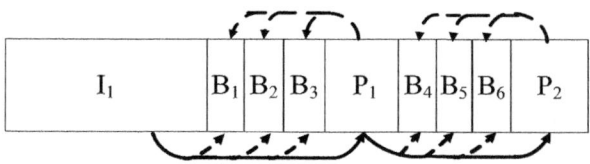

Display Order : $I_1 \to B_1 \to B_2 \to B_3 \to P_1 \to B_4 \to B_5 \to B_6 \to P_2$

Decode Order : $I_1 \to P_1 \to B_1 \to B_2 \to B_3 \to P_2 \to B_4 \to B_5 \to B_6$

Fig. 1. The relations between display order and decode order of a video stream

I1 and P1 first. For supporting streaming in BitTorrent with exists shared video files such as MPEG-4 coded files, a video's frames should be downloaded in the decode order instead of display order. In such a way, a user can watch instant video streams instead of downloading full video file.

Many video files in BitTorrent are using MPEG-4 file format. The algorithms introduced in this paper, however, aren't limited to this standard and could be applied to other frame-based video compression schemes.

3   Algorithms

The goal of our work is to minimize the transmission latency in playing streaming media and to achieve resource abundance of precious video frames. In this Section, we introduce our proposed algorithms in detail.

3.1   Decoding Order Frame First (DOFF)

Decoding order frame first (DOFF) frame selection algorithm selects downloading frames according to frame decode order, which makes a peer can successfully play out video frames in sequence when frames are steadily and continuously downloaded. In BitTorrent, a file is partitioned into multiple fixed-size chunks called pieces [5][7]. However, such a file partition way did not take into account the undivided completeness of a video frame. If the cut-off point of a video frame is not on the correct file position while doing file partition, a video frame cannot be decoded after transmitting a data piece in BitTorrent. The BitTorrent file partition method makes it hard to support video streaming in nature. To avoid transmission of an incomplete video frame, a single encoded video frame is transmitted as a basic transmission unit for video streaming in the proposed algorithms. In the proposed algorithms, a download sliding window is defined to regulate the stream receptions. The download sliding window is W frames wide. The leftmost end of the download sliding window is moving related the current download buffer state and video playout time. For video frames within the current download sliding window, such frames are downloaded using decoding order frame first (DOFF) frame selection algorithm. Figure 2 shows the

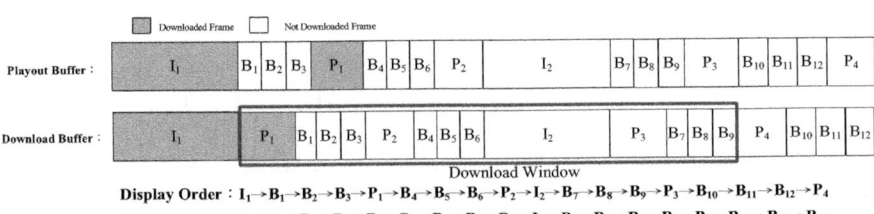

Fig. 2. The proposed download sliding window for retrieving video streams with decoding order frame first (DOFF) frame selection algorithm

proposed download sliding window for retrieving a video stream with decoding order frame first (DOFF) frame selection algorithm. In Figure 2, it shows that frames' downloading order is the same as the decoding order by using DOFF algorithm. Frame P1 references the preceding frame I1, frame B1 references the preceding frame I1 and successive frame P1. In order to decode the frame B1, a peer needs to download frames I1 and P1 first. A corresponding video play-out buffer is shown for comparison. Decoding order frame first (DOFF) sorts the video frames according to frames' decoding order and then downloads encoded frames progressively, which allows peers can successfully play out the video frames in time, compared with downloading frames in display order.

Algorithm 1. Decoding Order Frame First (DOFF)

```
WHILE (Frames of a video are not played out)
  Calculate downloadWindowSize
  Calculate number of GOPs in the downloadWindow
  Allocate downloadBuffer for storing the sorted picture frames
  Download frames to downloadBuffer by decoding order
  Mark the index of the downloaded frames in downloadBuffer
  IF (currentFrame is downloaded)
    Shift the downloadWindow
    Announce haveFramesList to neighbor peers
  END IF
END WHILE
```

3.2 Rarest I Frame First (RIFF)

Rarest I frame first (RIFF) frame selection algorithm selects downloading frames according to the frame's importance, e.g., I, P, and B picture frame. For MPEG-4 video streams, I picture frames are downloaded first in RIFF frame selection algorithm, followed by the P picture frame, and finally the B picture frame.

A MPEG-4 video stream consists of three types of frames: intra (I), predictive (P), and bidirectional predictive (B). I frame is coded by itself without any motion compensation, which has the largest amount of data for decoding. P frame is coded with motion compensation from a previous anchor frame, which has the fewer amount of data for decoding. B frame is coded with motion compensation both from a previous anchor frame and from a future anchor frame, which has the least amount of data for decoding. Since MPEG-4 uses preceding P or I frames to estimate the motion of P frames, I frame is the most important frame. Without I frame, the dependent P and B frames cannot be decoded. Therefore, I frames must be downloaded first if there has available bandwidth during video streaming. Rarest I frame first (RIFF) frame selection algorithm selects I picture frames for downloading first to ensure that rare I picture frames are replicated sufficiently. To avoid the lack of I picture frames and achieve resource abundance, rarest I frame first (RIFF) frame selection algorithm is used to speed up the distribution of most important I frames.

```
Algorithm 2. Rarest I Frame First (RIFF)

WHILE (Frames a video are not played out)
  Update absentFrameArray for storing the index of not played out frames
  Receive haveFramesList from neighbor peers
  absentFrameArrayI=SortLeastHavedFrame(absentFrameArray, haveFramesList
                  , I-Frame)
  absentFrameArrayP=SortLeastHavedFrame(absentFrameArray, haveFramesList
                  , P-Frame)
  absentFrameArrayB=SortLeastHavedFrame(absentFrameArray, haveFramesList
                  , B-Frame)
  indexFrame = FindNearestDownloadFrame(absentFrameArrayI, playTime)
  FOR i= indexFrame to Len(absentFrameArrayI)
    AddToDownloadJobQueue(absentFrameArrayI, i, downloadWindow)
  END FOR
  indexFrame = FindNearestDownloadFrame(absentFrameArrayP, playTime)
  FOR i= indexFrame to Len(absentFrameArrayP)
    AddToDownloadJobQueue(absentFrameArrayP, i, downloadWindow)
  END FOR
  indexFrame = FindNearestDownloadFrame(absentFrameArrayB, playTime)
  FOR i= indexFrame to Len(absentFrameArrayB)
    AddToDownloadJobQueue(absentFrameArrayB, i, downloadWindow)
  END FOR
  IF currentFrame is downloaded
    Update the index of currentFrame to haveFrameList
    Announce haveFramesList to neighbor peers
  END IF
END WHILE
```

4   Performance Evaluation

To evaluate the performance of the proposed algorithms, we use the NS2 network simulator to simulate the BitTorrent file sharing environment. Comparisons with standard BitTorrent protocol in NS2 simulator are performed. To simulate the standard BitTorrent protocol, the simulation is performed by using a modified flow-level simulator based on [3]. Our analysis to BitTorrent protocol is operating in a one-hop star topology.

To simulate MPEG-4 video streaming, we use a MPEG-4 video trace file named Verbose_StarWarsIV.dat which is based on [11]. The simulated MPEG-4 video file's relevant parameters are as follows: the file size is 200 MB, total frame number is 10006, the average data size of a video frame is about 20.47 KB, the video's length is 400 seconds, and the video's resolution is 176x144 with frame rate of 25 fps. In the video file, the number of I frame is 834, the number of P frame is 2502, the number of B frame is 6669.

In the simulation, the buffer time for smoothing the start-up delay is set to 40 seconds. The parameters used in the simulated LAN environment are referred to Chunghwa Telecom's ADSL bandwidth rate in Taiwan. The different ADSL bandwidth rates of Chunghwa Telecom are 256K/64K, 1M/64K, 2M/256K, and 8M/256K bits. To simulate BitTorrent file sharing system, the data size of a piece is set to 256 KB and the video file is partitioned into 800 pieces. There are 7 peers participant in the simulation environment, including 1 Seed and 6 Leechers. Each peer has 4 connections for packet transmissions. In the experiments, the size of the download buffer is set to 750 video frames, i.e., 30 seconds. The low-level threshold of the playout buffer is set to 250 video frames. The high-level threshold of the playout buffer is set to 500 video frames. The simulation runs with durations of 450 to 4000 seconds.

4.1   BitTorrent Protocol

Figure 3 shows the results of delivering video stream using BitTorrent rarest-first piece selection algorithm with ADSL data rate 256K/64K. The x-axis denotes the simulation time and the y-axis denotes the frame id. The yellow-line denotes the scheduled playout time of the video stream and the blue-line denotes the simulated frame arrival time of the BitTorrent rarest-first piece selection algorithm. For aggregated upload rates lower than the video bitrate, it is impossible for the peer to watch a video smoothly. Figure 4 shows that blue-line is below the yellow-line, which means that the video cannot be downloaded before its scheduled playout time, i.e., the bandwidth is not enough for video streaming. At time 59.59, the frame id of BitTorrent protocol is 171. At time 60.59, the frame id of BitTorrent protocol is 142. At time 971.536, the frame id of BitTorrent protocol is 2074. At time 972.381, the frame id of BitTorrent protocol is 3031. It shows that the frame id of BitTorrent protocol is out of sequence, which means that frames are arrived in random order. Using the rarest-first piece selection algorithm to download the data piece, BitTorrent's downloaded data pieces are stored in an out-of-order way. Such an out-of-order way makes the video stream cannot be decoded and displayed in sequence when a user is downloading frames.

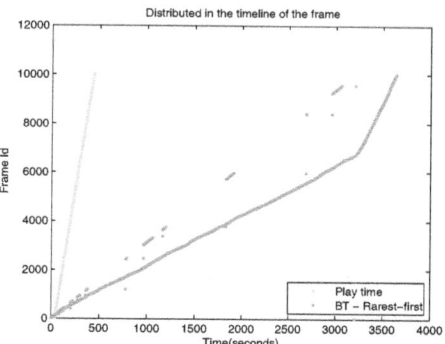

Fig. 3. The results of delivering video stream using BitTorrent's rarest-first piece selection algorithm with ADSL data rate 256K/64K

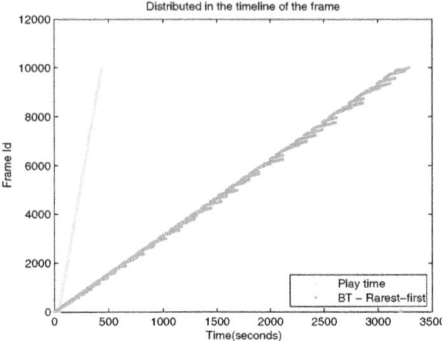

Fig. 4. The results of delivering video stream using BitTorrent's rarest-first piece selection algorithm with ADSL data rate 1M/64K

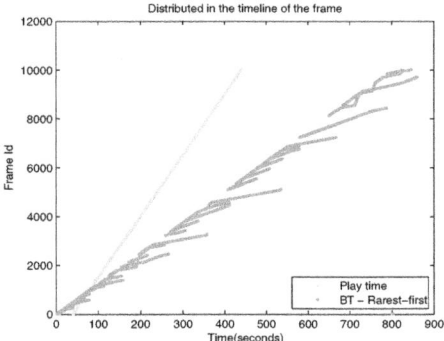

Fig. 5. The results of delivering video stream using BitTorrent's rarest-first piece selection algorithm with ADSL data rate 2M/256K

As a result, the user cannot watch a video smoothly. Figure 4 and 5 show similar results with different ADSL data rates. In Figure 6, it shows that blue-line is cross with the yellow-line, which means that the bandwidth is enough for video streaming with ADSL data rate 8M/640k. However, the frame id of BitTorrent protocol is still out of sequence, which means that rarest-first piece selection algorithm is not suitable for video streaming.

4.2 Dynamic Bandwidth Adaptation Algorithm

Figure 7, 8, 9, 10 shows the simulation results of the proposed dynamic bandwidth adaptation algorithm and BitTorrent protocol. The figures show the downloaded frame status in each peer. In the figures, each peer has 5 data fields: the number of successful played out frames, the frame number of not successful played out frames, the number of I/P/B frame in successful played out frames.

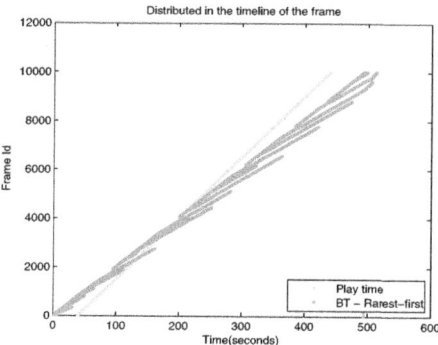

Fig. 6. The results of delivering video stream using BitTorrent's rarest-first piece selection algorithm with ADSL data rate 8M/640K

| | Dynamic bandwidth adaptation algorithm | | BitTorrent's rarest-first piece selection algorithm | |
| | Successful played frames / Not successful played frames | I/P/B frame in successful played frames | Successful played frames / Not successful played frames | I/P/B frame in successful played frames |
		I / P / B		I / P / B
Peer 1	410 / 9595	15 / 84 / 310	109 / 9896	10 / 27 / 71
Peer 2	247 / 9758	18 / 61 / 167	116 / 9889	10 / 27 / 78
Peer 3	291 / 9714	20 / 58 / 212	92 / 9913	8 / 23 / 60
Peer 4	292 / 9713	17 / 60 / 214	116 / 9889	11 / 31 / 73
Peer 5	402 / 9603	14 / 93 / 294	108 / 9898	10 / 26 / 71
Peer 6	409 / 9596	16 / 83 / 309	88 / 9918	7 / 23 / 57
Average	341 / 9664	16 / 73 / 251	104 / 9901	9 / 26 / 68

Fig. 7. The simulation results of the proposed dynamic bandwidth adaptation algorithm and BitTorrent protocol with ADSL data rate 256K/64K

| | Dynamic bandwidth adaptation algorithm | | BitTorrent's rarest-first piece selection algorithm | |
| | Successful played frames /Not successful played frames | I/P/B frame in successful played frames | Successful played frames /Not successful played frames | I/P/B frame in successful played frames |
		I / P / B		I / P / B
Peer 1	478 / 9527	13 / 107 / 357	129 / 9876	12 / 30 / 86
Peer 2	296 / 9709	18 / 71 / 206	120 / 9885	11 / 27 / 81
Peer 3	308 / 9697	15 / 75 / 217	94 / 9911	8 / 22 / 63
Peer 4	300 / 9705	10 / 80 / 209	114 / 9891	11 / 26 / 76
Peer 5	325 / 9680	14 / 82 / 228	95 / 9910	8 / 22 / 64
Peer 6	406 / 9599	16 / 90 / 299	108 / 9897	10 / 27 / 70
Average	352 / 9652	14 / 84 / 252	110 / 9895	10 / 25 / 73

Fig. 8. The simulation results of the proposed dynamic bandwidth adaptation algorithm and BitTorrent protocol with ADSL data rate 1M/64K

	Dynamic bandwidth adaptation algorithm		BitTorrent's rarest-first piece selection algorithm	
	Successful played frames /Not successful played frames	I/P/B frame in successful played frames I/ P /B	Successful played frames /Not successful played frames	I/P/B frame in successful played frames I/ P /B
Peer 1	1997 / 8008	128 / 431 / 1437	644 / 9361	52 / 163 / 428
Peer 2	1451 / 8554	117 / 342 / 991	795 / 9210	66 / 201 / 527
Peer 3	1435 / 8570	123 / 349 / 962	817 / 9188	68 / 206 / 542
Peer 4	1639 / 8366	114 / 392 / 1122	852 / 9153	71 / 194 / 566
Peer 5	1735 / 8270	105 / 407 / 1222	842 / 9163	70 / 213 / 558
Peer 6	1833 / 8172	118 / 423 / 1291	643 / 9362	54 / 161 / 427
Average	1682 / 8323	117 / 390 / 1170	765 / 9240	63 / 193 / 508

Fig. 9. The simulation results of the proposed dynamic bandwidth adaptation algorithm and BitTorrent protocol with ADSL data rate 2M/256K

	Dynamic bandwidth adaptation algorithm		BitTorrent's rarest-first piece selection algorithm	
	Successful played frames /Not successful played frames	I/P/B frame in successful played frames I/ P /B	Successful played frames /Not successful played frames	I/P/B frame in successful played frames I/ P /B
Peer 1	5368 / 4637	470 / 1322 / 3575	2819 / 7186	236 / 705 / 1877
Peer 2	5161 / 4844	460 / 1285 / 3415	3002 / 7003	257 / 767 / 1977
Peer 3	5175 / 4830	452 / 1284 / 3438	2781 / 7224	233 / 695 / 1852
Peer 4	5213 / 4792	451 / 1315 / 3446	2799 / 7206	250 / 744 / 1804
Peer 5	4984 / 5021	443 / 1245 / 3295	1573 / 8432	134 / 401 / 1037
Peer 6	5043 / 4962	449 / 1307 / 3286	1571 / 8434	132 / 394 / 1046
Average	5158 / 4847	454 / 1293 / 3409	2424 / 7581	207 / 506 / 1598

Fig. 10. The simulation results of the proposed dynamic bandwidth adaptation algorithm and BitTorrent protocol with ADSL data rate 8M/640K

The number of successful played out frames means that these frames can be successful displayed at peer's device on its scheduled playout time. The frame number of not successful played out frames means that these frames cannot be successful displayed at peer's device on its scheduled playout time due to packet loss and late arrival. The number of I/P/B frame in successful played out frames shows the different frame type in the played out frames, which can be used to observe the efforts of different frame selection algorithms.

Figure 7 shows the simulation results of the proposed dynamic bandwidth adaptation algorithm and BitTorrent protocol with ADSL data rate 256K/64K. In Figure 7, it shows that the number of total downloaded frame in the proposed dynamic bandwidth adaptation algorithm is 9664; the number of total downloaded frame in BitTorrent protocol is 9901. The results show that the BitTorrent's rarest-first piece selection algorithm can effectively download frames. However, the BitTorrent's rarest-first piece selection algorithm is not suitable for video streaming. In Figure 7, it shows the number of successful played out frames in the proposed dynamic bandwidth adaptation algorithm is 341; the number of successful played out frame in BitTorrent protocol is 104. The results show that the proposed dynamic bandwidth adaptation algorithm can effectively deliver video frames in sequence and display frames on their scheduled playout time. With DOFF and RIFF algorithms, the rarest I frames will be downloaded in start-up phases, which can protect the loss of cascaded P and B frames. At time 40, video frames are consumed by the peer's video device. When the number of frames in playout buffer is lower than the low-level threshold, the proposed dynamic bandwidth adaptation algorithm uses DOFF algorithm to continue download and display video frames. Figure 7 shows the P and B frames in proposed dynamic bandwidth adaptation have better opportunity to be successful displayed because of the using of DOFF and RIFF algorithms. Figure 7, 8, 9, 10 show the similar results in different ADSL data rates.

5   Conclusion

In this paper, we propose an adaptive video streaming algorithm for BitTorrent-based video systems. In order to support the video streaming for BitTorrent-based systems, the BitTorrent's original piece selection algorithms are changed to fit the nature of continues media, i.e., video frames should be downloaded sequentially. We proposed mechanisms to improve the original BitTorrent protocolG(1) frame selection algorithms named decoding order frame first (DOFF) and rarest I frame first (RIFF); (2) a dynamic bandwidth adaptation algorithm to allocate the available bandwidth adaptively for video streams. Decoding order frame first (DOFF) frame selection algorithm selects downloading frames according to the frame's decoding order, which makes a peer can successfully play out video frames in sequence when frames are steadily and continuously downloaded. Rarest I frame first (RIFF) frame selection algorithm selects downloading frames according to the frame's importance, e.g., I, P, and B picture frame. The dynamic bandwidth adaptation algorithm periodically checks the streaming buffer to have knowledge of downloaded frames, and then allocates the available bandwidth for adapting frame downloading jobs with DOFF and RIFF frame selection algorithms. Comparisons of the proposed mechanisms with traditional BitTorrent's piece selection algorithm are performed in the paper.

References

1. Bickson, D., Borer, R.: The bitcod client: A bittorrent clone using network coding. In: 7th IEEE International Conference on Peer-to-Peer Computing, pp. 231–232 (2007)
2. Daras, P., Kompatsiaris, I., Grinias, I., Akrivas, G., Tziritas, G., Kollias, S., Strintzis, M.G.: Mpeg-4 authoring tool using moving object segmentation and tracking in video shots. EURASIP Journal on Applied Signal Processing, 862–870 (2003)
3. Eger, K., Hoßfeld, T., Binzenhöfer, A., Kunzmann, G.: Efficient simulation of large-scale p2p networks: packet-level vs. flow-level simulations. In: 2nd workshop on Use of P2P, GRID and agents for the development of content network, pp. 9–16 (2007)
4. Erman, D., Ilie, D., Popescu, A.: Bittorrent traffic characteristics. In: International Multi-Conference on Computing in the Global Information Technology, p. 42 (2006)
5. Fan, B., Chiu, D.M., Lui, J.C.: Stochastic differential equation approach to model bittorrent-like p2p systems. In: Proceedings of IEEE International Conference on Communications, pp. 915–920 (2006)

6. Legout, A., Urvoy-Keller, G., Michiardi, P.: Rarest first and choke algorithms are enough. In: 6th ACM SIGCOMM conference on Internet measurement, pp. 203–208 (2006)
7. Liu, B., Cui, Y., Chang, B., Gotow, B., Xue, Y.: Bittube: Case study of a web-based peer-assisted video-on-demand system. In: 10th IEEE International Symposium on Multimedia, pp. 242–249 (2008)
8. Qiu, D., Srikant, R.: Modeling and performance analysis of bittorrent-like peer-to-peer networks. In: ACM Special Interest Group on Data Communication, pp. 367–377 (2004)
9. Sikora, T.: The mpeg-4 video standard verification method. IEEE Trans. Circuits Syst. Video Tech. 7(1), 19–31 (1997)
10. Skevik, K.A., Goebel, V., Plagemann, T.: Evaluation of a comprehensive p2p video-on-demand streaming system. The International Journal of Computer and Telecommunications Networking 53, 434–455 (2009)
11. Verbose_StarWarsIV.dat: Trace File (2009),
    http://www.tkn.tu-berlin.de/research/trace/ltvt.html
12. Wei, B., Fedak, G., Cappello, F.: Collaborative data distribution with bittorrent for computational desktop grids. In: 4th International Symposium on Parallel and Distributed Computing, pp. 250–257 (2005)
13. Tu, Y.-C., Sun, J., Hefeeda, M., Prabhaka, S.: An analytical study of peer-to-peer media streaming systems. Transactions on Multimedia Computing, Communications, and Applications 1, 354–376 (2005)
14. Choe, Y.R., Schuff, D.L., Dyaberi, J.M., Pai, V.S.: Improving vod server efficiency with bittorrnt. In: 15th International Conference on Multimedia, pp. 117–126 (2007)

Rough Sets Approximations for Learning Outcomes

Sylvia Encheva[1] and Sharil Tumin[2]

[1] Stord/Haugesund University College, Bjørnsonsg, 45, 5528 Haugesund, Norway
`sbe@hsh.no`
[2] University of Bergen, IT-Dept., P. O. Box 7800, 5020 Bergen, Norway
`edpst@it.uib.no`

Abstract. Discovering dependencies between students' responses and their level of mastering of a particular skill is very important in the process of developing intelligent tutoring systems. This work is an approach to attain a higher level of certainty while following students' learning progress. Rough sets approximations are applied for assessing students understanding of a concept. Consecutive responses from each individual learner to automated tests are placed in corresponding rough sets approximations. The resulting path provides strong indication about the current level of learning outcomes.

Keywords: Rough sets approximations, knowledge, intelligent systems.

1 Introduction

Extracting general rules from huge databases is not a task that can be easily completed by single individuals. Some classifications where rules can be automatedly obtained from a database, i.e. no preliminary knowledge about these rules are needed, can be done by applying rough sets theory. A rough logic classifier operates with lower and upper approximations while establishing whether an object belongs to any of the objects' classes to which the database is divided into. This under the assumption that there is no object that belongs to two different classes.

Evaluation of students' knowledge has been a subject of special interest to various research communities. In this respect automated tests appear to be among the most popular ways of providing immediate feedback to both students and test designers. A test designer has to give serious considerations to logical reasonings involved in the process of decision making. Use of Boolean logic limits system's responses to true or false and cannot therefore recognize other occurrences like for example partially correct or incomplete answers. Boolean logic appears to be quite sufficient for most everyday reasonings, but it is certainly unable to provide meaningful conclusions in presence of inconsistent and/or incomplete input, [5] and [8]. This problem can be resolved by applying methods from the theory of rough sets approximations.

The aim of this paper is to present an approach for following students' progress in obtaining new knowledge based on rough sets approximations. Consecutive responses to automated tests of each individual learner are placed in appropriate rough sets approximations. The resulting path provides strong indication about the current level of learning outcomes and points possible inconsistencies related to tests' contents.

G.S. Tomar et al. (Eds.): UCMA 2010, CCIS 75, pp. 63–72, 2010.

The rest of the paper is organized as follows. Section 2 contains definitions of terms used later on. Section 3 explains how to combine personal responses and Section 4 is devoted to a brief system description. Section 5 contains the conclusion of this work.

2 Background

2.1 Rough Sets

From a classical stand point of view a concept is well defined by a pair of intension and extension. Existence of well defined boundaries is assumed and an extension is uniquely identified by a crisp set of objects. In real life situations one has to operate with concepts having grey/gradual boundaries, like for example partially known concepts, [21], undefinable concepts, and approximate concepts,[10].

Rough Sets were originally introduced in [14]. The presented approach provides exact mathematical formulation of the concept of approximative (rough) equality of sets in a given approximation space, [15]. An *approximation space* is a pair $A = (U, R)$, where U is a set called universe, and $R \subset U \times U$ is an indiscernibility relation.

Equivalence classes of R are called *elementary sets* (atoms) in A. The equivalence class of R determined by an element $x \in U$ is denoted by $R(x)$. Equivalence classes of R are called *granules* generated by R.

The following definitions are often used while describing a rough set $X, X \subset U$:

- the *R-upper approximation* of X

$$R^{\star}(x) := \bigcup_{x \in U} \{R(x) : R(x) \cap X \neq \varnothing\}$$

- the *R-lower approximation* of X

$$R_{\star}(x) := \bigcup_{x \in U} \{R(x) : R(x) \subseteq X\}$$

- the *R-boundary region* of X

$$RN_R(X) := R^{\star}(X) - R_{\star}(X)$$

2.2 Assessment

A method enabling the instructor to do a post-test correction to neutralize the impact of guessing is developed in [7]. The theory and experience discussed in the above listed literature was used while developing our assessment tools.

A personalized intelligent computer assisted training system is presented in [13]. An intelligent tutoring system that uses decision theory to select the next tutorial action is described in [11]. A model for detecting student misuse of help in intelligent tutoring systems is presented in [2]. An investigation of whether a cognitive tutor can be made more effective by extending it to help students acquire help-seeking skills can be found in [9].

A proliferation of hint abuse (e.g., using hints to find answers rather than trying to understand) was found in [1] and [9]. However, evidence showing that when used appropriately, on-demand help can have a positive impact on learning was found in [16], [18], and [20].

A level-based instruction model is proposed in [12]. A model for student knowledge diagnosis through adaptive testing is presented in [6]. An approach for integrating intelligent agents, user models, and automatic content categorization in a virtual environment is presented in [17].

The Questionmark system [22] applies multiple response questions where a set of options is presented following a question stem. The final outcome is in a binary form, i.e. correct or incorrect because the system is based on Boolean logic [4], [19].

3   Combining Rough Sets and Understanding

The main focus in this section is on the idea of connecting correct, incorrect and partially correct responses, and rough sets approximations. A graphical representation of rough sets approximations can be seen in Fig. 1, based on five valued logic, [3].

Assessment of students' understanding of a concept is proposed. It employs multiple choice tests. The system is designed in a way that a new trial brings different questions and/or answer combinations but related to the same concept. A test related to a particular concept can be taken several times. In order to obtain a higher degree of certainty in the decision process on whether a concept is sufficiently understood we involve three different questions related to that concept. This gives an opportunity to the student to apply his/her understanding in different situations and decreases the chances of 'just a lucky guess'.

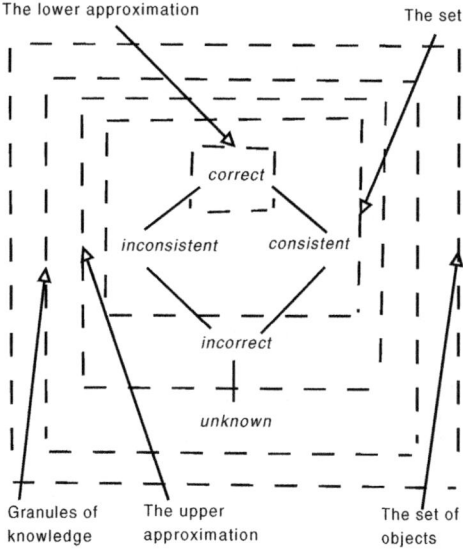

Fig. 1. Rough sets approximations and five truth values

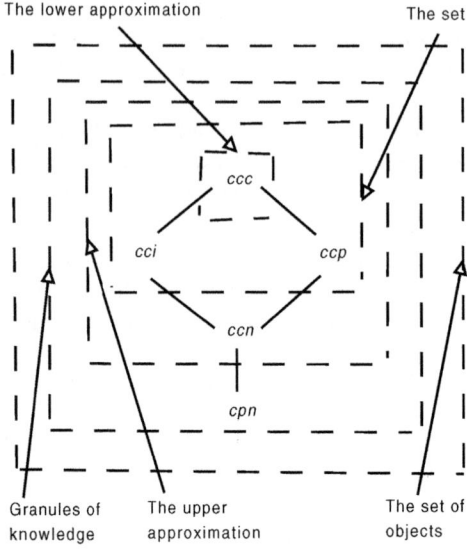

Fig. 2. Local rough set approximations related to correct responses

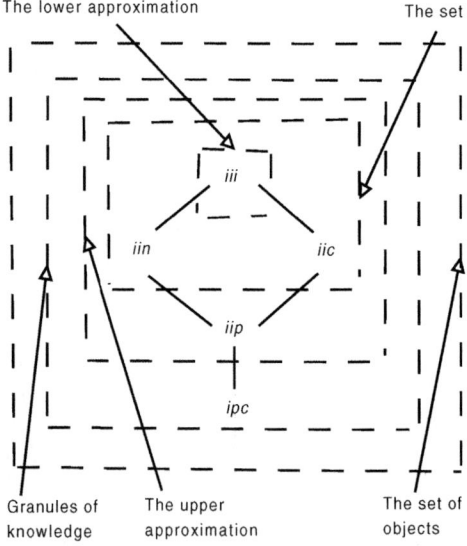

Fig. 3. Local rough set approximations related to incorrect responses

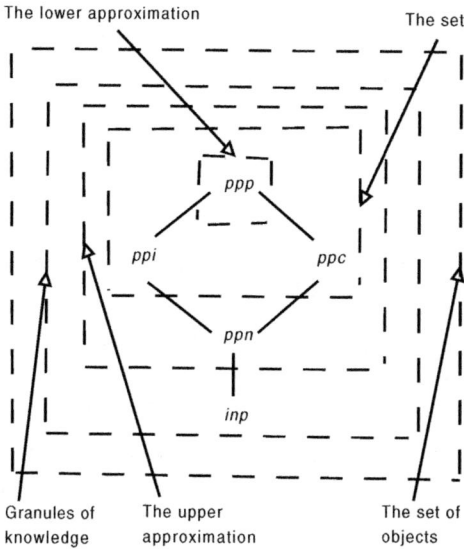

Fig. 4. Local rough set approximations related to possibly known but consistent responses

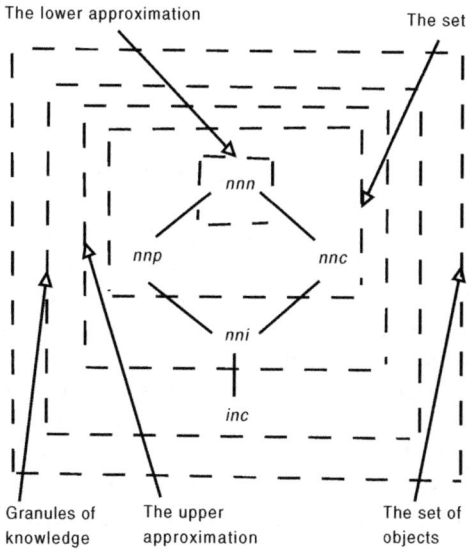

Fig. 5. Local rough set approximations related to inconsistent responses

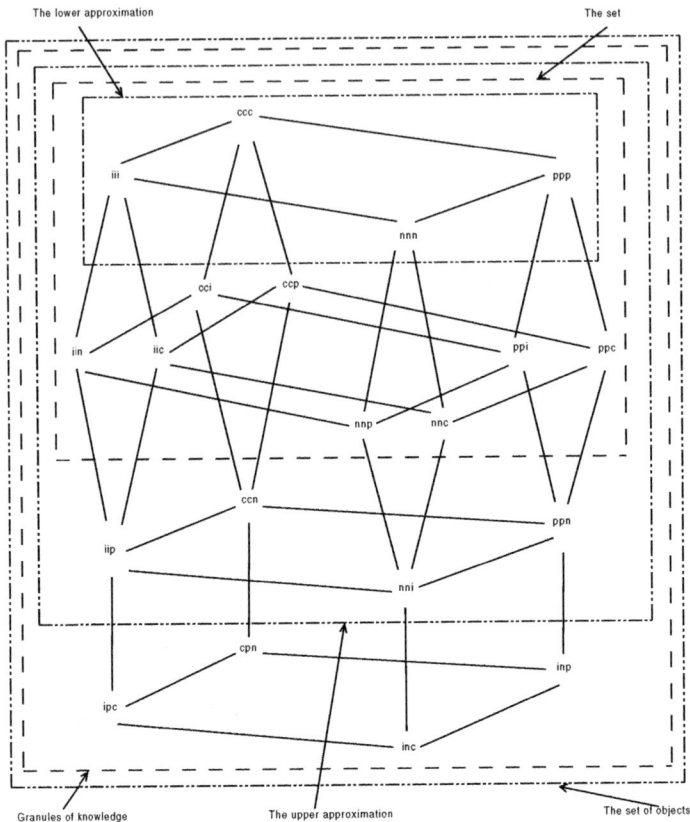

Fig. 6. Homogeneous and inhomogeneous granules

A test consists of three questions. Each question is followed by three alternative answers and a student can choose exactly one of them or skip that question. An alternative answer can be correct c, incorrect i or partially correct p and lack of a response is denoted by n. Thus an outcome of a test will be one of the twenty triplets: *ccc* - three correct answers, *ccp* - two correct answers and one partially correct answer, *ccn* - two correct answers and one unanswered question, *cci* - two correct answers and one incorrect answer, *cpp* - one correct answer and two partially correct answers, *cnn* - one correct answer and two unanswered questions, *cii* - one correct answer and two incorrect answers, *cpn* - one correct answer, one partially correct answer, one unanswered question, *cpi* - one correct answer, one partially correct answer, and one incorrect answer, *cni* - one correct answer, one unanswered question, and one incorrect answer, *ppp* - three partially answers, *ppn* - two partially answers and one unanswered question, *ppi* - two partially answers and one incorrect answer, *pnn* - one partially answer and two unanswered questions, *pii* - one partially answer and two incorrect answers, *pni* - one partially answer, one unanswered question and one incorrect answer, *nnn* - three unanswered questions, *nni* - two unanswered questions and one incorrect answer, *nii* - one unanswered question and two incorrect answers, *iii* - three incorrect answers.

In an attempt to obtain a clear presentation we first group all answer triples in four rough sets approximations as in Fig. 2, Fig. 3, Fig. 4, and Fig. 5 with respect to the number of correct answers and the level of consistency of each answer combination. The four granules in lower approximations Fig. 6 are 'homogeneous' (three answers of the same type, i. e. *ccc*, *iii*, *ppp*, *nnn*) and have no common elements, Fig. 6. The rest of the granules in lower approximations have similar structure, i.e. two answers of the same type. Any two connected by a line inhomogeneous granules have at least one common element.

Test results of a student can take place in the same rough set approximation or in different rough set approximations.

Moving from one 'homogeneous' granule to another 'homogeneous' granule in the lower approximation set indicates a serious change. A student who has such test results is strongly recommended to repeat the test in order to clarify the tendency.

Appearance of a single student consecutive test results in the lower approximation set is of a particular importance to the test designer. It might indicate serious inconsistencies with respect to level of difficulties, formulation and even contents of the pool of questions. Another place to look at is answer alternatives attached to each question. Some of them could be either too obvious, or too vague or simply misleading.

Moving from one 'inhomogeneous' granule to another 'inhomogeneous' granule indicates a moderate change. Appropriate reading materials are suggested before taking another trial.

4   System Description

A system prototype is build as a Web-based application using Apache HTTP server [23], mod_python module [24] and SQLite database [25]. The mod_python module provides programmable runtime support to the HTTP server using Python programming language. The whole application components are

1. Web-based users interface,
2. application logic and application interfaces written in Python, and
3. relational database.

The system architecture is presented in Fig. 7.

The system shown on Fig. 7 can be implemented as a typical three-tiers Web application server architecture. The presentation layer is handled by an Apache Web server. The logic layer is written in Python. The data layer is implemented using SQLite database engine. Python provides a programming environment for implementing script-based handler for dynamic content, data integration and users' software agents. The back end SQLite databases are used to store both static and dynamic data. Apache is a modular Web server that can incorporate a high level scripting language as a module such as for example mod_python. Using mod_python, python interpreter becomes a part of the Web server. SQLite is a small footprint, zero-administration and serverless database system.

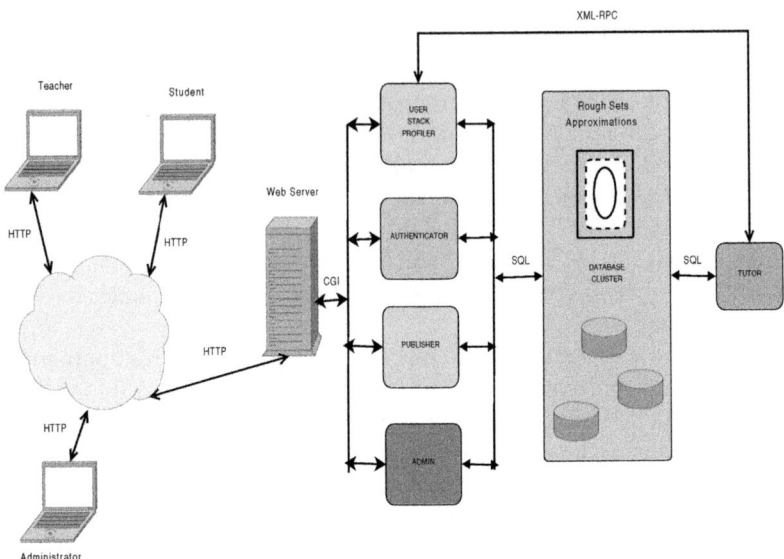

Fig. 7. System architecture

SQLite stores persistence data into files. SQLite thus provides a database platform for multiple databases.

The separation of these units makes it possible to modularly design and implement the system as loosely couple independent sub-systems. Communication framework based on XML-RPC is used to connect the Web application middleware and the intelligent assessment/diagnostic system together. The system is composed of sub-systems, all of which can be written in Python.

The document publisher sub-system dynamically compiles a page to be presented to the user. How the page will look is defined in a template object in relation to the user response, current state variables and activities history. Documents and template objects are read from a common documents database. Tests questions data is read from a common tests database.

The authenticator sub-system authenticates a user during login and creates initial session context in the system if the user provides correct credentials. This sub-system also provides user authorization during an active user's session and is also responsible for session cleanup at user's log off.

The stack profiler sub-system keeps track of user activities history in a stack like data structure in the user database. Each event, like for example response/result of a test or a change of learning flows after following a hint given by the system, is stored in this database. This sub-system provides the percepts to the intelligent tutorial sub-system. The stack profiler receives student's test responses and calculates the final result of the test. The stack profiler provides a user with immediate feed-back.

Analysis of the user's profile is given to the tutor sub- system. This subsystem runs in different processes but operates on the same user database. The tutor sub-system provides a student with intelligent diagnostics and the optimal study flow for that particular student based on her current profile. The hints and diagnostics are written into the user database. The stack profiler which is accessible by the user's browser reads the most recent messages from the tutor sub-system whenever hints or diagnostics are requested by the user. Using a rule-based method the tutor sub-system provides the student with the best study advice to facilitate students' progress in mastering new skills. Since the system is built on different sub-systems the independent sub-system can Be maintained and improved separately. These subsystems are operationally bounded with each other by the information stored in the multiple databases.

5   Conclusion

Evaluating knowledge is related to extracting information from imperfect, imprecise, and incomplete data. Therefore, precise reasoning rules are difficult and some times impossible to use. Applying rough sets approximations facilitates a balance between between accuracy and precision.

Rough set data analysis may be difficult to perform in the presence of a large boundary region.

References

1. Aleven, V., Koedinger, K.R.: Limitations of Student Control: Do Student Know when they need help? In: Gauthier, G., Van Lehn, K., Frasson, C. (eds.) ITS 2000. LNCS, vol. 1839, pp. 292–303. Springer, Heidelberg (2000)
2. Baker, R.S., Corbett, A.T., Koedinger, K.R.: Detecting student misuse of intelligent tutoring systems. In: Lester, J.C., Vicari, R.M., Paraguaçu, F. (eds.) ITS 2004. LNCS, vol. 3220, pp. 531–540. Springer, Heidelberg (2004)
3. Ferreira, U.: A Five-valued Logic and a System. Journal of Computer Science and Technology 4(3), 134–140 (2004)
4. Goodstein, R.L.: Boolean Algebra. Dover Publications, Mineola (2007)
5. Gradel, E., Otto, M., Rosen, E.: Undecidability results on two-variable logics. Archive of Mathematical Logic 38, 313–354 (1999)
6. Guzmàn, E., Conejo, R.: A model for student knowledge diagnosis through adaptive testing. In: Lester, J.C., Vicari, R.M., Paraguaçu, F. (eds.) ITS 2004. LNCS, vol. 3220, pp. 12–21. Springer, Heidelberg (2004)
7. Harper, R.: Correcting computer-based assessments for guessing. Journal of Computer Assisted Learning 19, 2–8 (2003)
8. Immerman, N., Rabinovich, A., Reps, T., Sagiv, M., Yorsh, G.: The boundary between decidability and undecidability of transitive closure logics. In: Marcinkowski, J., Tarlecki, A. (eds.) CSL 2004. LNCS, vol. 3210. Springer, Heidelberg (2004)
9. Koedinger, K.R., McLaren, B.M., Roll, I.: A help-seeking tutor agent. In: Lester, J.C., Vicari, R.M., Paraguaçu, F. (eds.) ITS 2004. LNCS, vol. 3220, pp. 227–239. Springer, Heidelberg (2004)
10. Marek, V.W., Truszczynski, M.: Contributions to the theory of rough sets. Fundamenta Informaticae 39(4), 389–409 (1999)
11. Mayo, M., Mitrovic, A.: Optimising ITS behaviour with Bayesian networks and decision theory. International Journal of Artificial Intelligence in Education 12, 124–153 (2001)

12. Park, C., Kim, M.: Development of a Level-Based Instruction Model in Web-Based Education. In: Luo, Y. (ed.) CDVE 2004. LNCS (LNAI), vol. 3190, pp. 215–221. Springer, Heidelberg (2004)
13. Pecheanu, E., Segal, C., Stefanescu, D.: Content modeling in Intelligent Instructional Environment. LNCS (LNAI), vol. 3190, pp. 1229–1234. Springer-, Heidelberg (2003)
14. Pawlak, Z.: Rough Sets. International Journal of Computer and Information Sciences 11, 341–356 (1982)
15. Pawlak, Z.: Rough Sets: Theoretical Aspects of Reasoning About Data. Kluwer Academic Publishing, Dordrecht (1991)
16. Renkl, A.: Learning from worked-out examples: Instructional explanations supplement self-explanations. Learning and Instruction 12, 529–556 (2002)
17. Santos, C.T., Osòrio, F.S.: Integrating intelligent agents, user models, and automatic content categorization in virtual environment. In: Lester, J.C., Vicari, R.M., Paraguaçu, F. (eds.) ITS 2004. LNCS, vol. 3220, pp. 128–139. Springer, Heidelberg (2004)
18. Schworm, S., Renkl, A.: Learning by solved example problems: Instructional explanations reduce self-explanation activity. In: Gray, W.D., Schunn, C.D. (eds.) Proceeding of the 24th Annual Conference of the Cognitive Science Society, pp. 816–821. Erlbaum, Mahwah (2002)
19. Whitesitt, J.E.: Boolean Algebra and Its Applications. Dover Publications, New York (1995)
20. Wood, D.: Scaffolding, contingent tutoring, and computer-supported learning. International Journal of Artificial Intelligence in Education 12, 280–292 (2001)
21. Yao, Y.Y.: Interval-set algebra for qualitative knowledge representation. In: Proceedings of the Fifth International Conference on Computing and information, pp. 370–374 (1993)
22. http://www.leeds.ac.uk/perception/v4_mrq.html
23. Apache HTTP Server Project, http://httpd.apache.org/
24. Python Programming Language, http://www.python.org/
25. SQLite, http://www.sqlite.org/

An Energy Efficient Instruction Prefetching Scheme for Embedded Processors

Ji Gu and Hui Guo

School of Computer Science and Engineering
The University of New South Wales
Sydney, NSW 2052, Australia
{jigu,huig}@cse.unsw.edu.au

Abstract. Existing instruction prefetching schemes improve performance with significant energy sacrifice, making them unsuitable for embedded and ubiquitous systems where high performance and low energy consumption are all demanded. In this paper, we reduce energy overhead in instruction prefetching by using a simple prefetching hardware/software design and an efficient prefetching operation scheme. Two approaches are investigated: one, Decoded Loop Instruction Cache based Prefetching (DLICP) that is most effective for loop intensive applications; two, enhanced DLICP with the popular existing Next Line Prefetching (NLP) for applications of a moderate number of loops. Our experimental results show that both DLICP and enhanced DLICP deliver improved performance at greatly reduced energy overhead. Up to 21% performance can be improved by the enhanced DLICP at about 3.5% energy overhead, as in comparison to the maximal 11% performance improvement and 49% energy overhead from NLP.

1 Introduction

On-chip cache has been widely used in modern microprocessors to bridge the speed gap between the processor and main memory. Cache exploits the spatial and temporal locality of memory reference to avoid the long latency of memory access from the processor. A high cache hit ratio plays a vital role in the overall system performance. This is especially essential for the instruction cache (I-cache) due to frequent instruction fetch operations; An instruction cache miss will cause the processor stall, hence slowing down the system.

Plenty of techniques have been proposed to reduce I-cache misses. Among them is the instruction prefetching [1][2]- fetching instructions from memory into the cache before they are used so that cache misses can be avoided. However, existing instruction prefetching schemes mainly focus on improving cache performance, often suffering significant energy losses due to a large amount of wasteful over-prefetching operations and/or complicated prefetching hardware components. Nevertheless, low energy consumption is one of the most important design constraints for embedded and ubiquitous systems, especially in the application domain of mobile and ubiquitous computing.

G.S. Tomar et al. (Eds.): UCMA 2010, CCIS 75, pp. 73–88, 2010.

In this paper, we aim to reduce energy overhead in instruction prefetching by using a simple prefetching hardware/software design and an efficient prefetching operation scheme. We investigate two approaches: the decoded loop instruction cache based prefetching (DLICP) and the enhanced DLICP.

The decoded loop instruction cache (DLIC) originates from the decoded instruction buffer (DIB) proposed in [3]. It is a small *tag-less* cache residing between the instruction decoder and the execution unit in the microprocessor to store decoded loop instructions so that fetching and decoding the same set of instructions for the following loop iterations can be avoided, hence reducing energy dissipation in the processor.

We extend this energy-saving technique to instruction prefetching by overlapping the execution of decoded loops with fetching instructions to the cache from memory so that most instructions are available in the cache when they are executed. This approach is effective for loop intensive applications. For applications with a small amount of loops, we enhance the design with the existing Next Line prefetching (NLP) scheme, which has been proved efficient in cache miss reduction for applications with a dominant sequential instruction execution flow [4].

The rest of the paper is organized as follows. Section 2 reviews some existing instruction prefetching methods for cache performance optimization. The structure and working principle of our DLICP scheme is given in Section 3, where the hardware/software codesign and the prefetching operation scheme are detailed. Section 4 presents the experimental setup, results and related discussions. The paper is concluded in Section 5.

2   Related Work

A variety of prefetching techniques have been proposed to improve the traditional instruction cache miss for performance improvement. These can be classified as software based prefetching and hardware based prefetching.

Software prefetching schemes [5][6][7] rely on the compiler to insert prefetch instructions into the program code before the application is executed, which requires a known memory access behavior and a dedicated compiler.

Hardware prefetching is transparent to the software and exploits the status of the program execution to dynamically prefetch instructions for future use. It is more flexible than the software based approach but incurs hardware overhead and increases the complexity of the processor architecture. The hardware based approaches mainly include sequential prefetching and non-sequential prefetching.

Next-Line prefetching [4] utilizes the spatial locality of the program execution is one of the sequential prefetch approaches. On an instruction cache miss, it fetches the current cache miss line and sequentially prefetches the next lines to reduce possible cache misses. The adaptive sequential prefetch method [8] prefetches varying number of cache lines based on different program execution behaviors.

The stream buffer prefetch [9] is another sequential prefetch approach designed specifically for the direct-mapped cache (where conflict cache misses may become a key problem). This approach places the prefetched cache line into a stream buffer and only writes it to the cache when it is actually referenced by the processor to reduce possible conflict cache misses. A downside of this approach is that, in case a referenced data item is missing in both the cache and buffer, the buffer will be flushed by the next cache line. This wastes many prefetched cache lines and makes the prefetch scheme ineffective.

Sequential prefetching is efficient for programs with sequential execution. To handle applications with a large amount of branches, Pierce et al [10] proposed a non-sequential Wrong-Path scheme that prefetches instructions for all branch directions. Stride-directed prefetching [11][12] is another non-sequential approach, which is based on the observation that if a memory address is accessed, the memory location some stride away from the address is likely to be accessed soon. This method examines the memory access behavior for such a potential stride. If the stride is found, cache lines to be prefetched are offset by such a distance. Shadow directory prefetching [13] associates each cache line with a shadow address that points to the next possible cache line. When a cache line is accessed and hit, its shadow-address pointed cache line will be prefetched.

Some non-sequential schemes utilize cache miss prediction for instruction prefetch. Joseph and Grunwald [14] proposed a prediction based prefetching technique, where a Markov model is used to correlate a stream of instruction misses. The predicted miss addresses are stored in the prediction table indexed by the related miss address. The instruction prefetch is triggered when a cache miss occurs. The tag-correlating prefetching [15] is a similar technique. However, they only store the tag bits of the missing instruction addresses to reduce its size. The fetch directed instruction prefetching scheme [16] uses a branch predictor to predict the program execution stream. The branch predictor generates a queue of prefetching targets and the prefetched cache lines are initially stored in an additional prefetch buffer. The prefetched instructions are only written into the cache when they are referenced. A cache miss due to the misprediction has to flush the prefetching target queue and the prefetched instruction buffer.

In branch history guided prefetching [17], Srinivasan et al. propose to correlate the instruction cache misses with branch instructions based on their execution history. They store the correlations in the prefetch table indexed by the address of branch instruction. The prefetches are triggered by the branch instructions when the same correlations are found later during the program execution. Zhang et al. propose the execution history guided prefetching [18] where they correlate the cache misses with every instruction according to the execution history. This scheme has finer granularity than [17]; any instruction (not only the branch instructions) can potentially be the prefetching trigger to allow more prefetching opportunities and effectiveness.

The above hardware-based prefetching schemes are popular techniques for cache performance improvement of the general purpose computer architecture. Most schemes are impractical in mobile or ubiquitous embedded systems, where low energy consumption is of ultimate importance.

In this paper, we aim to reduce energy consumption in instruction prefetching and further improve the prefetching efficiency by effectively paralleling instruction prefetching with the processor execution. We compared our approach with the Next Line Prefetching, which is the most power effective approach among existing prefetching schemes. Experimental results show that our design is more efficient in both power reduction and performance improvement.

3   DLIC-Based Instruction Prefetching

The system architecture with our proposed DLIC-based prefetching scheme is illustrated in Fig. 1. It contains a five-stage pipeline processor, with the decoded loop instruction cache (DLIC) sitting between the instruction decode (ID) stage and execution (EXE) stage; a two-level memory hierarchy, with the separate on-chip instruction cache and data cache, and off-chip main memory, and a memory controller. The memory controller controls memory access in two fashions each operated by *Fetcher* and *Prefetcher*, respectively. For the normal processor execution, *Fetcher* retrieves instructions from cache, or from memory if there is a cache miss; During execution of a decoded instruction loop, *Prefetcher* fetches instructions that are to be executed after the loop but are not yet in the cache.

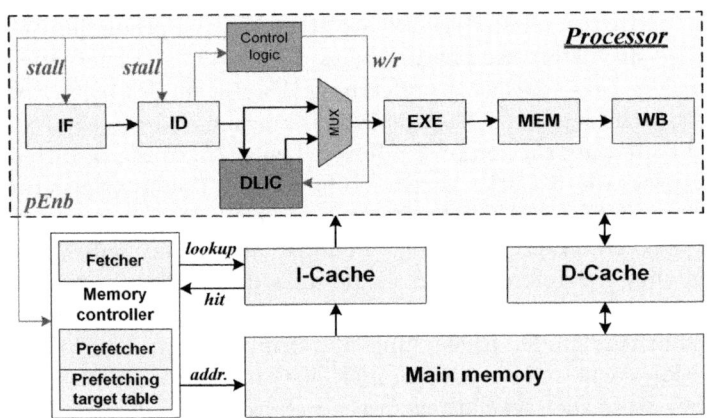

Fig. 1. Architecture for DLIC-based instruction prefetching

It is worth noting that the DLIC structure implemented in this paper has a more ability than the normal decoded instruction buffer. It allows to cache loops of indeterminate loop counts, rather than only cache loops of a known number of iterations in the traditional decoded instruction buffer design. The hardware/software design for the decoded loop instruction cache and an efficient strategy for prefetching operations are elaborated in the following subsections.

3.1   Hardware/Software Design of Decoded Loop Instruction Cache

For a given application, its loop execution behavior can be easily extracted, which makes it possible to use software approach to storing decoded loop instructions so

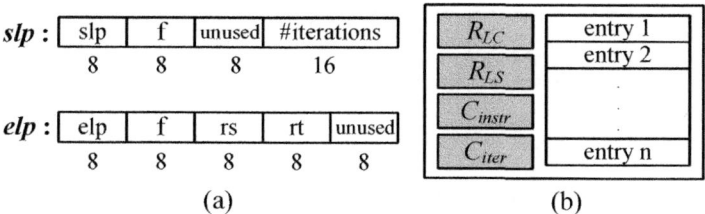

Fig. 2. (a) Formats of special instructions, (b) components in DLIC cache

that associated hardware component can be simplified, hence reducing hardware area cost and energy consumption. We aim at basic loops that are frequent and small in size, which is often the case in most embedded and ubiquitous systems [19]. For such loops, we define two special instructions:

$$\begin{cases} slp \ f, \ \#iterations \\ elp \ f, \ rs, \ rt \end{cases} \tag{1}$$

Instruction *slp* will be inserted at the top of loops, and instruction *elp* the end of loops, to control to store and execute the decoded loop instructions.

The formats of these two instructions (based on SimpleScalar PISA [20] architecture) are illustrated in Fig. 2(a) (More explanation will follow). The hardware components related to the cache operation are given in Fig. 2(b).

Apart from the multiple entries in the DLIC cache for storing decoded instructions, there are two special registers: R_{LC} (for loop count in terms of the number of loop iterations) and R_{LS} (for loop size in terms of the number of instructions in the loop), and two special counters: C_{instr} (for counting number of executed instructions in a loop) and C_{iter} (for counting number of executed loop iterations). The counters are initialized for each loop execution.

Depending on whether the loop count is known at compile time, the instruction pair will have two different treatments, which is controlled by flag *f* in the instruction.

CASE 1: Loops with Determinate Loop Counts

For the loop whose iteration count is known before execution, the flag *f* of the *slp* instruction is set to *0xFF* and the flag in instruction *elp* is set to *0x00*. Examples of such loops are given in Fig. 3 (a) and (b), where both *while-loop* and *for-loop* have a determinate loop count at compile time. Fig. 3 (c) demonstrates the corresponding instructions with the loop count equal to 10.

When executing *slp* with the *0xFF* flag value, the processor saves the *#iterations* value given in the instruction in register R_{LC} and enables the decoded instruction caching function. For each instruction executed in the first loop iteration, its decoded instruction value is sequentially stored in the DLIC cache and counter C_{instr} is incremented by 1. Therefore, at the end of the first iteration when instruction *elp* is encountered, C_{instr} records the number of instructions in the loop. This number is then saved in register R_{LS} (the register for loop

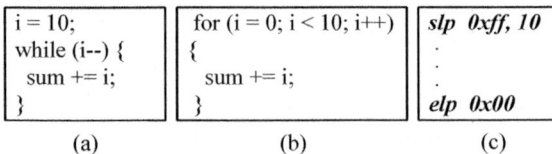

Fig. 3. Determinate loop count: (a) while-loop, (b) for-loop, (c) special instruction pair

size) and C_{instr} is reset to 0 for the next loop iteration. For each loop iteration, counter C_{iter} is incremented by 1 until it reaches the loop count value stored in register R_{LC}, which means the decoded instruction loop is finished and the processor is back to the normal execution state.

CASE 2: Loops with Indeterminate Loop Counts
For loops with unknown loop counts at compile time, as the examples shown in Fig. 4(a) and (b), the f flag for instruction slp is set to $0x00$ and for instruction elp instruction, it is set to $0xFF$.

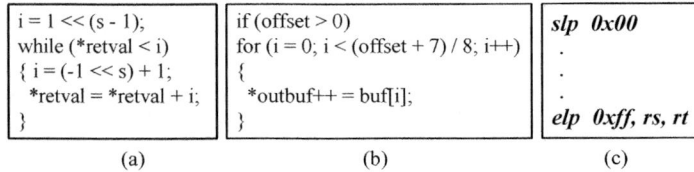

Fig. 4. Indeterminate loop count: (a) while-loop, (b) for-loop, (c) special instruction pair

During executing slp with the $0x00$ flag value, register R_{LC} and counter C_{iter} are not used. But register R_{LS} and counter C_{instr} work in the same way as in Case 1. R_{LS} stores the total number of decoded instructions that should be executed for each of loop iterations and C_{instr} counts the number of executed instructions for the current iteration. Unlike in Case 1, where elp is executed only once for a loop, elp in Case 2 will be executed at the end of each iteration to determine whether the loop is finished. When the condition that registers rs and rt have the same value is satisfied, the loop execution is terminated.

It is worth to note that by using the special instructions and related hardware design, the loop control instructions in the original program code can be removed, reducing the total instruction count of the application, hence improving performance.

3.2   Instruction Prefetching Control Scheme

Due to different program control flows, some prefetched instructions may not be actually used, which not only wastes time but also incurs unnecessary energy lost.

To improve the prefetching efficiency, we try to prefetch instructions on the execution path of high operating frequency. Take the execution control flow shown

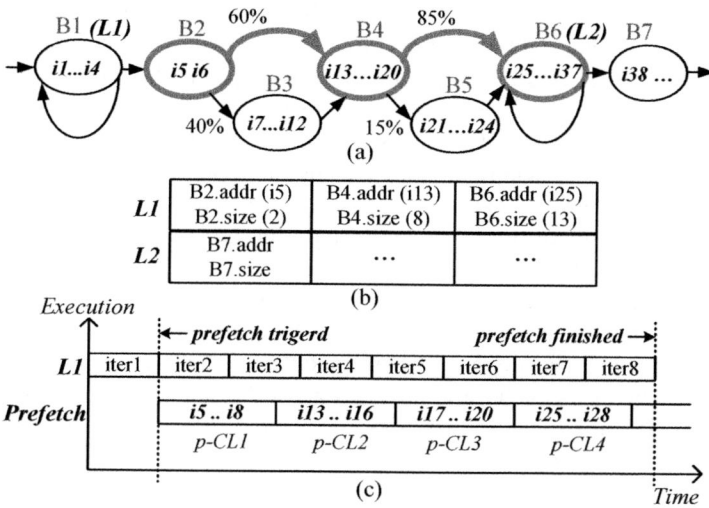

Fig. 5. (a) An example of execution control flow, (b) the corresponding prefetching target table, (c) execution diagram of the DLICP scheme

in Fig. 5 (a) as an example. It contains 7 basic blocks; each block consists of a sequence of instructions. Blocks *B1* and *B6* are loops (*L1, L2*), whose decoded instructions will be cached; between the two loops are four basic blocks connected by two branches, which leads to various execution paths. The frequencies of the branches to different targets are shown in the flow. Blocks *B2*, *B4*, *B6* form an execution path with a higher execution frequency. We, therefore, want to prefetch the instructions in those blocks during the *L1* execution.

The frequent execution path for each decoded loop can be found by profiling and is stored in a table, called prefetching target table (PTT). Each entry in the table associates with a decoded loop and holds the information of the instruction blocks on the frequent execution path. For each instruction block, its start address and size in terms of the number of instructions are provided so that all instructions of the block in the memory can be located by *Prefetcher*. Fig. 5 (b) illustrates the PTT table for the execution flow in Fig. 5(a). The first block in each table entry is always the immediate block of the related loop.

During execution of a decoded loop, we use the PTT table to find the instructions on the frequent execution path and to prefetch them from memory if they are not available in the cache. To explain, we use the execution of *L1* as an example (see Fig. 5 (c) for the execution timing diagram).

Assume L1 has 8 iterations. After the first iteration, all instructions in the loop have been decoded and saved in the DLIC cache. The processor is now in the state for the decoded loop execution, where the Program Counter (PC) is temporarily disabled with its value statically pointing to the instruction immediately after the loop (i.e. instruction *i5* in the example) during the whole decode loop execution.

When the L1 execution enters the second iteration, the instruction prefetching is triggered. The *Prefetcher* (see Fig. 1) searches the PTT table (based on the current PC value) for the first instruction block on the frequent execution path. The block is then checked to see whether instructions of the block are available in the cache, if not, the related cache line(s) will be prefetched; otherwise, continue to the next basic block. This process is repeated for the rest of the instruction blocks in the PTT entry until the execution of the decoded loop is finished, as illustrated in Fig. 5 (c), where a 4-word cache line is assumed and each instruction is one-word long. Here we also assume all instructions on the frequent execution path are not available in the cache and are prefetched in four cache lines (denoted by *p-CL1* to *p-CL4* inFig. 5 (c)).

As can be seen, the cache line size and duration of the decoded loop execution affect the number of instructions that can be prefetched. The larger the cache line and the longer the decoded loop execution, the more instructions can be fetched. But the large cache line may allow *Prefetcher* to fetch instructions that are not needed; for example, instructions *i7, i8* in block *B3* were brought along by prefetching the first cache line *p-CL1*.

3.3   Enhanced DLIC Prefetching

With the DLICP design, the prefetching operation is restricted by the availability of basic loops and distribution of these loops in the program. For an application with a small number of such loops, or the loops are located at the end of the program, only limited prefetching operations can be performed, hence limited cache miss savings. This limitation can be circumvented by incorporating the existing NLP prefetching scheme that always prefetches instructions on a cache miss.

It must be emphasized that the cache miss saving from DLICP does not incur performance overhead because of the parallel prefetching operations (see Fig 5(c)), while the saving from NLP is accompanied with the cache miss performance penalty. With DLIC, such penalties can be reduced. Therefore, combining both DLICP and NLP, we can achieve high cache miss reduction with a smaller performance overhead. This NLP scheme is implemented in the *Fetcher* memory control component in our system (see Fig 1).

4   Experimental Results

To examine the efficiency of our DLIC-based prefetching scheme, we applied it to a set of applications from Motorola's Powerstone [21] and MiBench [22] benchmark suites, which are widely used in the embedded application domain of automotive control, image processing, audio/vedio coding. The reference input data of each program are used in our experiments.

4.1   Experimental Setup

Fig. 6 shows our experimental setup. We selected the Simplescalar PISA [20] as the target processor instruction set architecture. An in-house VHDL model of PISA processor, generated using the commercial tool ASIPMeister [23], was

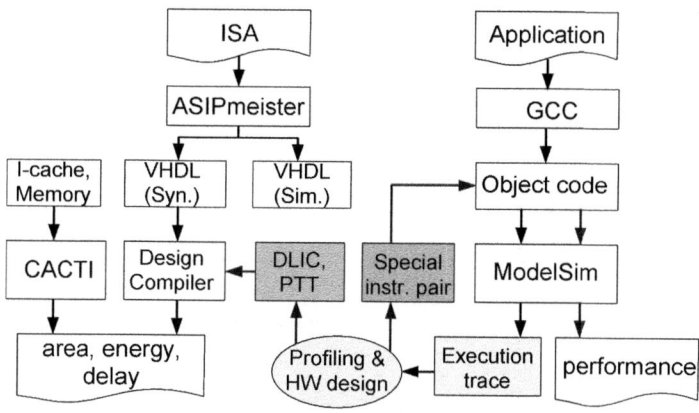

Fig. 6. Experimental setup

used as the platform for the application simulation. The experiment started with a given application written in C, compiled by the simplescalar-gcc cross compiler and then simulated on the VHDL model. The loop behavior of each application was extracted from the execution instruction trace, based on which the frequent basic loops were modified with special instruction pairs for decoded loop instruction caching. Hardware designs of the related prefetching schemes were then integrated to the processor model for evaluating their logic cost and energy overhead with Synopsys DesignCompiler. The area and energy consumption for the I-cache and main memory were obtained from CACTI 5 [24], which is a widely used cache and memory model for evaluation of access time, area, and energy consumption.

In our experiment, we assumed the on-chip I-cache was 2-way set associative of 2K bytes, with the line size of 32 bytes. The small 2K I-cache is suitable for ubiquitous embedded systems where the costs are very restrained.

4.2 Performance Improvement

Performance can be evaluated in terms of total execution time, which is the product of the total number of clock cycles used and the clock cycle time when running an application. Cache performance affects the execution clock cycles. Therefore, we first investigate the cache performance.

Cache Misses and Miss Penalties in Prefetching

With prefetching, apart from the two normal cache states (*cache hit* and *cache miss*), there is an extra case – the data requested is not yet in the cache, but is on the bus, being transferred from the memory to the cache by prefetching. We refer to this special case as **false miss** since it does not incur a new memory access.

Unlike a real cache miss, which has a fixed miss penalty, the false miss has a reduced and varying miss penalty due to the parallel operations of processor

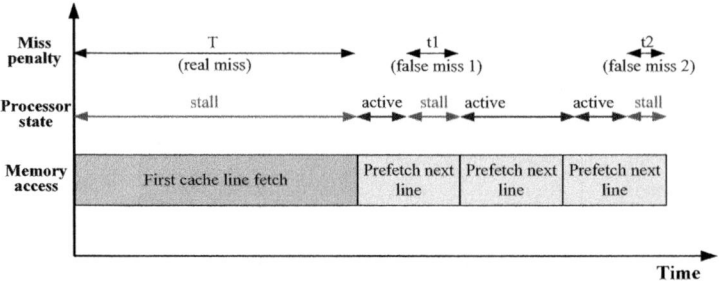

Fig. 7. Cache miss penalty

and prefetching, as illustrated in Fig. 7, where on a real miss, the miss penalty is fixed (T); for the false misses, the miss penalty varies (t_1 and t_2 in the example), depending on the relative time needed for the processor to finish available instructions during the next line prefetching.

Table 1 lists the measurements of real cache misses (namely, false misses being excluded) when running different applications under the three prefetching schemes (columns 3-5). For a comparison, the baseline design without prefetching is also given in the table (column 2). The baseline is a 2 way associative instruction cache of 2K bytes and has a cache line of 32 bytes. The cache access time is assumed as 1 clock cycle. The last row shows the average value. The normalized cache miss ratios as compared to the baseline design, are plotted in Fig. 8.

As can be seen from the measurements, NLP provides a better cache-miss reduction (an average of 34.6%) than DLICP (22.1%). This is due to the insufficient basic loops available. Therefore, fewer prefetching operations in DLICP were performed, hence less cache misses reduced. NLP is not restricted by the loop patterns in the application program. Two exceptions are the *salsa* and *seal* benchmarks, where there are a large amount of basic loops evenly distributed

Table 1. Cache Misses

	Baseline	NLP	DLICP	Ehd' DLICP
blit	59	34	49	31
crc	57	33	45	29
dijkstra	19774	12440	17845	17828
g3fax	1072	914	1028	992
jpeg	66186	52192	64849	64796
qsort	83	55	62	43
rc4	98	53	69	62
rijndael	1020	600	684	656
salsa	446	280	265	242
seal	1908	1278	1123	1114
sha	3197	2163	2581	2563
AVG	8536.4	6367.5	8054.5	8032.4

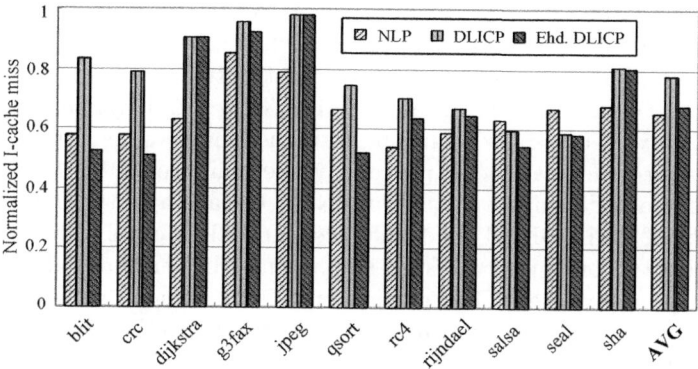

Fig. 8. Normalized I-cache miss ratio

in the program such that DLICP can reduce more cache misses than NLP by prefetching. With combined DLICP and NLP, we can, however, improve the cache miss reduction by an average of 32.4%.

Performance Improvement

Since prefetching does not affect the processor instruction set architecture and organization, all designs can have the same clock cycle time. NLP executes an equal number of instructions for a given application as the baseline design. DLICP and enhanced DLICP, however, need extra special instructions inserted in the program at compile time and thus the number of executed instructions are different from the baseline design. The system performance of the three designs can be, therefore, compared in terms of total execution clock cycles.

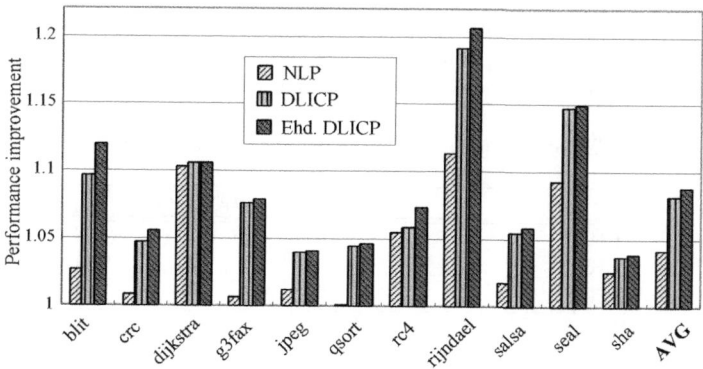

Fig. 9. Performance improvement

Fig. 9 shows the program total execution cycles normalized to the baseline design without instruction prefetching and the cache miss penalty is 32 clock cycles. As can be seen, both DLICPs present better results than NLP for all applications; For some applications, such as *blit*, *crc*, and *rijndael*, the enhanced DLICP achieves remarkably higher performance improvement than DLICP. Up to 21% performance can be improved by the enhanced DLICP, as compared to the maximal 11% improvement from NLP. On average, the performance improvements of NLP, DLICP and enhanced DLICP are 4.2%, 8.2% and 8.9%, respectively. The enhanced DPLCP is two times better than NLP in terms of performance improvement. The performance improvement is largely due to the savings of *false cache misses* which are significant in NLP. *False cache misses* suffer a longer processor stall than *cache hits*.

4.3   Implementation Costs and Energy Overhead Reduction

To evaluate the area costs and power consumption of prefetching, we have modeled the NLP, DLICP and enhanced DLICP designs in VHDL and each design are estimated using Synopsys Design Compiler. For the cache and memory, we first obtain their area costs and the energy consumption per access from CACTI 5 [24], based on which we then estimate the total energy overhead of the prefetching. Both the Synopsys Design Compiler and CACTI simulations are based on the 65nm technology.

Table 2 lists the simulation results. Rows 2 to 4 show the area cost of each prefeching logic and their energy consumption per memory access. The costs of the decoded instruction cache (DLIC) used by the two DLIC prefetching schemes are given in row 5; followed by the costs of the Prefetching target table (PTT) that is used by Enhanced DLICP. It is worth to mention that because most applications have loops with less than 32 instructions and each number of decoded control signals for each instruction is less than 192 in our instruction architecture, we therefore set the decoded cache size as 32×192 bits. The last two rows (Rows 7&8) present the area and energy consumption of cache and memory per memory access measured from CACTI.

As can be seen from the table the NLP scheme shows small overheads as compared to our two DLICP approaches, in terms of area cost and energy consumption per memory access. However, energy per access of the off-chip instruction

Table 2. Area Cost and Energy Consumption

	Area [μm^2]	Energy/Access [pJ]
NLP	1070	0.54
DLICP	3561	1.31
Eh'd. DLICP	3932	1.61
DLIC (32 x 192bits)	118958	20.41
PTT (32 x 40bits)	18915	3.62
I-cache (2KB)	184255	42.66
I-memory (2MB)	3652402	1871.44

memory is much higher than that of the on-chip I-cache, 50x times higher for a 2M memory over the 2KB cache, which results in the savings on the overall energy overhead.

Energy Overhead Reduction

Some instructions prefetched may never be used, namely never accessed by the processor before being flushed from the cache. Such useless prefetches do not aid performance improvement rather than waste valuable energy.

Table 3 shows our measurements of the total prefetches and useless prefetches when executing each application. As can be seen from the table, both DLICP schemes demonstrate low useless prefetches (336 and 350, respectively) as compared to the 4199 found in NLP.

Fig. 10 gives the percentages of useless prefetches over the total prefetches number, which shows the DLICP is most effective – of all prefetches, 39.5% are useless and the rest contribute to the cache hits (data accessed from cache instead of memory), hence performance improvement and energy reduction.

To calculate the energy overhead of the three prefetching schemes, we use the run-time profile of the I-cache, main memory, and the prefetching logic activities (number of accesses, number of hits/misses, number of useless prefetches, etc.) collected during simulation, together with the energy per access values as given in Table 2.

Fig. 11 shows the results when using the main memories of different sizes ranging from 64K to 4M bytes, where the energy overheads (displayed in lines) are normalized to the energy consumption of main memory access (in columns) of the baseline design without the prefetching function.

It can be seen from the plots, NLP consumes much higher energy than the other two schemes, consistently about 49% energy consumption over all different memory configurations. This is because such energy overhead is decided largely by the

Table 3. Useless Prefetches

	NLP		DLICP		Enh. DLICP	
	#pref.	useless	#pref.	useless	#pref.	useless
blit	34	9	12	2	34	6
crc	33	9	14	2	37	9
dijkstra	12440	5106	3108	1179	3130	1184
g3fax	914	756	162	118	215	135
jpeg	52192	38198	2339	1002	2414	1024
qsort	55	27	33	12	57	17
rc4	53	8	47	18	66	30
rijndael	600	180	564	228	627	263
salsa	280	114	415	234	454	250
seal	1278	648	1288	503	1301	507
sha	2163	1129	1012	396	1060	426
AVG	6367.5	4198.5	817.6	335.8	854.1	350.1

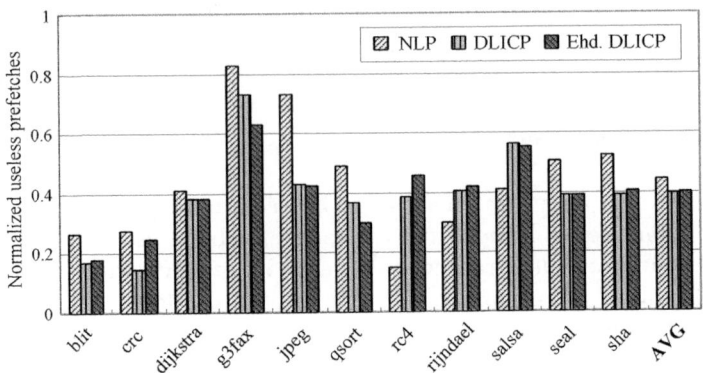

Fig. 10. Normalized useless prefetches

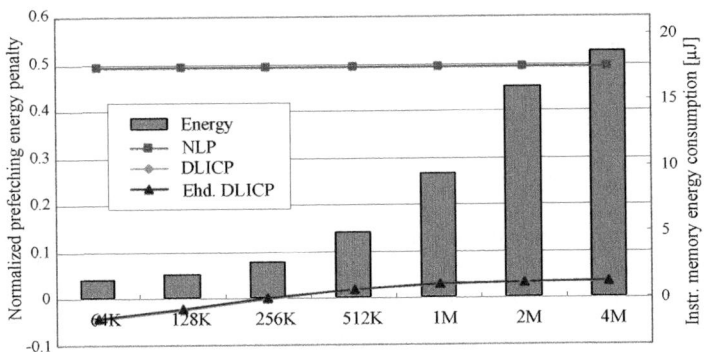

Fig. 11. Energy penalties of the three schemes normalized to the energy consumption of the instruction memory of the baseline design

useless prefetching, where the number of useless prefetchings of NLP is about 49% of the I-cache miss in the baseline design. On the other hand, the energy overheads of DLICP and enhanced DLICP are under 3.5%. When the main memory size is reduced to below 256KB, even energy savings can be observed. For example, a saving of 4.5% can be achieved when the main memory is as small as 64KB. This is because the energy overhead of DLICP prefetching can be canceled out by the energy savings due to fetching decoded loop instructions from the energy-efficient DLIC instead from the energy-expensive I-cache during execution.

5   Conclusions

Our experiment results show that even Next Line Prefetching (NLP), an existing low cost prefetching scheme, incurs a high energy overhead (around 49% of memory energy consumption), which is impractical for energy-aware embedded and ubiquitous systems.

In this paper, we presented an energy efficient instruction prefetching design for ubiquitous embedded systems with two-level memory hierarchy (on-chip cache and off-chip memory). We exploit the decoded loop cache and maximally parallelize the instruction prefetching with the decoded loop execution to reduce instruction cache misses while at a low energy overhead. The decoded loop cached based prefetching (DLICP) can be enhanced with the NLP approach for applications, where limited loops available for the decoded loop cache.

Our experiments show that both DLICP schemes outperform NLP with improved performance and much less energy overhead, an average of 3.5% extra energy consumption as compared to 49% extra energy consumed by NLP. For some applications, the enhanced DLICP scheme offers a markedly better performance than DLICP. Up to 21% performance can be improved by the enhanced DLCIP, as compared to the 11% performance improvement by NLP.

References

1. Smith, A.J.: Sequential program prefetching in memory hierarchies. Computer 11(12), 7–21 (1978)
2. Hennessy, J.L., Patterson, D.A.: Computer Architecture: A Quantitative Approach, 3rd edn. Elsevier Science Pte Ltd., Amsterdam (2003)
3. Bajwa, R.S., Hiraki, M., Kojima, H., Gorny, D.J., Nitta, K., Shridhar, A., Seki, K., Sasaki, K.: Instruction buffering to reduce power in processors for signal processing. IEEE Transactions on Very Large Scale Integration (VLSI) Systems 5(4), 417–424 (1997)
4. Smith, J.E., Hsu, W.C.: Prefetching in supercomputer instruction caches. In: Proceedings of the 1992 ACM/IEEE Conference on Supercomputing, pp. 588–597 (1992)
5. Gornish, E.H., Granston, E.D., Veidenbaum, A.V.: Compiler-directed data prefetching in multiprocessors with memory hierarchies. In: Proceedings of the 4th International Conference on Supercomputing, pp. 354–368 (1990)
6. Luk, C.K., Mowry, T.C.: Cooperative prefetching: compiler and hardware support for effective instruction prefetching in modern processors. In: Proceedings of the 31st Annual ACM/IEEE International Symposium on Microarchitecture, pp. 182–194 (1998)
7. Cristal, A., Santana, O., Cazorla, F., Galluzzi, M., Ramirez, T., Pericas, M., Valero, M.: Kilo-instruction processors: Overcoming the memory wall. IEEE Micro 25(3), 48–57 (2005)
8. Dahlgren, F., Dubois, M., Stenstroem, P.: Sequential hardware prefetching in shared-memory multiprocessors. IEEE Transactions on Parallel and Distributed Systems 6(7), 733–746 (1995)
9. Jouppi, N.P.: Improving direct-mapped cache performance by the addition of a small fully-associative cache and prefetch buffers. In: Proceedings of the 17th Annual International Symposium on Computer Architecture, pp. 364–373 (1990)
10. Pierce, J., Mudge, T.: Wrong-path instruction prefetching. In: Proceedings of the 29th Annual ACM/IEEE International Symposium on Microarchitecture, pp. 165–175 (1996)
11. Fu, J.W.C., Patel, J.H., Janssens, B.L.: Stride directed prefetching in scalar processors. ACM SIGMICRO Newsletter 23(1-2), 102–110 (1992)

12. Kim, S., Veidenbaum, A.V.: Stride-directed prefetching for secondary caches. In: Proceedings of the 1997 International Conference on Parallel Processing, pp. 314–321 (1997)
13. Charney, M.J., Puzak, T.R.: Prefetching and memory system behavior of the spec95 benchmark suite. IBM Journal of Research and Development 41(3), 265–286 (1997)
14. Joseph, D., Grunwald, D.: Prefetching using markov predictors. IEEE Transactions on Computers 48(2), 121–133 (1999)
15. Hu, Z., Martonosi, M., Kaxiras, S.: Tcp: Tag correlating prefetchers. In: Proceedings of the 9th International Symposium on High-Performance Computer Architecture, pp. 317–326 (2003)
16. Reinman, G., Calder, B., Austin, T.: Fetch directed instruction prefetching. In: Proceedings of the 32nd Annual ACM/IEEE International Symposium on Microarchitecture, pp. 16–27 (1999)
17. Srinivasan, V., Davidson, E.S., Tyson, G.S., Charney, M.J., Puzak, T.R.: Branch history guided instruction prefetching. In: Proceedings of the 7th International Conference on High Performance Computer Architecture, pp. 291–300 (2001)
18. Zhang, Y., Haga, S., Barua, R.: Execution history guided instruction prefetching. In: Proceedings of the 16th International Conference on Supercomputing, pp. 199–208 (2002)
19. Villarreal, J., Lysecky, R., Cotterell, S., Vahid, F.: A study on the loop behavior of embedded programs. Technical Report UCR-CSE-01-03, University of California, Riverside (2002)
20. Burger, D., Austin, T.: The Simplescalar Tool Set, Version 2.0. tech. report CS-TR-1997-1342, Dept. of Computer Science, Univ. of Wisconsin, Madison (1997)
21. Scott, J., Lee, L.H., Arends, J., Moyer, B.: Designing the low-power m-core architecture. In: International Sympsium on Computer Architecture Power Driven Microarchitecture Workshop, pp. 145–150 (1998)
22. Guthaus, M.R., Ringenberg, J.S., Ernst, D., Austin, T.M., Mudge, T., Brown, R.B.: Mibench: A free, commercially representative embedded benchmark suite. In: IEEE 4th Annual Workshop on Workload Characterization, pp. 83–94 (2001)
23. Itoh, M., Higaki, S., Takeuchi, Y., Kitajima, A., Imai, M., Sato, J., Shiomi, A.: Peas-iii: An asip design environment. In: Proceedings of the 2000 IEEE International Conference on Computer Design, pp. 430–436 (2000)
24. Thoziyoor, S., Muralimanohar, N., Ahn, J.H., Jouppi, N.P.: Cacti: An integrated cache and memory access time, cycle time, area, leakage, and dynamic power model. Technical Report HPL-2008-20, HP Laboratories (2008)

EFL/ESL Textbook Selection in Korea and East Asia - Relevant Issues and Literature Review

Robert C. Meurant

Director, Institute of Traditional Studies; Seojeong College University,
Yongam-Ri 681-1, Eunhyun-Myeon, Yangju-Si, Gyeonggi-Do, Seoul, Korea 482-863
Ph.: +82-10-7474-6226
rmeurant@me.com
http://web.me.com/rmeurant/INSTITUTE/HOME.html

Abstract. EFL/ESL departments periodically face the problem of textbook selection. Cogent issues are that non-native speakers will use L2 English mainly to communicate with other non-native English speakers, so an American accent is becoming less important. L2 English will mainly be used in computer-mediated communication, hence the importance of L2 Digital Literacy. The convergence of Information Communication Technologies is radically impacting Second Language Acquisition, which is integrating web-hosted Assessment and Learning Management Systems. EFL/ESL textbooks need to be compatible with blended learning, prepare students for a globalized world, and foster autonomous learning. I summarize five papers on EFL/ESL textbook evaluation and selection, and include relevant material for adaptation. Textbooks are major sources of contact with the target language, so selection is an important decision. Educators need to be systematic and objective in their approach, adopting a selection process that is open, transparent, accountable, participatory, informed and rigorous.

Keywords: EFL/ESL, Textbook evaluation and selection, online literacy assessment, L2 digital literacy, Second Language, SLA, Convergence, E-learning, Learning Management Systems, LMS, blending learning, autonomous learning, Information Communication Technologies, Korea, East Asia.

1 Introduction

EFL/ESL departments periodically face the problem of selecting a textbook series for their courses. In Section 2, I raise certain cogent issues that are relevant to the process of textbook selection, and which should be taken into consideration. These include firstly the kind of English taught, and the (lack of) importance of accent, given that most L2 English use is in communication with other non-native speakers. Secondly, L2 digital literacy is of emerging importance given that most L2 English use will be in computer-mediated communication. As I elsewhere address [1], the future of EFL pedagogy should also be taken into account, given the radical impact that Information Convergence Technologies and their Convergence are having on Second Language Acquisition, particularly the integration of newly developed web-based assessment

G.S. Tomar et al. (Eds.): UCMA 2010, CCIS 75, pp. 89–102, 2010.

systems such as Cognero [2], popular Learning Management Systems such as Moodle [3], and the rapid development of hybrid L2 education. The blending of textbooks with digital media should be considered, in tandem with the use of the computer and the Internet in the classroom and the growing importance of ancillary digital resources. Thirdly, the textbook selection process itself needs to be transparent and accountable, encourage teacher participation, and allow for a change in direction that offers students a more relevant preparation for a rapidly globalizing world that confronts students and new graduates with critical issues that urgently need to be addressed. Fourthly, the primary aims in textbook selection should be considered, and I suggest these include the importance of diversity, the recognition of multilingualism and bilingualism as normal, and the fostering of autonomous language learning.

In Section 3, I summarize five papers from the extensive literature on textbook evaluation and selection, with the intention of providing an entrée for teachers wishing to explore this literature further. Sample checklists and criteria are included which can readily be adapted for use with custom textbook evaluation and selection. I then conclude with general recommendations for the textbook selection process.

2   Relevant Considerations for the Choice of a Textbook Series for Native English Teacher EFL Programs in East Asia

2.1   Should Students Be Learning American or International English?

Graddol argues that, as the number of non-native speakers of English in the world surpasses the number of native speakers, non-native speakers are increasingly likely to use their English as a medium of communication with other non-native speakers, and *not* with native speakers - whose presence may in fact inhibit their use of English [4]. Korean learners of English express frustration at not being able to converse with native speakers; at a recent KATE conference, Professor Obari observed that in a similar Japanese situation, accent has become much less important, and Japanese EFL learners at Aoyama Gakuin University, Tokyo, are being taught International English, with a diverse range of accents from teachers of various nationalities [5].

2.2   What Is the Future of EFL Pedagogy?

Profound transformations throughout society, which stem from new Information Communication Technologies and their evolutionary Convergence, are beginning to radically impact EFL theory and practice.

a. My research [6] suggests that the primary use of English by non-Native speakers will increasingly be in *digital computer-mediated* communication - rather than face-to-face - and in *online* research, business and publishing. Hence, at a variety of conferences and publications, I am strongly advocating the intentional teaching of L2 English Digital Literacy skills within EFL/ESL pedagogy [7], [8], [9].
b. My experience in Korean EFL suggests that as yet only a few native English-speaking teachers (NEST) currently use Learning Management Systems (LMS). I use the Moodle LMS, together with the Cognero online assessment system

(which I am beta-testing), so that all tasks, quizzes and exams in all courses are computer-based [10], with all tests web-hosted. More native faculty will likely adopt LMS, so demand for classroom computer facilities and for Internet-friendly educational material will rapidly rise. Textbooks therefore need to be compatible with the developing provision of e-learning and m-learning, and publishers such as Cambridge University Press are already implementing LMS sites that complement texts [11].

c. It is critical therefore that the texts chosen are forwardly compatible with this profession-wide shift to computer-based LMS that enable blended learning environments. In a textbook choice made by Gyeongsang National University some years ago, publishers provided teachers with free exam-writing software together with question banks on the textbooks, which were useful to prepare quizzes and exams. A recent textbook choice made by Sejong University favored texts with digital resources such as interactive presentation whiteboard software and video DVDs.

d. In similar fashion, texts need to be technologically up-to-date, and Internet savvy, with scope for digital User Generated Content to be developed and integrated. Provision for multimedia presentation in class and online access to relevant study resources are similar factors that can greatly enhance textbook value.

2.3   How Are the Textbooks to Be Selected?

The textbook selection process provides an opportunity to signal a shift in political ambience in Korean educational culture, which has historically tended to place what Westerners may regard as a bewildering weight on non-productive administration at the expense of critically needed innovation [12]. This shift could encourage what Obama in his first speech as President identified as key factors of transparency and accountability. Important in this is the provision for and support of informed debate, recently identified by Shaffer at a recent KATE conference as a quality noticeably absent in the native English-speaking teacher education of English in Korea [13].

a. Thus, teacher involvement in the choice of textbook series should be encouraged. Gyeongsang National University faculty formed an ad hoc textbook committee to which any interested teacher could join. Staff individually and collectively explored options, and arranged presentations by interested publishers and distributors. Final recommendations were made, and acted upon by the Administration.

b. Does a single choice of textbook series even need to be made? An alternative would be to have a period of trying the best three recommendations in different classes and at different levels for perhaps a year; or even to decide to use diverse textbook series in different classes by different teachers.

c. This potential change of textbook offers an excellent opportunity for university departments to change direction and offer their students a more relevant discourse and preparation for an increasingly globalized world. It is now evident that *"steady as she goes"* and the concomitant *"après moi les deluge"* philosophies are simply inappropriate and even irresponsible when confronted with the pressing realities of global warming, global pollution, environmental degradation, the mass extinction of species, falling birth rates, aging societies in Korea and Japan, local and regional uncertainties including critical shifts in Korean attitudes and society, fluctuating tensions with North Korea concerning their nuclear weapon program and alternative de facto unification with South Korea, and the anticipated rise of China to Super-Power status. Textbook selection could and should favor content-based instruction that addresses such critical issues among others.

2.4   What Then Are the Primary Aims in Textbook Selection?

In addition to providing an excellent pedagogical tool, the textbook series would, I trust, celebrate and strengthen diversity, no easy matter given Korea's tradition of ethnic homogeneity [14].

a. As presented at Suzanne Flynn's keynote speech at SICOLI-2009, multilingualism and bilingualism are being recognized as natural and normal, with monolingualism emerging as merely a restricted case of multilingualism [15].
b. Selection of a suitable textbook series could help contribute to what Obari has identified as a key issue in second language acquisition - that of fostering autonomous learning in the foreign language classroom [16].

I do not regard these considerations as exhaustive, but trust they will contribute towards a helpful discussion and open debate. I turn now to a brief review of research literature that addresses the processes of textbook evaluation and selection.

Table 1. Garinger's Checklist for ESL Textbook Selection [17]

Yes/No   A. Program and Course

_____ Does the textbook support the goals and curriculum of the program?
_____ Is the textbook part of a series, and if so, would using the entire series be appropriate?
_____ Are a sufficient number of the course objectives addressed by the textbook?
_____ Was this textbook written for learners of this age group and background?
_____ Does the textbook reflect learners' preferences in terms of layout, design, and organization?
_____ Is the textbook sensitive to the cultural background and interests of the students?

　　　　　　　B. Skills

_____ Are the skills presented in the textbook appropriate to the course?
_____ Does the textbook provide learners with adequate guidance as they are acquiring these skills?
_____ Do the skills that are presented in the textbook include a wide range
of cognitive skills that will be challenging to learners?

　　　　　　　C. Exercises and Activities

_____ Do the exercises and activities in the textbook promote learners' language development?
_____ Is there a balance between controlled and free exercises?
_____ Do the exercises and activities reinforce what students have already learned
and represent a progression from simple to more complex?
_____ Are the exercises and activities varied in format so that
they will continually motivate and challenge learners?

　　　　　　　D. Practical Concerns

_____ Is the textbook available?
_____ Can the textbook be obtained in a timely manner?
_____ Is the textbook cost-effective?

3 A Survey of EFL Textbook Selection Literature Relevant to Korean and East Asian Native Teacher EFL/ESL Programs

There is an extensive literature on the process of textbook selection for EFL/ESL purposes. This section is intended to serve merely as an entrée to that literature, in the hope that the decision-making process may be better informed, and result in an appropriate choice that properly serves the needs of students and teachers. I summarize five papers on the selection of EFL/ESL textbooks, and include relevant checklists and criteria. The full papers can be accessed from the links provided.

3.1 Textbook Selection for the ESL Classroom

Dawn Garinger, Southern Alberta Institute of Technology.
Eric Digest, EDO-FL-02-10, December 2002.
http://www.cal.org/resources/Digest/0210garinger.html

Garinger [18], in a concise insightful guide, observes that researchers have advocated a variety of approaches, but in practice the process is often based on personal preference, and affected by factors unrelated to pedagogy including limited awareness of available texts, budget restrictions, and limited availability. A practical, thorough and straightforward method is to analyze the options according to program issues, working from broad to specific, and eliminating unsatisfactory texts at each stage.

Matching the Textbook to the Program and the Course. Educators should thoroughly examine the curriculum, and decide whether to choose a textbook series or to use individual texts for each course. They should then consider how well the text and course objectives match one another, and identify the appropriateness of the text for the intended learners. Layout, design and organization should be considered, as students and teachers want visually stimulating material that is well organized and easy to follow. Textbook content should be sensitive to cultural backgrounds, and allow for comfortable and safe discussion of cross-cultural experiences and concerns.

Review the Skills Presented in the Textbook. While improving learner language skills is generally the main purpose of ESL programs, the skills taught and how they are taught differs by course and program, so the effectiveness of each text in helping learners acquire necessary skills must be considered, by asking questions such as whether the text focus on the skills it claims to focus on, and whether it actually teaches these skills or merely provides practice for existing skills? The importance of cognitive skills should not be overlooked, particularly higher order skills of analysis, synthesis and evaluation. Several published evaluation checklists use Bloom's taxonomy [19] to assess the processes and skills that textbooks require learners to perform.

Review Exercises and Activities in the Textbook. Four key questions need to be answered: Do the exercises and activities contribute to learners' language acquisition? Are the exercises balanced in their format, containing both controlled and free practice? Are the exercises progressive as students move through the textbook? Are the exercises varied and challenging?

Weighing Practical Considerations. Such issues, including availability and cost, are often deciding factors and must be acknowledged.

Garinger concludes that the textbook selection decision affects teachers, students and the overall classroom dynamic, and it is probably *one of the most important decisions facing ESL educators.* She provides a checklist (see Table 1 above) that may be adapted as a tool to help ESL educators decide which textbooks may be most appropriate for their classes.

Table 2. Ansary and Babii's Set of Universal Features of EFL/ESL Textbooks [20]

APPROACH
- Dissemination of a vision (theory or approach) about
  - o the nature of language
  - o the nature of learning
  - o how the theory can be put to applied use

CONTENT PRESENTATION
- Stating purpose(s) and objective(s)
  - o For the total course
  - o For individual units
- Selection and its rationale
  - o Coverage
  - o Grading
  - o Organization
  - o Sequencing
- Satisfaction of the syllabus
  - o To the teacher
    - ▪ Providing a guide book
    - ▪ Giving advice on the methodology
      - ▪ Giving theoretical orientations
      - ▪ Key to the exercises
    - ▪ Supplementary materials
  - o To the student
    - ▪ Piecemeal, unit-by-unit instruction
    - ▪ Graphics (relevant, free from unnecessary details, colorful, etc.)
    - ▪ Periodic revisions
    - ▪ Workbook
    - ▪ Exercise and activities
      - ▪ In the classroom
      - ▪ Homework
      - ▪ Sample exercises with clear instructions
      - ▪ Varied and copious
    - ▪ Periodic test sections
    - ▪ Accompanying audio-visual aids

PHYSICAL MAKE-UP
- Appropriate Size & weight
- Attractive layout
- Durability
- High quality of editing and publishing
- Appropriate title

ADMINISTRATIVE CONCERNS
- Macro-state policies
- Appropriate for local situation
  - o Culture
  - o Religion
  - o Gender
- Appropriate Price

Table 3. Ansary and Babii's Scheme #1 of Tucker's Criteria [21]

C. A. Tucker (1975)

I. INTERNAL CRITERIA	VS	MS
PRONUNCIATION CRITERIA		
Completeness of presentation		
Appropriateness of presentation		
Adequacy of practice		
GRAMMAR CRITERIA		
Adequacy of pattern inventory		
Appropriate sequencing		
Adequacy of drill model & pattern display		
Adequacy of practice		
CONTENT CRITERIA		
Functional load		
Rate & manner of entry & reentry		
Appropriateness of contexts and situations		
II. EXTERNAL CRITERIA		
Authenticity of language		
Availability of supplementary materials		
Adequate guidance for non-native teachers		
Competence of the author		
Appropriate level for integration		
Durability		
Quality of editing and publishing		
Price & Value		

Table 4. Ansary and Babii's Scheme #2 of Ur's Criteria [22]

ELT Textbooks Evaluating Scheme

Penny Ur (1996)

Criterion	importance	
Objectives explicitly laid out in an introduction, and implemented in the material		
Approach educationally and socially acceptable to the target community		
Clear attractive layout; print easy to read		
Appropriate visual materials available		
Interesting topic and tasks		
Varied topics and tasks, so as to provide for different learners levels, learning styles, interests, etc.		
Clear instructions		
Systematic coverage of syllabus		
Content clearly organized and graded (sequenced by difficulty)		
Periodic review and test sections		
Plenty of authentic language		
Good pronunciation explanation and practice		
Good vocabulary explanation and practice		
Good grammar explanation and practice		
Fluency practice in all four skills		
Encourages learners to develop own learning strategies and to become independent in their learning		
Adequate guidance for the teacher, not too heavy preparation load		
Audio cassettes		

3.2   Universal Characteristics of EFL/ESL Textbooks:
A Step Towards Systematic Textbook Evaluation

Hasan Ansary and Esmat Babaii, Shiraz University.
The Internet TESL Journal, Vol. VIII, No. 2. February 2002.
http://iteslj.org/Articles/Ansary-Textbooks/

Ansary and Babaii [23] outline a summary of common-core characteristics of standard EFL/ESL textbooks, after investigating whether a de facto consensus exists over what makes a good text. They scrutinize textbook reviews and evaluation checklists, hoping to achieve a "canonizing discourse", which may lead to universal textbook evaluation schemes.

Checklist Approach to Textbook Evaluation. Any textbook should be used judiciously; teachers have not been confident about judgment methods and qualifying decisions, and textbook selection has generally been made in haste and with a lack of systematically applied criteria. The literature on textbook selection and/or evaluation procedure is considerable, with scholars suggesting different ways to help teachers become more systematic and objective in their approach. Checklists have been offered based on generalizable criteria, using various methods of assessment. They compare two checklist approaches as samples, and identify the fundamental problem of such checklists as being their dependence on swings of the theoretical pendulum.

The Current Study. They consider prior checklists to have had little practical utility, and textbook selection so far to have been ad hoc: teachers make decisions on unreliable and simplistic criteria such as appropriateness of grammar presentation, functional load, competence of the author, and even popularity. They indirectly explore whether a de facto consensus exists over what makes a good EFL/ESL textbook, aiming to lead to the development of universal textbook evaluation schemes.

Method. Ten EFL/ESL textbook evaluation schemes and ten EFL/ESL textbook reviews served as their corpus and were carefully scrutinized, with points made by reviewers for and against being recorded. The same procedure identified the elements that checklist producers introduce as important evaluation and selection criteria. Common summary characteristics were sought.

Results. They present a set of features they consider universal to EFL/ESL textbooks (refer Table 2 above, see also Tables 3 and 4 above), according to Approach, Content Presentation, Physical Make-up, and Administrative Concerns.

Discussion and Application. While no neat formula or system provides a definitive way to judge, the application of a set of universal characteristics may help make textbook evaluation coherent, systematic and thoughtful. A system of textbook evaluation should thus include:

- a predetermined data-driven theory-neutral collection of universal characteristics of EFL/ESL textbooks, discrete and precise enough to help define one's preferred situation-specific criteria,
- a system within which one may ensure objective, quantified assessment,
- a rating method that can provide the possibility for a comparative analysis,
- a simple procedure for recording and reporting the evaluator's opinion,
- a mechanism by which the universal scheme may be adapted and/or weighted to suit particular requirements,

- a rating trajectory that makes possible a quick and easy display of the judgments on each and every criterion, and
- a graphic representation to provide a visual comparison between the evaluator's preferred choices as an archetype and their actual realizations in a particular textbook under scrutiny.

Ansary and Babaii conclude with a reminder that there is a limit to what teaching materials can do, as texts are just simple tools. What is important is what teachers can do with them - the emphasis being not on providing interesting materials, but on doing interesting things with those materials.

3.3 ESL Textbook Evaluation Checklist

Joshua Miekley, University of Cincinnati.
The Reading Matrix, Vol. 5, No. 2, September 2005.
http://www.readingmatrix.com/reading_projects/miekley/project.pdf

Miekley [24] provides educators with valuable checklists for evaluating ESL/EFL reading textbooks, and explains how to use them, with the intention of making the textbook selection process more efficient and reliable. Textbook choice is important, as teachers spend much time using textbooks in class. Checklist questions are based on recent research or developed checklists.

Checklist Approach to Textbook Evaluation. While textbooks have dramatically improved in quality, the selection process has not become easier. The vast array of textbooks means textbook selection gravitates between the two extremes of educators asking too many questions, and of educators choosing a textbook with little or no evaluation - which then becomes the center of the curriculum until another haphazardly chosen textbook replaces it. In contrast, his checklists provide administrators and teachers with the tools necessary for making an informed evaluation, balancing the need for thorough evaluation with the need for efficiency. These checklists are based on recent second language instruction research, and on checklists for general textbook evaluation. The most vital aspect is Byrd's emphasis [25] on the text being a good fit for teachers, students and the curriculum.

Miekley's checklists I. Textbook and III. Teacher's Context are provided here in Table 5 (space does not permit replicating his useful II. Teacher's Manual checklist); although these are specifically tailored for the evaluation of ESL *reading* textbooks, they could readily be adapted for general EFL texts. He concludes by recognizing that while his checklists are effective as is, educators should add additional questions when appropriate. Each context will require adaptation. Since reading is so important in second language learning, research on L2 reading should be utilized both in classroom instruction and during the textbook selection process, and these checklists provide valuable assets towards accomplishing that goal.

3.4 Textbook Evaluation and ELT Management: A South Korean Case Study

David R. A. Litz, UAE University Al Ain.
Asian EFL Journal, 2005.
http://www.asian-efl-journal.com/Litz_thesis.pdf

Table 5. Miekley's Textbook Evaluation Checklists: Textbook [26] and Context [27]

I. TEXTBOOK	Excellent	Good	Adequate	Poor	Absent	Mandatory	Optional	N.A.
A. Content								
i. Is the subject matter presented either topically or functionally in a logical, organized manner? (1,2,3)	4	3	2	1	0	M	O	N
ii. Does the content serve as a window into learning about the target language culture (American, British, etc.)? (2,18)	4	3	2	1	0	M	O	N
iii. Are the reading selections authentic pieces of language? (5,10)	4	3	2	1	0	M	O	N
iv. Compared to texts for native speakers, does the content contain real-life issues that challenge the reader to think critically about his/her worldview? (1,2,3,7,21)	4	3	2	1	0	M	O	N
v. Are the text selections representative of the variety of literary genres, and do they contain multiple sentence structures? (1,13)	4	3	2	1	0	M	O	N
B. Vocabulary and Grammar								
i. Are the grammar rules presented in a logical manner and in increasing order of difficulty? (1,2,3)	4	3	2	1	0	M	O	N
ii. Are the new vocabulary words presented in a variety of ways? (2,3,12)	4	3	2	1	0	M	O	N
iii. Are new vocabulary words presented at an appropriate rate so the text is understandable and students able to retain new vocabulary? (1,2,3,5)	4	3	2	1	0	M	O	N
iv. Are the new vocabulary words repeated in subsequent lessons to reinforce their meaning and use? (1,2,3)	4	3	2	1	0	M	O	N
v. Are students taught top-down techniques for learning new vocabulary words? (7,8,9,11)	4	3	2	1	0	M	O	N
C. Exercises and Activities								
i. Are there interactive and task-based activities that require students to use new vocabulary to communicate? (1,2,3,5)	4	3	2	1	0	M	O	N
ii. Does the textbook instruct students to read for comprehension? (6)	4	3	2	1	0	M	O	N
iii. Are top-down and bottom-up reading strategies used? (17)	4	3	2	1	0	M	O	N
iv. Are students given sufficient examples to learn top-down techniques for reading comprehension? (7,8,9,10)	4	3	2	1	0	M	O	N
v. Do the activities facilitate students' use of grammar rules by creating situations in which these rules are needed? (1,2,3)	4	3	2	1	0	M	O	N
vi. Does the text make comprehension easier by addressing one new concept at a time instead of multiple new concepts? (2,3)	4	3	2	1	0	M	O	N
vii. Do the exercises promote critical thinking of the text? (2)	4	3	2	1	0	M	O	N
D. Attractiveness of the Text and Physical Make-up								
i. Is the cover of the book appealing? (1,2,3)	4	3	2	1	0	M	O	N
ii. Is the visual imagery of high aesthetic quality? (1,2,3,14)	4	3	2	1	0	M	O	N
iii. Are the illustrations simple enough and close enough to the text that they add to its meaning rather than detracting from it? (1)	4	3	2	1	0	M	O	N
iv. Is the text interesting enough that students will enjoy reading it? (15)	4	3	2	1	0	M	O	N
III. TEACHER'S CONTEXT								
A. Is the textbook appropriate for the curriculum? (1,2,19,20)	4	3	2	1	0	M	O	N
i. Does the text coincide with the course goals? (1,2,3,19,20)	4	3	2	1	0	M	O	N
B. Is the textbook appropriate for the students using it? (1,2)	4	3	2	1	0	M	O	N
i. Is the text free of material that might be offensive? (1,6,16)	4	3	2	1	0	M	O	N
ii. Are the examples and explanations understandable? (1)	4	3	2	1	0	M	O	N
iii. Will students enjoy reading the text selections? (1,2,3,15)	4	3	2	1	0	M	O	N
iv. Will the content meet students' felt needs for learning English or can it be adapted for this purpose? (2,3)	4	3	2	1	0	M	O	N
C. Are the textbook and teacher's manual appropriate for the teacher who will be teaching from them? (1,2,4)	4	3	2	1	0	M	O	N
i. Is the teacher proficient enough in English to use the teacher's manual? (1)	4	3	2	1	0	M	O	N

Table 6. Litz's Teacher Textbook Evaluation Form [28]

TEACHER TEXTBOOK EVALUATION FORM
*** PLEASE NOTE:1 = HIGHLY DISAGREE   10 = HIGHLY AGREE ***

1	2	3	4	5	6	7	8	9	10

A   *Practical Considerations:*
1. The price of the textbook is reasonable.
2. The textbook is easily accessible.
3. The textbook is a recent publication.
4. A teacher's guide, workbook, and audio-tapes accompany the textbook.
5. The author's views on language and methodology are comparable to mine
   (Note: Refer to the 'blurb' on the back of the textbook).

B   *Layout and Design:*
6. The textbook includes a detailed overview of the functions,
   structures and vocabulary that will be taught in each unit.
7. The layout and design is appropriate and clear.
8. The textbook is organized effectively.
9. An adequate vocabulary list or glossary is included.
10. Adequate review sections and exercises are included.
11. An adequate set of evaluation quizzes or testing suggestions is included.
12. The teacher's book contains guidance about how the textbook can be used to the utmost advantage.
13. The materials objectives are apparent to both the teacher and student.

C   *Activities:*
14. The textbook provides a balance of activities (Ex. There is an even distribution of
    free vs. controlled exercises and tasks that focus on both fluent and accurate production).
15. The activities encourage sufficient communicative and meaningful practice.
16. The activities incorporate individual, pair and group work.
17. The grammar points and vocabulary items are introduced in motivating and realistic contexts.
18. The activities promote creative, original and independent responses.
19. The tasks are conducive to the internalization of newly introduced language.
20. The textbook's activities can be modified or supplemented easily.

D   *Skills:*
21. The materials include and focus on the skills that I/my students need to practice.
22. The materials provide an appropriate balance of the four language skills.
23. The textbook pays attention to sub-skills -
    i.e. listening for gist, note-taking, skimming for information, etc.
24. The textbook highlights and practices natural pronunciation (i.e. - stress and intonation).
25. The practice of individual skills is integrated into the practice of other skills.

E   *Language Type:*
26. The language used in the textbook is authentic - i.e. like real-life English.
27. The language used is at the right level for my (students') current English ability.
28. The progression of grammar points and vocabulary items is appropriate.
29. The grammar points are presented with brief and easy examples and explanations.
30. The language functions exemplify English that I/my students will be likely to use.
31. The language represents a diverse range of registers and accents.

F   *Subject and Content:*
32. The subject and content of the textbook is relevant to my (students') needs
    as an English language learner(s).
33. The subject and content of the textbook is generally realistic.
34. The subject and content of the textbook is interesting, challenging and motivating.
35. There is sufficient variety in the subject and content of the textbook.
36. The materials are not culturally biased and they do not portray any negative stereotypes.

G   *Conclusion:*
37. The textbook is appropriate for the language-learning aims of my institution.
38. The textbook is suitable for small-medium, homogeneous, co-ed classes of university students.
39. The textbook raises my (students') interest in further English language study.
40. I would choose to study/teach this textbook again.

Litz [29] observes ELT textbooks play an important role in language classrooms, but there has been widespread debate in the ELT profession on their actual role. Texts need to be of acceptable quality, and appropriate to the learners for whom they are being used. It is essential therefore to establish and apply a wide variety of relevant and contextually appropriate criteria for textbook evaluation. A complex evaluation process undertaken at SungKyunKwan University was used to determine the overall pedagogical value and suitability of the book towards their specific language program.

Appendices include forms for Student Profile, Student Needs Analysis, Student Textbook Evaluation Form (with Practical Considerations, Layout and Design, Activities, Skills, Language Type, Subject and Content, and Overall Consensus), and in Table 6 above, Teacher Textbook Evaluation Forms (with similar headings). (N.B. numerical scales of 1-10 for each item are not included here for reasons of space). These could readily be adapted for further research, evaluation and selection.

3.5   Examining the Importance of EST and ESL Textbooks and Materials: Objectives, Content and Form

> Nooreen Noordin and Arshad Abdul Samad, Universiti Putra Malaysia.
> International Educators Program (no date).
> http://rumutha.ru.funpic.de/Examining_the_Importance
> _of_EST_and_ESL_Textbooks_and_Materials.doc

Noordin and Samad [30] examine just how far the prescribed textbooks used in ESL classrooms provide the necessary tools in preparing learners for the transition of language skills across disciplines. For most teachers, textbooks provide the foundation for the content of lessons, the balance of the skills taught, and the kinds of language practice the students engage in during class activities. The textbook becomes the major source of contact ESL learners have with the language, apart from teacher input.

Under *Framework*, they cover Syllabus, Progression, Integration of Skills, and Cohesion; under *The Units*, Length of Unit, Presentation, Practice, Variety and regularity, and Clarity of purpose; under *Subject Matter*, Interest; under *Form*, Visual Appeal, and Illustrations. They conclude that EST materials must create an interest that will assist learners in acquiring linguistic competence and increase their confidence levels. Although the goals of EST (English for Science and Technology) include increasing language proficiency, the materials used in its teaching should not be completely language based. Instead it should have a prominent visual bias. EST materials need to enhance students' visual literacy, and audio-visual elements such as video clips and sound files should be a compulsory element in all EST materials.

4   Conclusion

I have first raised a number of general considerations that are relevant to the evaluation and selection of EFL/ESL textbooks, and which I trust will stimulate debate. Issues that should be considered include the kind of English taught whether American or International, the need for L2 Digital Literacy in English, the future of EFL pedagogy and the radical impact of Information Communication Technologies and their Convergence. These effects include blended language education, digital media, and online assessment and learning management systems. Diversity, multilingualism and autonomous learning are also relevant issues. There is a wide scope of research literature addressing the evaluation and selection for textbooks for EFL/ESL purposes, of which I have then provided just a brief survey, with the intention of providing interested teachers with an entrée to the field. This research is pertinent to the selection processes of textbook series (or individual textbooks) for Korean and East Asian native teacher programs, and should inform them. Bearing in mind that - other than native teacher input - the textbook is the major source of contact with the target language, textbook selection is clearly one of the most important decisions facing EFL/ESL educators. That process benefits from teachers becoming more systematic and objective in their approach. I therefore argue that the selection process should be - and needs to be - open, transparent, accountable, participatory, informed and rigorous.

References

1. Meurant, R.C.: Applied Linguistics and the Convergence of Information Communication Technologies. The Opoutere Press, Auckland (2010)
2. Cognero: Cognero Full-Circle Assessment, http://www.cognero.com/
3. Moodle: Welcome to the Moodle Community! http://moodle.org/
4. Graddol, D.: The future of English? (Electronic version). britishcouncil.org, British Council English (2002), http://www.britishcouncil.org/english/pdf/future.pdf
5. Obari, H.: Integration of e-learning and m-learning in teaching EFL in Japan. In: The KATE 2009 International Conference: Across the Borders: Content-based Instruction in the EFL Contexts, p. 249 (2009)
6. Meurant, R.C.: Second Survey of Korean College EFL Student Use of Cell Phones, Electronic Dictionaries, SMS, Email, Computers and the Internet to address L1:L2 Language Use Patterns and the Associated Language Learning Strategies Used in Accessing Online Resources. In: Advances in Information Sciences and Services - Special Issue on ICCIT 2007, vol. 2, pp. 240–246. Advanced Institute of Convergence Information Technology (AICIT), Gyeongju (2007)
7. Meurant, R.C.: The Key Importance of L2 Digital Literacy to Korean EFL Pedagogy: College Students Use L2 English to Make Campus Video Guides with Their Cell Phone Videocams, and to View and Respond to Their Videos on an L2 English Language Social Networking Site. IJHIT: the International Journal of Hybrid Information Technology 1(1), 65–72 (2008); SERSC (Science and Engineering Research Support Center), Daejeon
8. Meurant, R.C.: The Significance of Second Language Digital Literacy - Why English-language Digital Literacy Skills Should be Fostered in Korea. In: CPS Series Proceedings of ICCIT 2009, pp. 369–374. IEEE Computer Society, Los Alamitos (2009)
9. Meurant, R.C.: Developing Critical L2 Digital Literacy through the Use of Computer-Based Internet-Hosted Learning Management Systems such as Moodle. In: Communications in Computer and Information Science CCIS #60: Multimedia, Computer Graphics and Broadcasting, pp. 76–83. Springer, Heidelberg (2009)
10. Meurant, R.C.: Computer-based Internet-hosted Assessment of L2 Literacy: Computerizing and Administering of the Oxford Quick Placement Test in ExamView and Moodle. In: Communications in Computer and Information Science CCIS #60: Multimedia, Computer Graphics and Broadcasting, pp. 84–91. Springer, Heidelberg (2009)

11. English 360, in partnership with Cambridge University Press,
    http://www.english360.com/
12. Kohls, L.R.: Learning to Think Korean: A Guide to Living and Working in Korea. Intercultural Press, Yarmouth (2001)
13. David Shaffer, D.: Discerning the Characteristics of the Professional Development-Inclined NEST. In: The KATE 2009 International Conference: Across the Borders: Content-based Instruction in the EFL Contexts (2009)
14. Breen, M.: The Koreans Who They Are, What They Want, Where Their Future Lies, 2nd edn. Thomas Dunne Books, St. Martin's Griffin (2004)
15. Flynn, S.: Multilingualism and the Human Capacity for Language. In: Current Issues in Linguistic Interfaces, Proceedings of the SICOLI-2009 Seoul International Conference on Linguistic Interfaces. Hankook Munhwasa, Seoul (2009)
16. Obari, H., Goda, Y., Shimoyama, Y., Kimura, M.: Mobile Technologies and Language Learning in Japan - Learn Anywhere, Anytime (n.d.)
17. Garinger, D.: Textbook Selection for the ESL Classroom, Eric Digest, EDO-FL-02-10, p. 2 (2002), http://www.cal.org/resources/Digest/0210garinger.html
18. Ibid, pp. 1–2
19. Bloom, B.S. (ed.): Taxonomy of educational objectives: The classification of educational goals: Handbook I, cognitive domain. Longmans Green, New York (1956)
20. Ansary, H., Babii, E.: Universal Characteristics of EFL/ESL Textbooks: A Step Towards Systematic Textbook Evaluation. The Internet TESL Journal VIII(2), 6–7 (2002), http://iteslj.org/Articles/Ansary-Textbooks/
21. Ansary, Babii, op. cit., Appendix 1
22. Ansary, Babii, op. cit., Appendix 2
23. Ansary, Babii, op. cit., pp. 1–9
24. Miekley, J.: ESL Textbook Evaluation Checklist. The Reading Matrix 5(2) (2005), http://www.readingmatrix.com/reading_projects/miekley/project.pdf
25. Byrd, P.: Textbooks: Evaluation and selection and analysis for implementation. In: Celce-Murcia, M. (ed.) Teaching English as a second or foreign language, 3rd edn. Heinle & Heinle, Boston (2001)
26. Miekley, op. cit., p. 4
27. Miekley, op. cit., p. 5
28. Litz, D.R.A.: Textbook Evaluation and ELT Management: A South Korean Case Study. Asian EFL Journal, 43–45 (2005), http://www.asian-efl-journal.com/Litz_thesis.pdf
29. Ibid
30. Noordin, N., Samad, A.A.: Examining the Importance of EST and ESL Textbooks and Materials: Objectives, Content and Form. International Educators Program (n.d.), http://rumutha.ru.funpic.de/Examining_the_Importance_of_EST_and_ESL_Textbooks_and_Materials.doc

Fujisaki Model Based Intonation Modeling
for Korean TTS System

Byeongchang Kim[1], Jinsik Lee[2], and Gary Geunbae Lee[2]

[1] School of Computer and Information Communication Engineering,
Catholic University of Daegu, Gyeongbuk, South Korea
bckim@cu.ac.kr
[2] Department of Computer Science and Engineering,
Pohang University of Science and Technology (POSTECH), Pohang, South Korea
{palcery,gblee}@postech.ac.kr

Abstract. One of the enduring problems in developing high-quality TTS (text-to-speech) system is pitch contour generation. Considering language specific knowledge, an adjusted Fujisaki model for Korean TTS system is introduced along with refined machine learning features. The results of quantitative and qualitative evaluations show the validity of our system: the accuracy of the phrase command prediction is 0.8928; the correlations of the predicted amplitudes of a phrase command and an accent command are 0.6644 and 0.6002, respectively; our method achieved the level of "fair" naturalness (3.6) in a MOS scale for generated F0 curves.

Keywords: intonation modeling, pitch contour generation, Fujisaki model, speech synthesis.

1 Introduction

1.1 Intonation in Korean

So far, several methods have been used to produce high-quality speech in TTS(Text-To-Speech) systems. Some prosodic properties in the produced speech increases intelligibility and naturalness of the speech itself. In general, prosody means audible changes in pitch, loudness and syllable length.

In [1], the intonation structure of standard (=Seoul) Korean has two prosodic units: intonational phrase (IP) and accentual phrase (AP). An IP is marked by a boundary tone with final lengthening. Based on the shape of F0 contour on the IP final syllable, at least nine boundary tones have been identified (L%, H%, LH%, HL%, LHL%, HLH%, HLHL%, LHLH%, LHLHL%). On the other hands, an AP is marked by a phrasal tone, THLH (T=H if the AP initial segment is aspirated or tense, T=L otherwise) without final lengthening.

Also, F0 tends to gradually decline in the course of an utterance (declination), which is separate from the F0 movement inside each phrase. Thus, it is desirable for an intonation model to have two different components: long- and short-term components. The long-term component should be able to model F0 declination and its reset

G.S. Tomar et al. (Eds.): UCMA 2010, CCIS 75, pp. 103–111, 2010.

which may appear at major phrasal boundaries. The short-term component should reflect local F0 variations induced by boundary and phrasal tones.

1.2 Fujisaki Model

Fujisaki model [2] provides means for such a representation of F0 curve. In the model, F0 contour is mathematically formulated as the superposition of two filters as the following equations.

$$\ln F_0(t) = \ln F_b + \sum_{i=1}^{I} A_{p_i} G_p(t - T_{0_i})$$
$$+ \sum_{j=1}^{J} A_{a_j} \left[G_a(t - T_{1_j}) - G_a(t - T_{2_j}) \right] \tag{1}$$

$$G_p(t) = \begin{cases} \alpha^2 t \exp(-\alpha t) & t \geq 0 \\ 0 & t < 0 \end{cases} \tag{2}$$

$$G_a(t) = \begin{cases} \min[1 - (1 + \beta t) \exp(-\beta t), \ \gamma] & t \geq 0 \\ 0 & t < 0 \end{cases} \tag{3}$$

Phrase and accent commands are used as excitations to produce a slow-varying long-term phrase component G_p and a fast-varying short-term accent component G_a, respectively. The symbols in the equations stand for

F_b : baseline value of F0
I : number of phrase commands,
J : number of accent commands,
A_p : amplitude of a phrase command,
A_a : amplitude of an accent command,
T_0 : timing of a phrase command,
T_1 : onset of an accent command,
T_2 : offset of an accent command,
α : natural angular frequency of the phrase control,
β : natural angular frequency of the accent control,
γ : relative ceiling level of accent components.

2 Methods

Fujisaki model has been successfully applied on several languages such as Japanese, Chinese, English, German, Greek, Korean, Spanish, and Swedish [3]. Until now, however, linguistically motivated language specific knowledge has not been incorporated. The following subsections provide the linguistic knowledge investigated for Korean and adapted in the Fujisaki framework.

2.1 Fujisaki Parameter Extraction

There is no analytic solution to the inverse of Fujisaki model. Thus, to infer the phrase and accent commands, usually approximation techniques are adopted. In [4], a multi-stage approach is proposed, which performs a spectral decomposition in low and high frequency components of F0 contour.

(1) The first step is a quadratic spline stylization of the curve. F0 values for un-voiced and short pauses are interpolated, and micro-prosodic variations are smoothed. (2) Then, the smoothed F0 contour is decomposed into two components by passing through high- and low-pass filters. Onsets and offsets of an accent command are de-tected in high frequency contour, and the onsets of a phrase command are detected in low frequency contour. (3) Finally, this initial command parameter sequence is refined by a hill-climbing search to minimize the overall mean square error.

However, regardless of linguistic knowledge, the estimated command parameter sequence may not represent a prosodic phenomenon effectively, even though it is suitable for generating a F0 curve close to original one. Thus, considering linguistic features, the following two constraints are used to reconsider the initial command parameter sequence before entering step (3), which is illustrated in **Fig. 1**.

The reset of F0 declination may appear at major phrasal boundaries; a phrase command is moved to the nearest IP boundary.

A phrasal tone appears on each syllable in an AP, and so does a boundary tone at the IP final syllable; an accent command is imposed on each syllable.

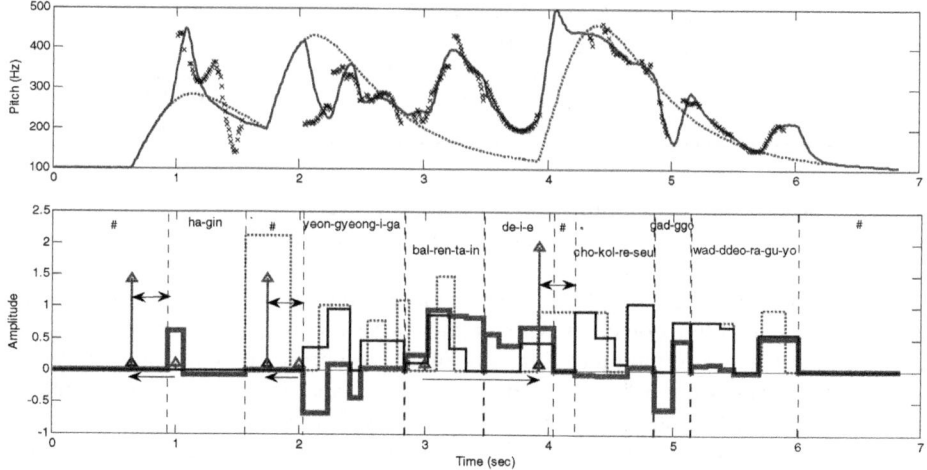

Fig. 1. Reconfiguration and refinement of an initial command parameter sequence for a sentence "In fact, Yeon-gyeong brought a chocolate in Valentine's Day'. In the upper one, ex-tracted pitch values (blue 'x' signs) are represented along with the corresponding Fujisaki curve: a red dotted line – phrase components; a green solid line – phrase components plus ac-cent components. In the lower one, phrase commands (stems) and accent commands (stairs) are represented. Initial command parameters (red dotted) are reconfigured (to blue solid) and then refined (to green thick solid). Phrase commands are moved to 0.3 seconds before (bi-direction arrows) the nearest IP boundary (uni-direction arrows).

2.2 Machine Learning Features

In [5] and [6], amplitudes (A_p and A_a) and timings (T_0, T_1, and T_2) are predicted using artificial neural networks with text and speech features. Various features contribute performance improvement, but most of the features are irrelevant to command parameters (no significant correlation, especially with timings). In this work, the features including linguistic ones are explored and employed in prediction. A major difference with the related works is that timings do not have to be considered, because phrase and accent commands are set to be assigned on a near IP boundary and each syllable, respectively.

Table 1 shows the set of features to predict the presence of a phrase command with their correlations. For each space-delimited orthographic word[1], the absence and presence of a phrase command are coded as 0 and 1. In fact, some of the features do not have an individually significant correlation, but they contribute to prediction improvement by ensemble. An explanation of the features in Table 1 follows:

Table 1. Set of features F and their correlations r for the presence of a phrase command P (PC: phrase command)

F #	Description	r (F, P)
1	Index # of word in sentence from begin.	0.0298
2	Index # of word in sentence from end	0.1445
3	Length of sentence in seconds	0.1275
4	Length of preceding pause in seconds	0.2680
5	Distance to preceding PC in seconds	0.1387
6	Distance to preceding PC in syllables	0.0526
7	Preceding orthographic mark	0.1339
8	Preceding part-of-speech tag	0.1087

F1-F3. The position of a word in a sentence is represented; an absolute position is directly represented by F1 and F2, and a relative position is indirectly represented by F1, F2, and F3.

F4. It indicates that the reset of F0 declination, which corresponds to the presence of a phrase command, often coincides with a major phrasal boundary (a long pause).

F5-F6. The distance to the preceding and following phrase command is an important feature. However, since a local classifier predicts a label for each time slice, the distance to the preceding phrase command is alternatively considered.

F7. Codification is from lower to higher correlation as the following order: no mark, other marks, "...", and comma. Note that the same shall apply hereinafter.

F8. It is coded as the following order: adnomial, nominal, predicate, exclamation, ending, affix, particle, and the others.

Table 2 and Table 3 show the sets of features and their correlations with amplitude of phrase and accent commands. Amplitude of a phrase command is inferred on which a classifier predicts as the presence of a phrase command. On the other hand, amplitude of an accent command is inferred on every syllable.

---

[1] The space in between orthographic words is a candidate for a major phrasal boundary.

An explanation of the features in **Table 2** follows:

Table 2. Set of features F and their correlations r for amplitude of a phrase command A_p

F #	Description	$r\,(F, A_p)$
1	Index # of word in sentence from begin	-0.2490
2	Index # of word in sentence from end	0.0954
3	Length of sentence in seconds	-0.0906
4	Length of preceding pause in seconds	0.4824
5	Distance to preceding PC in seconds	-0.2213
6	Distance to preceding PC in syllables	-0.2610
7	Distance to following PC in seconds	0.3389
8	Distance to following PC in syllables	0.3772

F1-F2. A_p is higher in the beginning of a sentence and lower in the end of a sentence.
F3. A_p is lower for a long sentence. It reflects a slowly declined F0 curve lasting long utterance. Note that higher A_p makes F0 curve steep.
F4. A_p is higher for a long pause. It indicates that, to reset F0 declination or to utter the following phrase with higher F0 than before, a long pause is necessarily followed.
F5-F8. It indicates that the following phrase command is affected by the preceding phrase command, and vice versa.

To predict amplitude of an accent command, some of the features used in the previous work [6] have too small correlations for our data. For example, duration of a syllable and a vowel is 0.0045 and 0.0013, respectively. Thus, such features are excluded. An explanation of the features in **Table 3** follows:

Table 3. Set of features F and their correlations r for amplitude of an accent command A_a

F #	Description	$r\,(F, A_a)$
1	Type of syllable	0.0246
2	Type of vowel	0.0765
3	Type of first consonant	0.0838
4	Distance to beginning of phrase in sec.	0.4903
5	Distance to beginning of phrase in syll.	0.4267
6	Distance to end of phrase in seconds	-0.2145
7	Distance to end of phrase in syllables	-0.1860
8	Distance to beginning of word in sec.	0.1373
9	Distance to beginning of word in syll.	0.1227
10	Distance to end of word in seconds	-0.0523
11	Distance to end of word in syllables	-0.0237

F1. According to the consonant (C) and vowel (V) sequence in a syllable, it is coded as the following order: V-C, V, and C-V-C, C-V.
F2. According to the height (H: high, M: mid, L: low), backness (F: front, B: back), and roundness (N: no rounding, R: rounding) of a vowel, it is coded as the following order: H-F-N, M-B-N, L-B-N, H-B-N, L-F-N, M-F-N, M-F-R, H-B-R, H-F-R, and M-B-R. Rounding vowels are positively correlated to the amplitude.

F3. The first consonant of the initial syllable of a word, which possibly is an AP initial segment, constrains the phrasal tone. It is coded as the following order: the others, tense, /s/, /h/, and aspirated.

F4-F11. The distance to the phrase and word boundary of a syllable is represented.

3 Experiments

3.1 Corpus

A speech corpus used in experiments is 28-hour-long (including silent pauses) conversational speech uttered by a single female professional announcer, which contains 25,400 sentences or 118,815 words. To extract F0 values and estimate the length of a syllable and pause, Praat[7] and HTK[8] were adopted. For extracting linguistic features, a part-of-speech tagger [9] was used. The data set is divided into two portions: training (90%) and test (10%).

3.2 Prediction of Phrase and Accent Commands

For prediction of presence of a phrase command, four classifiers were adopted: a decision tree (C4.5), a multinomial logistic regression (Logistic), a polynomial kernel Support Vector Machine (SVM), and a multi-layer perceptron (MLP). For evaluation, the following measures are used: accuracy, precision rate, recall rate, and F-score. The result is given in **Table 4**, and shows that C4.5 and MLP outperforms the others.

For prediction of amplitude of a phrase and an accent command, two regression models were adopted: a linear regression (LinearReg) and a multi-layer perceptron (MLP). For evaluation of the regression models, correlation coefficient (r) and root mean squared error (RMSE) are used. The result is given in **Table 5**. MLP shows the better result in prediction of A_p, but LinearReg shows the better result in terms of RMSE in prediction of A_a.

3.3 Evaluation of Predicted F0

Based on the experiments in Section 3.2, all possible combinations of models are used to predict the presence of a phrase command as well as amplitude of a phrase and an accent command in a cascaded manner. Then, using predicted Fujisaki parameters, a sequence of F0 values is generated.

Generated F0 curves are evaluated quantitatively and qualitatively. The result of quantitative evaluation is given in **Table 6**. The combination "Logistic-MLP" shows the best performance in terms of a correlation coefficient, and so does "Logistic-LinearReg" in terms of RMSE. For qualitative evaluation, MOS (mean opinion score) test was performed (Very natural = 5; Natural = 4; Fair = 3; Unnatural = 2; Very unnatural = 1) on two combinations mentioned above. Ten sentences having various r and RMSE were chosen from the test set, and nine native Korean speakers evaluated them. Test samples were resynthesized from the original speech using "Manipulation (overlap-add)" in Praat. For a fair comparison, the order of appearance of test samples is randomized, and the highest and lowest scores are excluded to average scores. The result is given in **Table 7**, and shows that the synthesized speech is "somewhat natural".

Table 4. Classification performance on the prediction of the presence of a phrase command on test data

	Accuracy	Precision	Recall	F-score
C4.5	**0.8928**	**0.9416**	0.7533	0.8370
Logistic	0.8440	0.8934	0.6506	0.7529
SVM	0.8450	0.9385	0.6163	0.7440
MLP	0.8923	0.9348	**0.7581**	**0.8372**

Table 5. Regression performance on the prediction of amplitude of a phrase and an accent command on test data

	LinearReg		MLP	
	r	RMSE	r	RMSE
A_p	0.6274	0.3474	**0.6644**	**0.3431**
A_a	0.5093	**0.5066**	**0.6002**	0.6836

Table 6. The quantitative evaluation of generated F0 curves

Presence	Amplitude	r	RMSE (Hz)
C4.5	LinearReg	0.2603	89.66
	MLP	0.3526	119.62
Logistic	LinearReg	0.2754	**83.60**
	MLP	**0.4075**	112.33
SVM	LinearReg	0.2509	89.22
	MLP	0.3972	113.96
MLP	LinearReg	0.2851	83.70
	MLP	0.3667	117.01

Table 7. The qualitative evaluation of generated F0 curves

Sent #	Logistic-LinearReg			Logistic-MLP		
	r	RMSE	Score	r	RMSE	Score
1	0.6711	61.96	1.9	0.7870	108.62	3.1
2	0.1912	113.73	1.3	0.3723	120.58	2.1
3	0.2219	86.43	3.0	0.3658	140.85	3.3
4	0.5693	56.04	3.0	0.6619	105.70	4.4
5	0.1791	96.82	3.4	0.5184	147.48	4.0
6	0.1963	83.33	2.6	0.4798	102.28	3.6
7	0.2453	78.12	3.3	0.2700	132.45	3.6
8	0.7220	59.14	3.3	0.8380	98.49	4.3
9	0.2034	49.59	4.0	0.1100	106.80	3.4
10	0.1660	69.97	3.4	0.3185	103.71	4.6
Avg.	0.3366	75.51	3.1	0.4722	116.70	3.6

3.4 Analysis

According to the result in **Table 4**, the combinations of C4.5 and MLP might show the better performance than those of Logistic in **Table 6**, but actually they did not. This is because the numbers in **Table 6** are more sensitively affected by the amplitude rather than the presence of a phrase command. Even if the phrase command is wrongly inserted or missed, reasonably estimated amplitudes of phrase and accent commands complement the generation of F0 curve.

In **Table 5**, MLP shows the better result in terms of r, and so does LinearReg in terms of RMSE, which is reflected in **Table 6**.

To evaluate the synthesized speech, r and RMSE to the original speech are usually used. However, in the actual perceptual test on naturalness, the lower RMSE and the higher r do not necessarily guarantee the higher naturalness (see Logistic-LinearReg of sentence #1 in **Table 7**). The common opinion between assessors is that an abrupt pitch up results in unnaturalness, which is mainly caused by incorrect prediction of amplitude of a phrase command. **Table 7** shows that the quality of synthesized speech is on the level of "fair" (3.1 and 3.6).

4 Discussion

The initial command parameters are refined by a two-step hill-climbing algorithm: (1) the estimation of phrase components and (2) the estimation of accent components. It is designed that phrase components shall be placed on the raw pitch curve and accent commands be positively or negatively imposed on each syllable. In [3], the polarity of an accent command for Korean was grouped into "positive only", but in our point of view, it is more natural to be grouped into "positive and negative" by intuition. This makes the accent commands to reflect desired properties of each syllable (e.g., H or L phrasal tones) and to be feasibly predicted. For reference, following to [3], preliminary experiments were performed as in **Table 6**, and r and RMSE of all combinations respectively ranged from 0.1 to 0.2 and 100 to 150, which is caused by poor prediction of amplitude of an accent command.

It is not directly comparable to the related works, since methods and corpora used in experiments are different. However, it is meaningful to show that our method really works. Compared to the related work [6], this work (*) shows the comparable results (P: 0.893* vs. 0.893; A_p: 0.664* vs. 0.654; A_a: 0.600* vs. 0.602; MOS: 3.6* vs. 3.2).

To generate the final F0 curve, the command parameters are predicted in a cascaded manner. That is, incorrect prediction may adversely affect on the next-step prediction. Thus, it can be considered that all the parameters are jointly inferred in one step. To verify this, preliminary experiments were performed, but a significantly better performance cannot be achieved. This is because phrase and accent commands are independent.

Even though the presence of a phrase command does not much affect on the result in **Table 6**, it is still important. In fact, this problem can be treated as IP boundary (or major phrase break) prediction, which has been widely studied. In the future, sophisticated methodologies and refined features can be incorporated.

5   Conclusions

This paper presents a method for intonation modeling via Fujisaki model for Korean. Using the characteristic of Korean, parameter extraction algorithm is adjusted, which is feasibly predictable and intuitive. Also, various machine learning features with classifiers and regression models are explored. By incorporating the linguistically motivated language specific knowledge, a simple and effective system is developed; in our method, timing is not required to predict as in [5] and [6], and both quantitative and qualitative tests show the comparable results.

Acknowledgements

This work was supported by the National Research Foundation of Korea (NRF) grant funded by the Korea government (MEST) (No. R01-2008-000-20651-0).

References

1. Jun, S.-A.: K-ToBI (Korean ToBI) Labelling Conventions (version 3.1),
   http://www.linguistics.ucla.edu/people/jun/ktobi/
   K-tobi.html (accessed on Feburary 10, 2010)
2. Fujisaki, H., Hirose, K.: Analysis of voice fundamental frequency contours for declarative sentences of Japanese. Journal of the Acoustical Society of Japan (E) 5(4), 233–242 (1984)
3. Fujisaki, H., Ohno, S.: The use of a generative model of F0 contours for multilingual speech synthesis. In: Proc. of the 4th International Conference on Signal Processing, pp. 714–717 (1998)
4. Mixdorff, H.: A novel approach to the fully automatic extraction of Fujisaki model parameters. In: Proc. of ICASSP, pp. 1281–1284 (2000)
5. Teixeira, J.P., Freitas, D., Fujisaki, H.: Prediction of Fujisaki Model's Phrase Commands. In: Proc. of Eurospeech, pp. 397–400 (2003)
6. Teixeira, J.P., Freitas, D., Fujisaki, H.: Prediction of Accent Commands for the Fujisaki Intonation Model. In: Proc. of Speech Prosody, pp. 451–454 (2004)
7. Boersma, P., Weenink, D.: Praat: doing phonetics by computer,
   http://www.fon.hum.uva.nl/praat/ (accessed on Feburary 10, 2010)
8. Machine Intelligence Laboratory in Cambridge University Engineering Department, Hidden Markov Model Toolkit (HTK), http://htk.eng.cam.ac.uk/ (accessed on Feburary 10, 2010)
9. Lee, G.G., Cha, J., Lee, J.-H.: Syllable pattern-based unknown morpheme segmentation and estimation for hybrid part-of-speech tagging of Korean. Computational Linguistics 28(1), 53–70 (2002)

Review: Security in Wireless Technologies in Business

F.Y. Sattarova and Tai-hoon Kim[*]

Multimedia Engineering Department, Hannam University,
133 Ojeong-dong, Daeduk-gu, Daejeon, Korea
mymail6585@gmail.com, taihoonn@hnu.kr

Abstract. Wireless technology seems to be everywhere now - but it is still relatively in its infancy. New standards and protocols continue to emerge and problems and bugs are discovered. Nevertheless, wireless networks make many things much more convenient and it appears that wireless networks are here to stay. The differences and similarities of wireless and wired security, the new threats brought by mobility, the security of networks and devices and effects of security, or lack of it are shortly discussed in this review paper.

1 Introduction

Many businesses have seen dramatic changes in recent years as Internet and networked business models have changed the way companies conduct their businesses today. As the competition has got tougher many companies have implemented their own e-business strategies to gain new efficiency. Electronic business, as we know it now, started mainly in the United States in the 1990's in the wired networks. In the recent times the new wave of the wireless Internet boom has started from the Western Europe and Japan. By 2006 it is estimated that the number of mobile Internet users worldwide will be over 920 million and is by that time more than the number of fixed Internet users. [Parker & McQueen, 2001, p. 228]

There is a wide number of books, articles, and other sources of knowledge of different technologies, services and data security separately. Still there is only quite few of them combining all to compact piece of knowledge.

Although wireless technology is often linked to mobile phones, the term "wireless" actually refers to a portfolio of different technologies and architectures that enable a variety of devices to connect to each other offering the ability to exchange and synchronize data between them.

A driving force of the wireless revolution is the rapidly rising number of people who work at home or in mobile offices, often in collaboration with virtual items that are connected by computer networks. For sales and field service employees in particular, wireless devices allow them to stay connected and retrieve the information they need to conduct their daily business without having to return to the office to "recharge". [Barbero, 2001, p. 10]

Companies that take the lead in the wireless revolution can position themselves as being innovative and at the forefront of the advanced technology, giving them

---

[*] Corresponding author.

G.S. Tomar et al. (Eds.): UCMA 2010, CCIS 75, pp. 112–120, 2010.

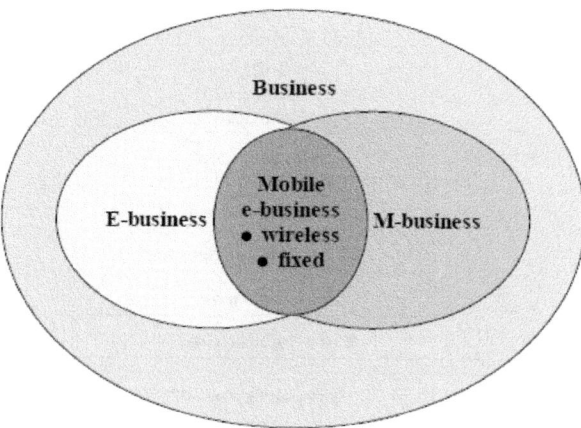

Fig. 1. The convergence of E- and M-Businesses

substantial marketing leverage. Implementing wireless technology can also give organizations a competitive advantage or, at the very least, retain a level playing field with their competition. [Barbero, 2001, p. 11]

A company can adopt new innovations that are:

1. The innovation is based on mobility and wireless, or
2. The innovation is impossible to implement without wireless technology.

In the first one, the new innovation is based on the benefits and possibilities of wireless technologies, but can also be implemented with traditional technologies. Still using the traditional technologies for the implementation of the innovation can lead to higher costs and vanishing benefits. In the second one, the new innovation is based solely on wireless technology and cannot be implemented with traditional technologies. These innovations can lead to new business ideas and models.

This paper's focus is on the differences and similarities of wireless and wired security, the new threats brought by mobility, the security of networks and devices and effects of security, or lack of it. Also the ways of handling the threats will be discussed.

2 Mobile Service Layers and Categories, Security

Mobile services can be divided into seven layer model in figure 8. introduced by Ward [Ward, 1998, p. 56].

Wireless or mobile services can be divided into two sections: business and consumer market oriented services. In the scope this study we should mainly concentrate on business market oriented services (b2b-concentration) but as consumer market oriented services include some services that are covered by the business-to-employee perspective, also those will be covered.

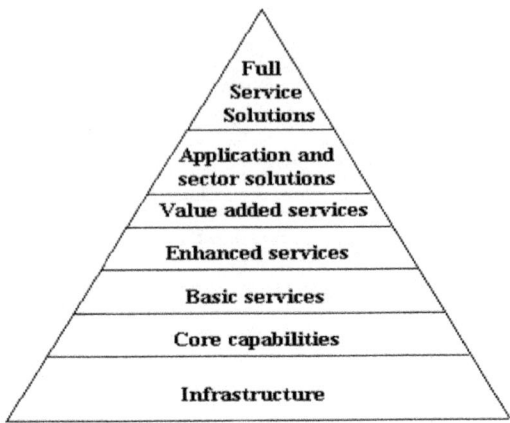

Fig. 2. Seven-layer service model [Ward, 1998, p. 56]

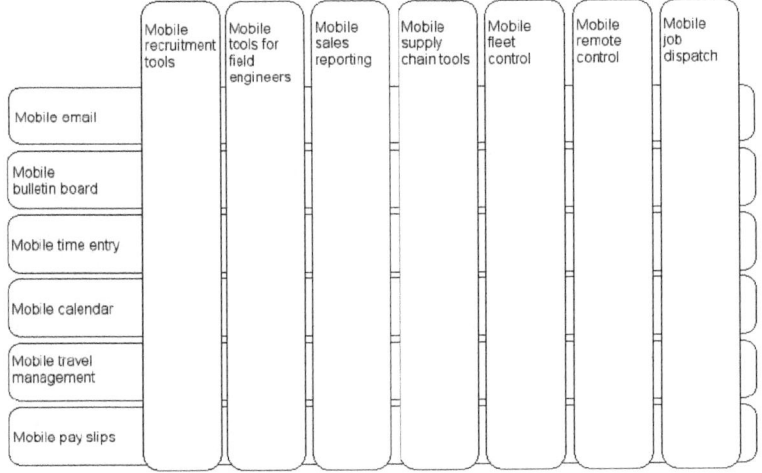

Fig. 3. Vertical and horizontal applications [Paavilainen, 2001, p. 139]

Business Market Orientated Services
- Intranet Access
- Internet Browsing
- Mobile Office
- Vertical Applications
- Email Access
- Machine to Machine (M2M)

Consumer Market Orientated Services
- Messaging
- Games and Entertainment
- Banking/Finance

- Location Based Services
- Internet Access (Mobile Phone)
- Information Services
- Remote Diagnostics
- Mobile Advertising
- Public Services
- Personal Health and Security [Snellman, 2001]

Müller-Veerse et al. [2001] categorizes business applications to three groups. All of these can be built into services that a company offers to its own workers or to the company's partners or they can be outsourced to service providers by integrating them to their services. On the horizontal line can be seen the business-to-business interaction and on the vertical line the business-toemployee and machine-to-machine interactions of the company.

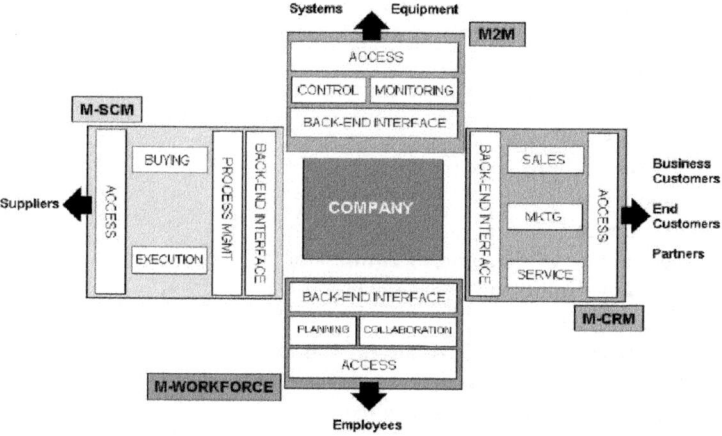

Fig. 4. Business applications overview. [adapted from Müller-Veerse et al., 2001, p. 105].

3 Wireless Security

Wireless security is in many occasions comparable with the security of its wired equivalent. But still the mobility and increasing amount of wireless devices and networks bring new threats and make many of the old ones even bigger.

As the workforce is becoming increasingly mobile the security matters will rise to new dimensions. As the workplace is not necessarily inside the corporate premises in controlled and secured locations where no unauthorized persons can enter, the mobile workforce will do their work in places where also others can obtain access like public places. Still the mobile workers have needs to get access remotely to corporate intranets and databases with their mobile devices.

Basic security goals can be defined as follows:

- Availability
- Integrity
- Confidentiality

Availability consists of the information availability to the users that have the access right to that certain piece of information. For the user that has been granted the access to the information, the information should always be accessible without extra efforts made to retrieve it. Integrity is the assurance that information can only be accessed or modified by those authorized to do so. Measures taken to ensure integrity include controlling the physical environment of networked terminals and servers, restricting access to data, and maintaining rigorous authentication practices. Data integrity can also be threatened by environmental hazards, such as heat, dust, and electrical surges. Confidentiality is much of privacy and trust; confidential information stays along the ones that have the rights to access that information – the data is kept private.

The same basic security threats are confronted in fixed and wireless networks, but the wireless and mobility brings a new aspect for all of them. Due to the high and ever increasing number of wireless and mobile devices the affects can be exponential to those of the fixed ones.

The basic types and threats are:

- **attacks**
- intellectual property theft
- identity theft
- brand theft
- destruction of data and/or equipment
- **Privacy violations**
- surveillance
- databases collecting private information
- traffic analysis
- massive electronic surveillance
- **Publicity attacks**
- disturbance or interception of communication
- "denial-of-service" attacks
   [Schneier, 2000, pp. 23-41]

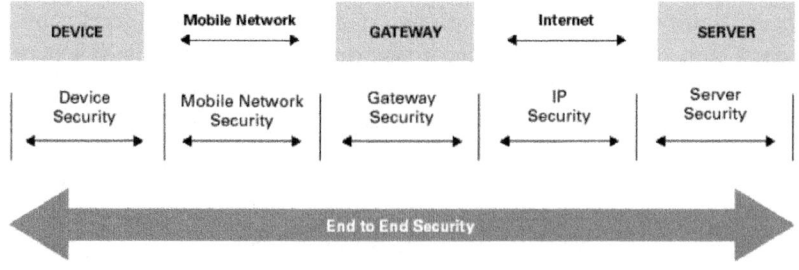

Fig. 5. End -to-end mobile security. [Müller-Veerse et al., 2001, p. 74].

To address current concerns the wireless product developers (including hardware and software vendors) and mobile service providers markets will have to provide end-to-end security, that goes from the user to the server and backwards. As mobile networks converge with the IP world to unified data architectures, security concerns of both areas should be viewed from an integrated perspective rather than as separate issues. The following key elements should be considered:

    - Device security
    - Network security
    - Gateway security
    - IP security
    - Server security
    [Müller-Veerse et al., 2001, p. 73]

From devices point-of-view there are features to point out that are generally causing security problems. These are:

- As they are wireless and mobile, they can be taken almost anywhere, not just in locked corporate premises;
- Typically they are small and light making them easy to lose or steal;
- As the amount of the devices is rising they are becoming a more attractive target for attackers;
- Hardware features set the limitations for certain security software to be used on the device itself (CPU, memory, battery life, etc.);
- Increasing features enable to store more confidential information on the device itself

For data security reasons almost all wireless networks have to have some degree of network security with their own security (encrypting) algorithms or mechanisms. The degree of the security within the network without outside encrypting depends on the network. For example, GSM communication is encoded with a 128k algorithm to ensure secure wireless transport. Each of the users is assigned a temporary code that enables them to receive only the digital signal sent to them. In an eavesdropping scenario the time required to crack the code is usually longer than the life of the temporary key. The security offering capability of the upcoming UMTS system is going to be higher due to the higher data rates and more complex modulation schemes [Müller-Veerse et al., 75 2001, p. 74].

The security of a public or private IP network is a problem that is not directly related to the mobile space. Still, this is a very important component of an end-toend mobile data security infrastructure. The proliferation of mobile devices also imposes additional requirements on corporate network management. Large companies are starting to incorporate mobile device security features into their enterprise security products. Tivoli, for example, has upgraded its SecureWay Policy Director software to centralize the security management of cell phones, PDAs and other handheld devices. [Müller- Veerse et al., 2001, p. 74]

Computer security is difficult, to the vendors of software and hardware products, but also to the users of those products. Even if the hardware, the software and network were secure, the complete system could still be jeopardized by one user that does not care enough about security.

To be able to gain security's three goals, availability, integrity and confidentiality, there are different tools. The tools of security are largely based on mathematical science (e.g. cryptography) and analysis of the content (e.g. Antivirus software).

Modern cryptography is concerned with the following four objectives:

> 1. *Confidentiality* (the information cannot be understood by anyone for whom it was unintended)
> 2. *Integrity* (the information cannot be altered in storage or transit between sender and intended receiver without the alteration being detected)
> 3. *Non-repudiation* (the creator/sender of the information cannot deny at a later stage his or her intentions in the creation or transmission of the information)
> 4. *Authentication* (the sender and the receiver can confirm each other's identity and the origin/destination of the information) [Whatis?com, 2002b]

Firewalls have generally been used to separate corporate intranets from the Internet by providing access control. A properly configured firewall prevents unauthorized access to or from private networks, especially Intranets. All messages (i.e. all IP traffic) entering or leaving the Intranet pass through the firewall, which examines each message and blocks messages that do not meet the specified security criteria. A Firewall is one of the fundamental components of a secure network.

Functions of a firewall can include:

> • The firewall examines each packet entering or leaving the network and accepts or rejects it based on a predetermined list of criteria.
> • The firewall provides an applications gateway that can apply security mechanisms to applications such a FTP (File Transfer Protocol) or Telnet servers.
> • Circuit-level gateways apply security when a Transmission Control Protocol (TCP) or User Datagram Protocol (UDP) connection is established.
> • A proxy server intercepts all messages entering and leaving the network, while hiding the true network address. [Intel, 2002]

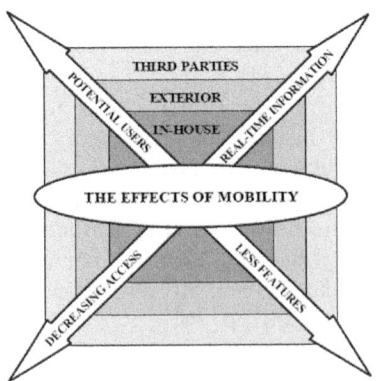

Fig. 6. The effects of mobility

The situation with wireless technologies, services, security, managing and all this together will be discussed analytically and some future visions will be reviewed. In the end there will be a discussion about this study and further points to study will be suggested.

Security will be far more important as the possibilities for different scenarios arise due to the rise of the amount of the devices themselves. Also the wider scale of different terminal types and connection types will bring their own aspects to planning good security.

Also due to the nature of wireless, anyone can in theory listen to someone else's communications; it is recommendable not to rely purely on security provided by the networks themselves. As these things are known, security matters have to be solved out before businesses in wireless networks really start to happen. That is why it is easy to understand the success of VPN solutions as it is always advisable to use network independent security solutions, such as VPN, for extremely confidential data transfers.

Much of the security is about the users also with wireless technologies. Even when we could build a totally secure systems, one user could still easily cause a leak in that system if he or she did not follow secure working methods; one could easily print classified documents from corporate intranet and then forget them into a public place like an airport lounge. Maybe the most important thing still is to educate the users the right attitude for security matters and remind them   periodically: security starts from the user. In the wake of Internet time and the attacks against security many companies have risen to acknowledge the problems with security and have formed security policies. But still it seems that there has not been enough education as we just look back the last few years and think of all the viruses and worms spread through emails: people still open emails and attachments sent to them without hesitation. On the other hand in some companies the security measures might have been too restrictive that it even makes working more complex and inflexible. In many companies there has been absolute restriction of using PDAs in corporate networks as they might open security holes. It is easy to deny everything in the sake of security, but it also makes the users to try other ways round it and it can be even more hazardous.

4 Conclusion

Wireless technologies bring many new possibilities for companies to achieve flexibility and competitiveness or even make possible things that were earlier impossible to do. The main obstacle in utilization of wireless technologies will be the imagination, or more importantly, the lack of it. But as the new technologies may sound a little heaven on Earth, they can become a nightmare if certain things like security and the management of those technologies are not considered, planned and implemented well. For sure, these new technologies will reshape the ways of doing work, business or services, maybe not all, but many of them.

Acknowledgement. This work was supported by the Security Engineering Research Center, granted by the Korean Ministry of Knowledge Economy.

References

1. Kytölä, O.: Wireless Technologies in E-Business:Services, Security and Management. LAP-PEENRANTA (June 19, 2002)
2. Ward, E.: World-class telecommunications service development, p. 260. Artech House (1998) ISBN 0-89006-922-0
3. Paavilainen, J.: Mobile Commerce Strategies, p. 252. IT Press (2001), ISBN 951-826-253-5
4. Müller-Veerse, et al.: UMTS report – An Investment Perspective. p. 141. Durlacher Research Ltd. (2001)

Emerging Approach of Natural Language Processing in Opinion Mining: A Review

Tai-hoon Kim[*]

Hannam University
Daejeon, Korea
taihoonn@empal.com

Abstract. Natural language processing (NLP) is a subfield of artificial intelligence and computational linguistics. It studies the problems of automated generation and understanding of natural human languages. This paper outlines a framework to use computer and natural language techniques for various levels of learners to learn foreign languages in Computer-based Learning environment. We propose some ideas for using the computer as a practical tool for learning foreign language where the most of courseware is generated automatically. We then describe how to build Computer Based Learning tools, discuss its effectiveness, and conclude with some possibilities using on-line resources.

Keywords: Translation Support System, Speech Technology, Parsing.

1 Introduction

The conversion of text in language study is not a new idea. Natural-language-understanding systems convert samples of human language into more formal representations that are easier for computer programs to manipulate. And that is going to be fed to the further process of language processing in the field of Opinion Mining [2]. Extraction of opinion expression from text, eventually including relations with the rest of content. It develops an in-depth understanding of both the algorithms available for the processing of linguistic information and the underlying computational properties of natural languages [3].

Computational linguists dealing with syntax and semantics of languages have long dealt with the problem of making sense of the message conveyed in a narrative [1]. The syntax, in general, is relatively easy to understand and interpret, but the semantics always posed a comparatively complex problem. The problem is compounded by the fact that word usage in any language is full of ambiguity, where the same word may have many senses depending on the context of the narrative.

2 Existing Techniques

Based on the above initial experiments we believe that reordering of the target language phrases improve substantially by tapping the available resources for English [4].

---

[*] Corresponding author.

G.S. Tomar et al. (Eds.): UCMA 2010, CCIS 75, pp. 121–128, 2010.

In theory, natural-language processing is a very attractive method of human-computer interaction. Early systems such as SHRDLU, working in restricted blocks worlds with restricted vocabularies, worked extremely well, leading researchers to excessive optimism, which was soon lost when the systems were extended to more realistic situations with real-world ambiguity and complexity.Natural-language understanding is sometimes referred to as an AI-complete problem, because natural-language recognition seems to require extensive knowledge about the outside world and the ability to manipulate it [5]. The definition of understanding is one of the major problems in natural-language processing. These areas being the key focus of most research done in NLP and will continue to increase in complexity in the future [15].

The techniques those are reviewed in this paper are explained as follows:

2.1 Translation Support System (English to Hindi)

Another way to model the construction of the dependency tree is using finite state machines or transition systems [14]. A transition system for dependency parsing is a quadruple S = (C; T; cs;Ct) where,

1. C is a set of configurations, each of which contains a bu_er of (remaining) nodes and a set A of dependency arcs,
2. T is a set of transitions, each of which is partial function T:C -> C
3. cs is an initialization function, mapping a sentence x = w0;w1; : : :wn to a configuration with _ = [1; : : : ; n],
4. Ct _ C is a set of terminal configurations.

This technique are shown in figure 1.

The translation system from English to Hindi i.e. from a foreign to a regional language consists of many problems. Any natural language is a free language, i.e. its structure is not fixed. Especially, for a language like English which has syntactic parsers of high quality, it is always desirable to tap these existing resources. The structure can keep changing as the user wishes. Hence a good translation system will

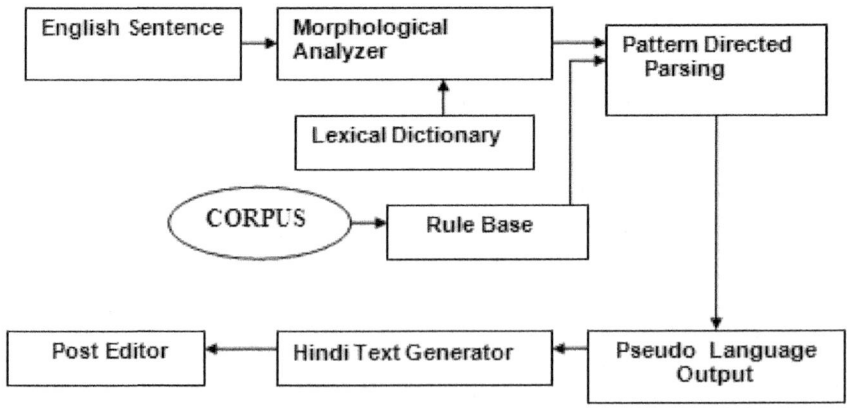

Fig. 1. Translation Support System (English to Hindi)

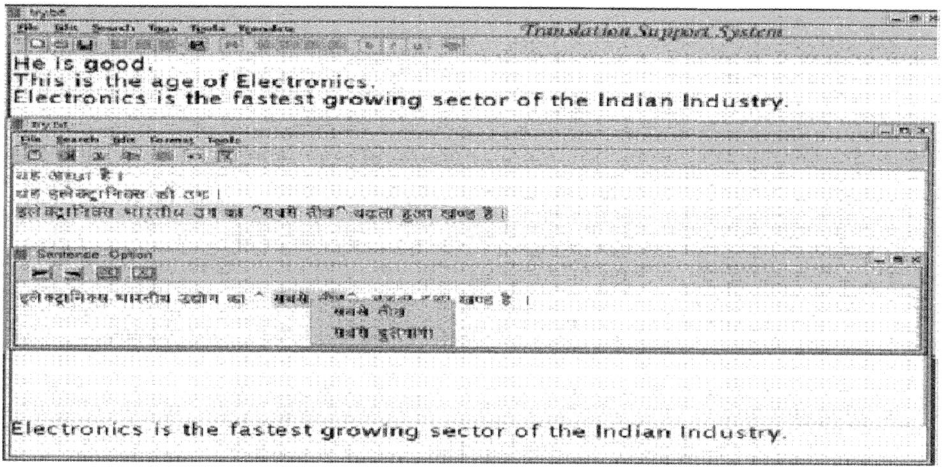

Fig. 2. Translation Support System

have to handle as many grammar constructs as possi ble [10]. Thus our purpose is to develop a Translation System that can translate English text into Hindi, with a special reference to "Weather Narration" in Translation support system.This translation technique are shown in figure 2.

2.2 Speech Technology and Tools

Speech Technology (also known as automatic speech technology or computer speech technology) converts spoken words to machine-readable input (for example, to key presses, using the binary code for a string of character codes) [7]. This technique is shown in the figure 3.

The goal of machine translation is to automatically translation translate a document from one language to another. The purpose of Speech Technology in syntactic analysis is to determine the structure of the input text [12].

Computations based on the input can be written with attribute grammar specifications that are based on an abstract syntax. The abstract syntax describes the structure of an abstract syntax tree, much the way the concrete syntax describes the phrase structure of the input. This text to speech synthesis is shown in the figure 4.

2.3 Parsing

2.3.1 Dependency Parsing

- In computer science and linguistics, parsing, or, more formally, syntactic analysis, is the process of analyzing a sequence of tokens to determine their grammatical structure with respect to a given more or less formal grammar [11]. Parsing is also an earlier term for the diagramming of sentences of natural languages, and is still used for the diagramming of inflected languages, such as the Romance languages or Latin. Assigning a syntactic and logical form to an input sentence

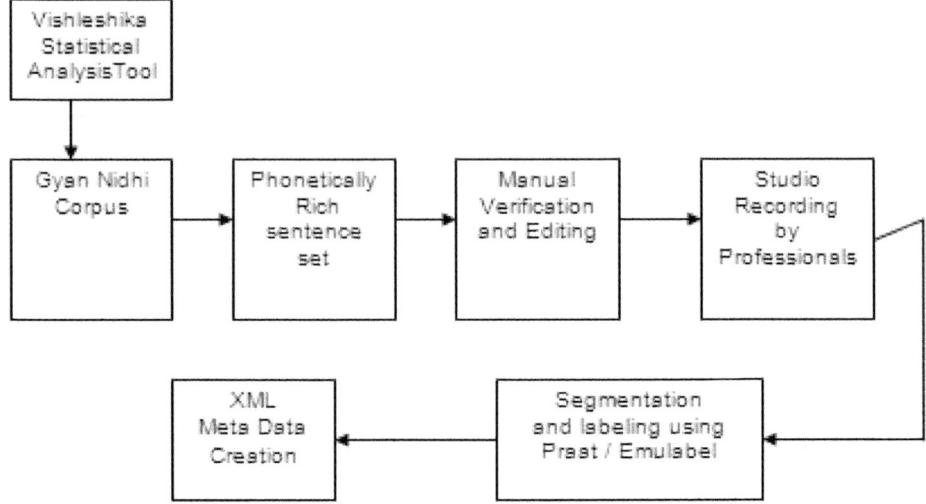

Fig. 3. Speech Technology and tools

- uses knowledge about word and word meanings (lexicon)
- uses a set of rules defining legal structures (grammar)

The term parsing comes from Latin pars, meaning part of speech. The long parsing times are the consequences of using a scripting language for the development and testing of the parser [13]. The results should reduce by a factor of several tens or even hundreds if the parser was implemented on a natively compilable language [9].

Parsing is the problem of constructing a derivation tree for an input string from a formal definition of a grammar. Parser which provides the ways and means to predict the words and sentences confined to the patterns and grammar of a language [16].

The Ranking algorithm is essentially embodied by the following pseudo-code:

a. Populate the list with every state for every word.
b. Sort the list by their probability scores.
c. Set pointer at the first state in the list.
d. While the list contains un-combined states:
e. Set pivot as the next most probable state.
f. Return if pivot state is a terminal state.
g. Combine pivot with all adjacent states with higher probability.
h. Insertion sort all newly created states in to the list.
i. Return failure

2.3.2 Phrase Parsing
We proposed a new technique of phrase parser in natural language processing. The research on the parser relatedness reported here is very much a work in progress.

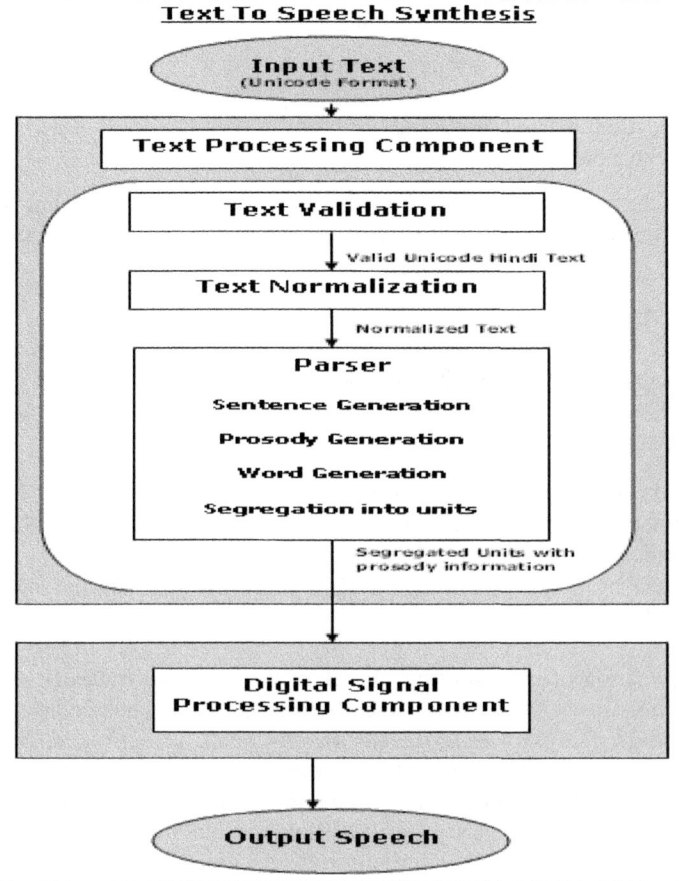

Fig. 4. Speech Technology and tools

In this course we will introduce statistical techniques for inferring structure from text. The aim of the course is to introduce existing techniques in statistical NLP and to stimulate thought into bettering these:

Translation system to improve the quality of the translation for a 'distant' language pair like English-Hindi. We proposed new techniques for efficient reordering. A slight improvement over the baseline is reported using these techniques. Kevin Ryan [6] claims also that the domain model produced by NLP means may be incomplete, because some information that is thought to be "common domain knowledge" is omitted in the requirements text. But this is exactly one of the tasks of the We also show that a simple pre-processing step can improve the quality of the translation significantly.

- We are mapping between surface, underlying forms
- Sometimes, information is 'invisible' (I.e., erased e, or a ununderlying/surface 0)
- There is ambiguity (more than one parse)

Parsing for fsa's: keep track of what 'next state' we could be in at each step

NB: *ambiguity* = > 1 path through network
= > 1 sequence of states (*'parses'*)
= > 1 'syntactic rep' = >1 'meaning'
fruit flies like a banana

In our approach, we convert natural human Language into any other human Language in Opinion Mining research field.we are using parsing technique into bettering these.

4 Results and Discussions

We consider parsing technique & also discuss Grammar.we draw full attention of word categories & syntactic structure.

Our target application shows:

- Many words have many meanings or senses.
- We need to resolve which of the senses of an ambiguous word is invoked in a particular use of the word.
- I made her duck. (made her a bird for lunch or made her move her head quickly downwards?)

With the application of this ordering, the algorithm allowed for early termination of the search, since the newly created states (being of equal or lesser probability) must be inserted below the pivot state due to the cascading effect of the product of the probability. Any terminal state found later would have a lower probability than the first one that was found, so the algorithm guarantees the retrieval of the most probable state without having to exhaustively search all possible combinations. By only using a single list to maintain all possible derivation of the states, traversals and maintenance of the ordering of the list used up a lot of valuable time. The algorithms we consider include mechanisms for ordering that reduce the search cost without loss of completeness or accuracy as well as mechanisms that prune the space and may result in eliminating valid parses or returning a suboptimal as the best parse. To counteract this, we re-introduce a charting behaviour as the second improvement to the algorithm. We implemented a table, called the indexed table, in which all the states that were in the used section were placed, rather than keeping them in the same list. The table also grouped together the states that occupied the same starting and ending positions, to simplify the decision process in determining which states were adjacent to the pivot state. Actually The phrase parser constructs phrases that can be reliably described as a regular language. The ranked list was replaced by a table, which we called the sorted table that handled the push and pop manipulations to simplify and to modularise the algorithm for future use. parsing is applied with the head words in the constituent structures of NL sentences and better performance is achieved [8]. This Lexicalized and Statistical Parsing with immediate head parsing technique and hybrid language model covers the advantages of free ordering of words, focus on syntax with semantics and long term relationship.

5 Future Work

The proposed three distinctions for opinions in online reviews are defined as follows:

- Machine Translation
    - Standardization Lexware Database design.
    - Working on the global approach 'BhashaSetu' which is a amalgamation of different approaches to squeeze the best of each approach
    - Development of Translation system Test Bed.

- Knowledge Management
    - Automatic Text Summarization tool for Hindi and other Indian languages.
    - Standardization of Parts of Speech TagSet for Hindi extendible to other Indian languages.
    - Parts of Speech Tagger development for Indian languages.
    - Automated Terminology Development tools.
    - Sentence alignment tool for Indian languages.
    - Development of manually tagged parallel corpus up to word level.

- Speech Technology
    - Speech to Speech Translation System.
    - Development of Semi-automated speech annotation tools.

6 Conclusion

In our paper we proposed a novel approach in Opinion Mining which enhances traditional Natural Language Processing techniques by exploiting valuable information extracted from response graphs based on the interactions of users [5].

This Algorithm clearly explained about the problem of dependency parsing and showed how it can be expressed as a classification problem. All the required learning algorithms for classification were also discussed. The graph-based models and transition system based models were also explained in the context of dependency parsing. We investigate several optimization approaches to reduce the search space for finding an accurate parse of a sentence where individual words can have multiple possible syntactic categories, and categories and phrases can combine together in different ways. The process of deriving computer programs starting with a natural language text implies a plethora of sophisticated language processing tools – such as syntactic parsers, clause detectors, argument structure identifiers, semantic analyzers, methods for coreference resolution, and so forth – which can be effectively put at work and evaluated within the framework of natural language programming. The promising results have reinforced our expectations that such an application can be easily adapted to any future Opinion Mining task in the election domain.

References

1. http://www.ccsenet.org/journal/index.php/mas/article/viewFil e/838/816 (as visited on 7/10/2009)
2. http://www.csc.liv.ac.uk/~wda2003/Papers/Section_II/Paper_7. pdf (as visited on 8/10/2009)
3. http://see.stanford.edu/see/materials/ainlpcs224n/exams.aspx (as visited on 8/10/2009)
4. http://ltrc.iiit.ac.in/nlptools2008/nlpToolsPapers/icon- 2008-iiithyd.pdf (as visited on 8/10/2009)
5. http://www.inf.u-szeged.hu/~rfarkas/wseas_OM_final.pdf (as visited on 9/10/2009)
6. Ryan, K.: The role of natural language in requirements engineering. In: IEEE International Symposium on Requirements Engineering, vol. 1992, pp. 240–242. IEEE Computer Society Press, Los Alamitos (1992) (as visited on 9/10/2009)
7. http://en.wikipedia.org/wiki/Speech_recognition (as visited on 9/10/2009)
8. http://en.wikipedia.org/wiki/Part-of-speech_tagging (as visited on 10/10/2009)
9. Collins, M.J.: Head-Driven Statistical Models for Natural Language Parsing, University of Pennsylvania, Ph.D. Dissertation (1999) (as visited on 10/10/2009)
10. http://sciencelinks.jp/j- ast/article/200419/000020041904A0636116.php (as visited on 10/10/2009)
11. http://www.aclweb.org/anthology/H/H94/H94-1025.pdf (as visited on 11/10/2009)
12. http://eli-project.sourceforge.net/elionline/syntax_toc.html (as visited on 11/10/2009)
13. http://en.wikipedia.org/wiki/Parsing (as visited on 11/10/2009)
14. http://www.oti.com/oti/patent/20061207-2006277332-US-A1 (as visited on 11/10/2009)
15. http://www.google.com/search?q=translation+support+system (as visited on 11/10/2009)
16. http://en.wikipedia.org/wiki/Parsing (as visited on 11/10/2009)

Power Management Scheduling for Low Rate Wireless Sensor Networks

Xiao Hong[1], Michael J. Plyler[2], Ji Jun[3], and Yang Xiao[2,*]

[1] Computer Basic Teaching Centre
Changchun Institute of Technology
Kuan Ping Road 395,
Changchun, Jilin Province, China. Post code:130012
[2] Department of Computer Science
The University of Alabama
Tuscaloosa, AL 35487-0290 USA
yangxiao@ieee.org
[3] School of Electrical Engineering and Information Techonlogy,
Changchun Institute of Technology,
Kuan Ping Road 395, Changchun, Jilin Province, China. Post code:130012

Abstract. Wireless Personal Area Networks (WPANs) are used to spread information over personal operating spaces (POSs) and typically among only a few clients. These connections involve little or no infrastructure. Because of this, they offer small, inexpensive, power efficient solutions that can be implemented for a wide range of wireless-capable hardware. This paper looks at a power management algorithm for a wireless network. The purpose of IEEE 802.15.4 is to provide a low rate, low complexity, low cost wireless connection with fixed or movable devices that use what is referred to as "ultra low" power consumption. It is essential to come up with ways for the sensors to conserve power in these networks so that not all devices are using power and covering the same area of the network. The main idea of the algorithm that will be presented is to conserve power by reducing redundant devices in the network.

Keywords: Lightweight Deployment-Aware Scheduling (LDAS), device (DEV), ST, BT, CT, number of working neighbors (NWN), completely redundant sensors, partially redundant sensors, global positioning systems (GPSs), location based algorithms, evenly distributed networks, sparse and dense networks, 1-hop neighbors, wireless sensor networks, IEEE 802.15.4 networks.

1 Introduction

Based on the work in [1], this paper has created a simulation based on the Lightweight Deployment-Aware Scheduling (LDAS) algorithm for wireless sensor networks. Many of the mathematical proofs were overlooked and accepted as true based on the work in [1].

---

* Corresponding author.

G.S. Tomar et al. (Eds.): UCMA 2010, CCIS 75, pp. 129–141, 2010.

The reason for attempting to design a power saving network is clear. In the case of an IEEE 802.15.4 wireless sensor network, almost all of the devices (DEVs) are battery powered [2-40]. Most of the applications for these DEVs are for data collection. When one of the DEVs runs out of energy, it is disposed of. These inexpensive DEVs are not worth the trouble of recharging them. Most of the applications that do not take into effect some sort of geographical information also use densely populated networks [2].

These types of networks can be large or small scaled. The sensors monitor the surrounding environment and send this data and smaller transmissions to each other.

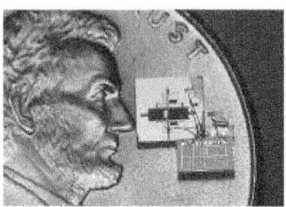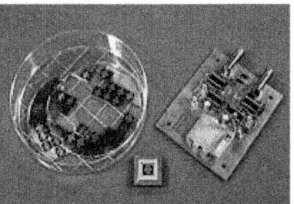

Fig. 1. These are several examples of wireless sensors that can be used in the types of networks that are being discussed in this paper

Each of these DEVs has limited transmission and reception functionality. Even though this is true, they are extremely small and light, which means that they can be easily deployed. Fig. 1 shows an example of such sensors that are being described. Because of this flexibility, the networks have almost limitless applications [1].

These types of networks could use geographical information for power management, but this would require much overhead. Using something like a Global Positioning System (GPS) would cost too much. Each DEV would have to obtain information such as location, direction, and distance. These costs are too high for small wireless sensors [1].

In these types of networks, there are a few important issues. The first is channel access. Although this doesn't play an enormous role with the topic of this paper, it does influence energy consumption. For this reason, we assume that we are using an 802.15.4 network [2-40]. Security is another important issue in any wireless network but is beyond the scope of this paper. That leaves us with the central issue of power management, which will be the main concentration of this paper.

The algorithm to be used should assume that there is no geographical information. This will enable the network to be randomly distributed for deployment and will conserve some energy by not using something like GPS.

In order to achieve some level of lower energy consumption, this research did primarily one thing: it cut off redundant sensors to conserve energy. As long as there is some type of reasonable coverage of a static network, it is not important for a densely populated network to stay on all of the time [1]. Maintaining a sufficient sensing area can be done by turning off redundant sensors, which gives the network a longer life. The proposed method of doing this is the LDAS algorithm.

The mathematical proofs and research for this paper have been strongly based on the acceptance of the findings of [1]. Based on the theoretical analysis of redundant probabilities, LDAS uses a weighted random voting mechanism to decide which DEVs will fall asleep.

Before we can discuss the program, or simulation, we must first look at some of the terms and some of the things that we assume about the network.

2   Ontology and Assumptions

There are a few items that must be understood before going any further with this paper. First, when talking about neighbors, there are many kinds. Fig. 2 shows a typical network. Every node that is attached to another by some communication flow is a neighbor. A 1-hop neighbor is a direct neighbor. This is the neighbor that is in direct communication with another DEV. This is the type of neighbor that we will deal with in the simulation in this paper.

A DEV's sensing range is the greatest distance at which a sensor can perceive another sensor [1]. Each DEV in an 802.15.4 network has a sensing range of about 10 meters. In fact, with devices, there are two different ranges involved in communication; a transmission range and a reception range. To keep confusion to a minimum, we assume that both ranges are 10 meters [2].

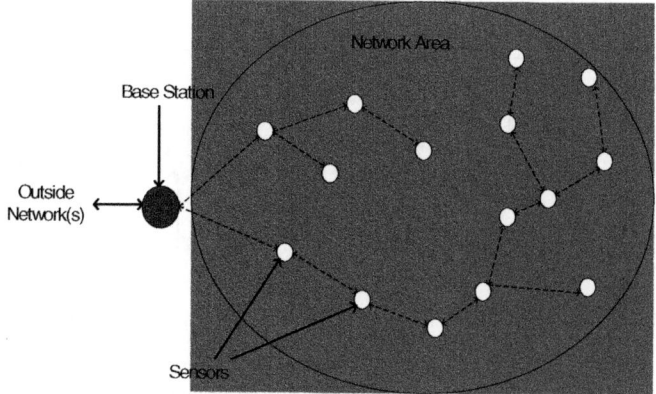

Fig. 2. This is an example of a wireless sensor network. The communication flow is shown by the dotted arrows. There are several node stations, but there is only one base station.

The Quality of Service (QoS) for these networks is the percentage of a given deployment region that can be monitored [1]. For this study of the LDAS algorithm, there were three different levels of QoS used: 85%, 90%, and 95%.

There are two different types of redundant sensors: completely redundant and partially redundant sensors. Completely redundant sensors are named so if their region of influence is covered by neighboring DEVs completely. A partially redundant sensor is one where the coverage area is partially covered by its neighbors [1].

Table 1 shows the mathematics behind the probability of a sensor being redundant [1]. These probabilities, based on the number of neighbors, are what will be used to test the network simulation.

Table 1. Redundancy with different number of neighbors [1]

Number of Neighbors	Probability of Complete Redundancy	Percentage of the Redundant Area (=)
5	31.22%-37.01%	91.62%
7	64.29%-65.21%	96.89%
9	82.97%-83.09%	98.85%
11	~92.28%	99.57%

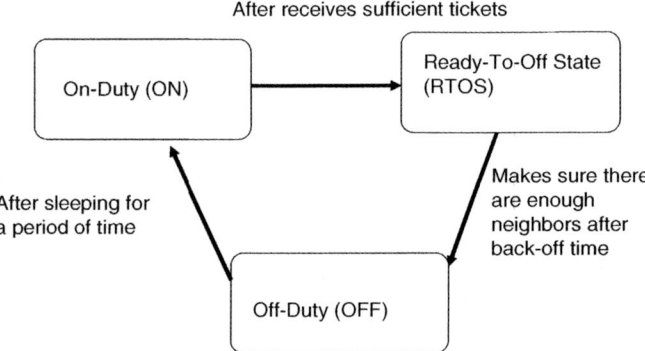

Fig. 3. Finite state machine to show the states of the network DEVs in this implementation

There are three basic functions that the network will perform for the power management functions: BT, CT, and ST. A BT is a beacon transmission. This is the interval at which information is updated by the network. The CT is a check time which is the interval at which a DEV will check its neighbor table (NT) and information. A DEV's NT stores information about the DEV's neighbors. It takes the form of Table 2. It has fields for neighbor identification (ID), device state (State), number of working neighbors (NWN), last update time, and the row (used as a pointer for fast access in the simulation) [1]. The third function of the DEVs is the ST. This is a sleep check time which is the interval at which a DEV checks to see if it can go to Off-Duty mode [1].

A few assumptions about the network are that there is no geographical information available (this is just too costly) that, the sensors are deployed at random (with uniform distribution), and that each sensor has mechanisms to sense the other devices in its range (a transceiver or other perceptual hardware). Every DEV is assumed to have an ID, status (mode and a state), neighbors, tickets, and general time checking variable members for event updates.

Table 2. This is an example of a DEV's neighbor table (NT)

ID	State	NWN	Last Update Time	Row
12	1	5	3	6
25	0	4	2	14

The status of the DEV has been broken into mode and state categories. The mode of a DEV is what part of the finite state machine in Fig. 3 that the DEV is currently in. There is an On-Duty (ON) state, Ready-To-Off-State (RTOS), and an Off-Duty (OFF) state [1]. Once a DEV receives a certain number of tickets, it will go into the RTOS mode. From here, the DEV checks to make sure that it has enough NWN so that it can switch to the OFF mode. If there are not enough neighbors, it stays in the RTOS until there are enough neighbors to go to SLEEP. After a DEV is in the OFF state, it sleeps for a period of time and then goes back to an ON state after clearing out the ticket counter [1].

The state of a DEV is simply ON (working) or OFF (not working, asleep). This is used in the NT when DEVs are calculating the NWN. The last update time is the time at which the DEV last updated the NT [1]. The row, again, is just a pointer for the simulation.

One of the last assumptions is that the network will use a random weighted voting mechanism to handle sparsely or densely populated networks [1].

In Fig. 4, we can see why this would be necessary. We can see that the DEV M in this case would not need to go to SLEEP as often as the neighbors of DEV E. The weighted voting would send tickets to DEVs that have more neighbors, essentially evening out a sparsely or densely populated network. This is an important step in the

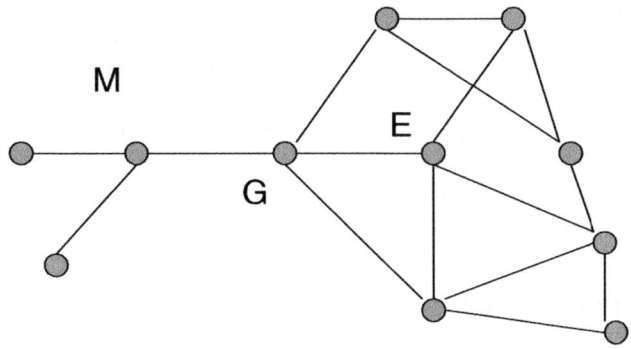

Fig. 4. This is a representation of a network with sparse and densely populated DEVs

network in order to keep the QoS levels at their requirements. It also lengthens the network's lifetime, especially if it is a densely populated network. In order to obtain the weight values, the DEVs essentially total up their number of neighbors and then use that as a basis for a random order in which to send out tickets [1].

3 Scheduling Algorithm and Parameters

This section talks about how the discrete event simulation was set up. The algorithm that was used differs only slightly from [1]. The steps in the network algorithm are as follows. First, the DEVs are deployed randomly. This is done by assigning an x and y coordinate value to each DEV. This is only used in order to randomly distribute the DEVs. The next step in the simulation is to find the number of required neighbors for a given QoS. In this case a lower bound formula from [1] was used:

$$1 - 0.609^r - (\frac{r}{6} - 0.109) * 0.109^{r-1} \tag{1}$$

This was used to find the minimum requirement. This gives us approximately the values from Table 1.

After this was done, a table array was set up to find the distance between all of the DEVs in order to distinguish which DEVs were neighbors. Once this information was gathered, it was then put into the NT. From here, the DEVs updated this information every BT period of time.

The next step in the simulation was to find the number of neighbors for every DEV in order to calculate a ticket threshold. The ticket threshold would be the maximum number of tickets a DEV could receive before going into the RTOS state. The formula is as follows:

$$(n-r) - \sqrt{-2(n-r)\ln \frac{r}{n=1}} \tag{2}$$

Here, n is the number of working neighbors and r is the number of required neighbors based on (1) [1].

The next step in the network cycle was to activate the BT, CT, and ST functions according to the event handler of each DEV [1]. A DEV would then check its battery life, status, and mode. This was done to collect data in order to plot results on a graph. The last step in the process was to increment the cycle counter.

The parameters that were used for the simulation were the time (set to values of 150, 200, 300, and 500s), the number of DEVs (800, 1200, 1600, and 200), the network size (150m X 150m), the QoS requirement (85%, 90%, and 95%), BT (1s), CT (1, 2s), ST (2, 4,5,8s), sleeptime (2,5,8,11s), ticket threshold, and the Wmax (12, 22, 32). The Wmax is the upperbound of the amount of time that a DEV will wait to try to go into the OFF state from a RTOS state based on the number of working neighbors.

4 Simulation Results

We ran our programs through several different tests which were divided into six cases. Each case used different parameters that will be indicated in the appropriate subsection. It is also important to note that all results are an average of at least 3-6 runs per variable tested. This helps to accurately portray the random deployment and DEV operations.

4.1 Relationship between QoS and Working Nodes

In Fig. 5, we can see the relationship between the QoS and the number of working nodes. The number of working nodes increases as the QoS requirement increases.

4.2 Case 1: QoS

In Case 1, BT was set to 1, CT set to 2, ST set to 3, sleeptime to 2, Wmax to 32, simulation time to 150s, and there were 2000 DEVs deployed. The key to Fig. 5 shows the three different QoS levels that were tested. As you can see in the graph, the DEVs set

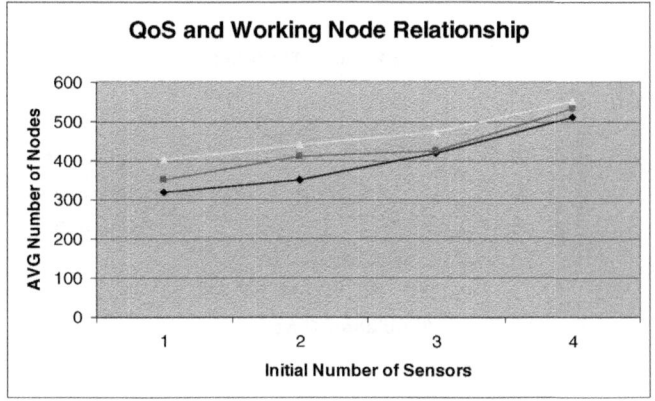

Fig. 5. The relationship between QoS and working nodes

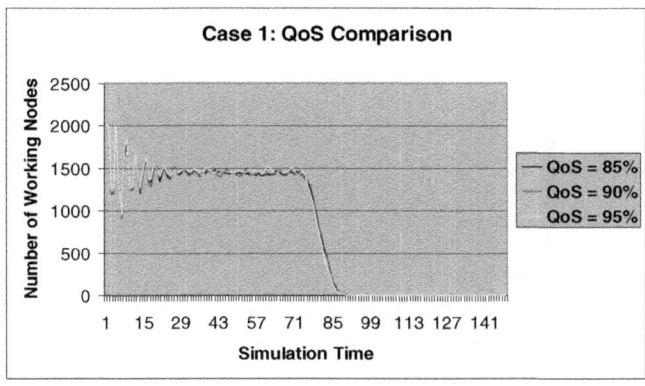

Fig. 6. This graph represents the first case of a comparison of QoS levels. The levels are indicated in the chart key.

at these different QoS levels operated in a similar fashion. The number of working nodes is greater if the QoS is higher. In the graph, the "steady state" shows that the coverage area has been kept constant.

4.3 Case 2: Ticket Threshold

In this case, BT =1, CT=2, ST=2, DEV = 2000, simulation time = 150s, sleep time = 2s, and Wmax = 32. In Fig. 7, the chart shows the average Ticket Threshold for time t. For a lower QoS, there is a higher ticket threshold. Several different variables were used to test the ticket threshold, all of which returned results similar to Fig. 7.

4.4 Case 3: ST

In Case 3, the ST was the variable that was tested. It was done at intervals of 2, 5, and 8s. ST = 1, CT = 1, DEV = 2000, simulation time = 200s, Wmax = 32, and QoS = 85%.

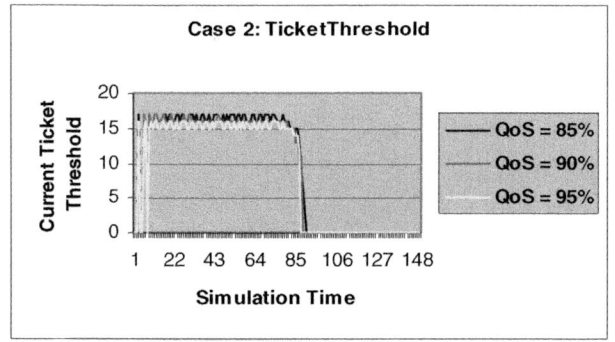

Fig. 7. This graph shows the result of the simulation that was run with different ticket threshold values

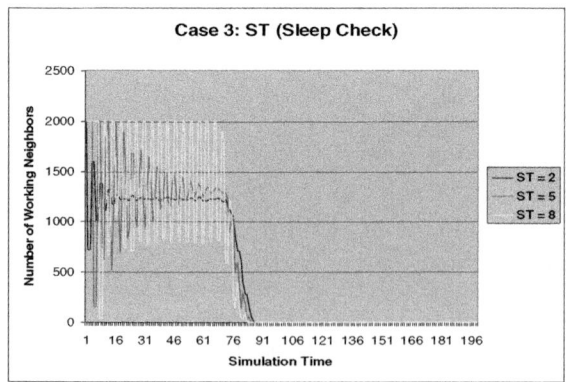

Fig. 8. This graph shows the result of the ST variable that was changed for this run of the simulation

With a higher check rate, there seem to be many DEVs that change from the ON to the Off-Duty state more frequently. The more frequent the ST, the better the energy consumption that is seen from the network. Notice the oscillations in Fig. 8. This shows the DEVs switching between states.

4.5 Case 4: Sleep Time

In this case, the sleep time was set to different intervals of 2,5,8, and 11. This is indicated in Fig. 9. BT was set to 1, CT = 2, ST = 3, DEV = 2000, time = 300s, Wmax = 32, and the QoS = 85%. In the figure, we can see that the sleep time seems to affect the lifetime of the DEV enormously. This can be attributed to the fact that the DEVs are sleeping for longer periods of time, thus conserving more energy. It was also noticed in a run of the simulation, that the greater the sleep time interval, the lower the average number of tickets for the ticket threshold.

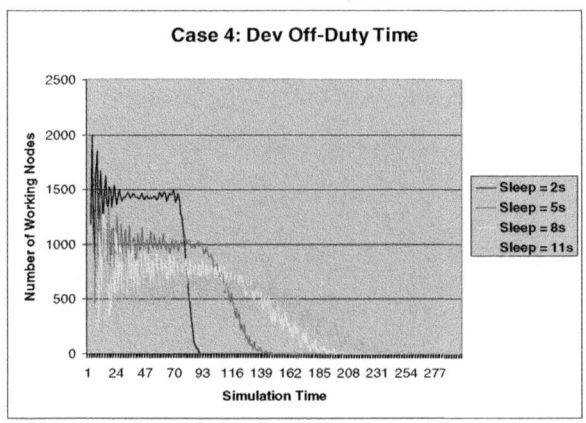

Fig. 9. This graph represents Case 4 where the off-duty time was studied

4.6 Case 5: Wmax

In this case, the Wmax was set to 12, 22, and 32 to see if it was a factor in the network's life. BT = 1, CT = 2, and ST = 3. The number of DEVs that were deployed was 2000. The sleep time for the DEVs was 2 seconds. The QoS level was set to 85%. Looking at Fig. 10, we can see that all of the Wmax intervals have about the same effect on network life and the number of working DEVs. It doesn't seem to affect it all that much.

4.7 Case 6: No Scheduling

In this case, we looked at a no sleep/no power scheduling method. In Fig. 11, you can see this indicated by the yellow line on the graph. Also plotted on this graph is a LDAS network using BT = 1, ST = 3, CT = 2, 2000 DEVs, sleep time of 2 seconds,

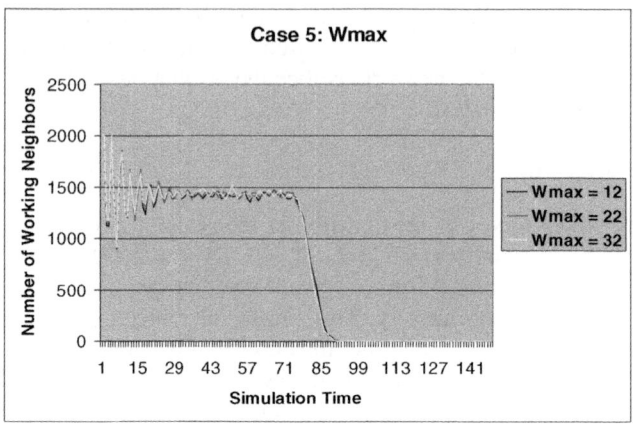

Fig. 10. This graph shows the results of a study on the variable Wmax

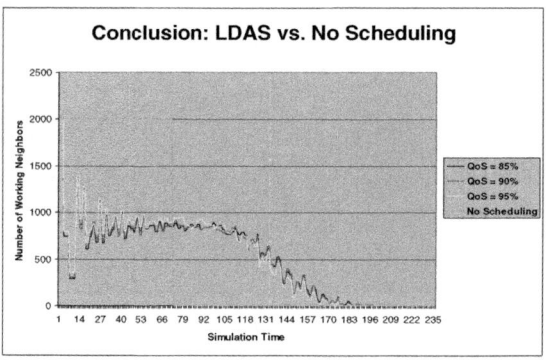

Fig. 11. This shows the result of a comparison of a network that doesn't use power management and a network that does use power management (LDAS)

simulation time of 1000s, and Wmax set at 32. Here the results are simple but astounding. LDAS is significantly favorable to a non-schedule network. The three different levels of QoS all do better than the no-schedule algorithm. This shows that it is viable to look into power scheduling to devise an efficient means of implementing it.

4.8   Other Findings

To see if this network algorithm was truly scalable, we ran a simulation using BT = 1, CT = 2, ST = 3, 2000 DEVs, an area of 300m X 300m, simulation time of 300s, sleep time of 8 seconds, Wmax = 32, and QoS = 85%. As you can see in Fig. 12, this algorithm worked on this network in a similar fashion to how it worked in the previous simulation examples with an area of 150m x 150m. This power scheduling algorithm is truly scalable.

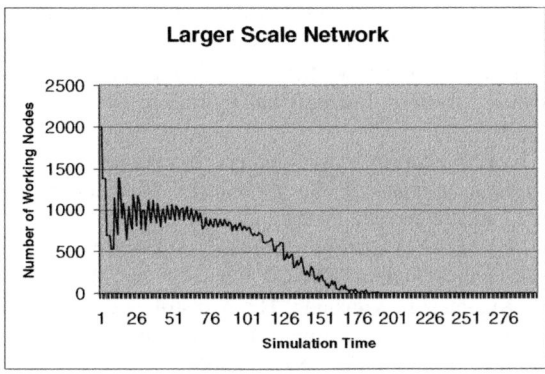

Fig. 12. This graph shows LDAS implemented on a larger network area

5 Conclusion

After studying [1] and implementing a simulation to emulate the study, several conclusions can be drawn. The first is that LDAS is better than no power management
scheduling. In all of the cases that LDAS was used, the number of working DEVs was
reduced to a steady value after a certain period of time. This was after several time
cycles which allowed the DEVs to collect information about each other and their
immediate neighbors.

It seems that the most influential factors on the network were the ST and the sleeping time. The sleep check time and the period of time the DEV sleeps are important
parts of power conservation, as these two variables seem to affect the network the
most. One of the factors that seemed not to affect the network in any way was
the Wmax. Remember, the Wmax is the upper bound of the backoff interval for the
RTOS to Off-Duty states.

A non-location based algorithm was found that could be implemented in wireless
sensor networks such as IEEE 802.15.4. The redundant sensors in the simulated network were eliminated. This provided more network life and reduced energy costs.

References

[1] Wu, K., Gao, Y., Li, F., Xiao, Y.: Lightweight Deployment-Aware Scheduling for Wire-
less Sensor Networks. In: ACM/Springer Mobile Networks and Applications (MONET),
Special Issue on Energy Constraints and Lifetime Performance in Wireless Sensor
Networks, December 2005, vol. 10(6), pp. 837–852 (2005)

[2] LAN/MAN Standards Committee of the IEEE Computer Society, Part 15.4: Wireless
Medium Access Control (MAC) and Physical Layer (PHY) Specifications for Low Rate
Wireless Personal Area Networks (LR-WPAN) (October 2002)

[3] Li, G., Znati, T., Gopalan, A.: REAP: ring band-based energy adaptive protocol for information dissemination and forwarding in wireless sensor networks. International
Journal of Sensor Networks 1(1/2), 103–113 (2006)

[4] Nguyen, C.K., Kumar, A.: Energy-efficient medium access control with throughput op-
timisation for wireless sensor networks. International Journal of Sensor Networks 1(3/4),
125–133 (2006)

[5] Sha, K., Du, J., Shi, W.: WEAR: a balanced, fault-tolerant, energy-aware routing protocol in WSNs. International Journal of Sensor Networks 1(3/4), 156–168 (2006)

[6] Tezcan, N., Wang, W.: TTS: a two-tiered scheduling mechanism for energy conservation in wireless sensor networks. International Journal of Sensor Networks 1(3/4), 213–228 (2006)

[7] Li, G., Znati, T.: RECA: a ring-structured energy-efficient clustering architecture for robust communication in wireless sensor networks. International Journal of Sensor Networks 2(1/2), 34–43 (2006)

[8] Zhao, S., Tan, L., Li, J.: A distributed energy efficient multicast routing algorithm for WANETs. International Journal of Sensor Networks 2(1/2), 62–67 (2006)

[9] Yuanyuan, Z., Xiaohua, J., Yanxiang, H.: A distributed algorithm for constructing energy-balanced connected dominating set in wireless sensor networks. International Journal of Sensor Networks 2(1/2), 68–76 (2006)

[10] Shen, S., O'Hare, G.M.P.: Wireless sensor networks, an energy-aware and utility-based BDI agent approach. International Journal of Sensor Networks 2(3/4), 235–245 (2007)

[11] Liang, Q., Wang, L., Ren, Q.: Fault-tolerant and energy efficient cross-layer design for wireless sensor networks. International Journal of Sensor Networks 2(3/4), 248–257 (2007)

[12] Watfa, M.K., Commuri, S.: A framework for assessing residual energy in wireless sensor network. International Journal of Sensor Networks 2(3/4), 256–272 (2007)

[13] Cagri Gungor, V.: Efficient available energy monitoring in wireless sensor networks. International Journal of Sensor Networks 2(1), 25–32 (2008)

[14] Kumar, S., Kambhatla, K.K.R., Zan, B., Hu, F., Xiao, Y.: An energy-aware and intelligent cluster-based event detection scheme in wireless sensor networks. International Journal of Sensor Networks 3(2), 123–133 (2008)

[15] Cardei, I., Cardei, M.: Energy-efficient connected-coverage in wireless sensor networks. International Journal of Sensor Networks 3(3), 201–210 (2008)

[16] Cai, L., Shen, X.: Editorial: Energy-efficient algorithm and protocol design in sensor networks. International Journal of Sensor Networks 4(1/2), 1–2 (2008)

[17] Lecuire, V., Duran-Faundez, C., Krommenacker, N.: Energy-efficient image transmission in sensor networks. International Journal of Sensor Networks 4(1/2), 37–47 (2008)

[18] Cheng, M.X., Yin, L.: Energy-efficient data gathering algorithm in sensor networks with partial aggregation. International Journal of Sensor Networks 4(1/2), 48–54 (2008)

[19] Zou, S., Nikolaidis, I., Harms, J.: Efficient aggregation using first hop selection in WSNs. International Journal of Sensor Networks 4(1/2), 55–67 (2008)

[20] Wang, Y., Li, F., Dahlberg, T.A.: Energy-efficient topology control for three-dimensional sensor networks. International Journal of Sensor Networks 4(1/2), 68–78 (2008)

[21] Chen, M., Kwon, T., Mao, S., Yuan, Y., Leung, V.C.M.: Reliable and energy-efficient routing protocol in dense wireless sensor networks. International Journal of Sensor Networks 4(1/2), 104–117 (2008)

[22] Kim, S., Wang, X., Madihian, M.: Energy efficiency of a per-hop relay selection scheme for sensor networks using cooperative MIMO. International Journal of Sensor Networks 4(1/2), 118–129 (2008)

[23] Gavalas, D., Pantziou, G., Konstantopoulos, C., Mamalis, B.: ABP: a low-cost, energy-efficient clustering algorithm for relatively static and quasistatic MANETs. International Journal of Sensor Networks 4(4), 260–269 (2008)

[24] Yeh, L., Wang, Y., Tseng, Y.: iPower: an energy conservation system for intelligent buildings by wireless sensor networks. International Journal of Sensor Networks 5(1), 1–10 (2009)

[25] Tan, L., Ge, F., Li, J., Kato, J.: HCEP: a hybrid cluster-based energy-efficient protocol for wireless sensor networks. International Journal of Sensor Networks 5(2), 67–78 (2009)

[26] Chen, M., Kwon, T., Mao, S., Leung, V.C.M.: Spatial-Temporal relation-based Energy-Efficient Reliable routing protocol in wireless sensor networks. International Journal of Sensor Networks 5(3), 129–141 (2009)

[27] Jeong, W., Nof, S.Y.: Design of timeout-based wireless microsensor network protocols: energy and latency considerations. International Journal of Sensor Networks 5(3), 142–152 (2009)

[28] Liu, J., Hong, X.: An online energy-efficient routing protocol with traffic load prospects in wireless sensor networks. International Journal of Sensor Networks 5(3), 185–197 (2009)

[29] Su, I.-F., Lee, C., Ke, C.: Radius reconfiguration for energy conservation in sensor networks. International Journal of Sensor Networks 5(4), 256–267 (2009)

[30] Chiang, M., Byrd, G.T.: Adaptive aggregation tree transformation for energy-efficient query processing in sensor networks. International Journal of Sensor Networks 6(1), 51–64 (2009)

[31] Xiao, Y., Chen, H., Wu, K., Sun, B., Zhang, Y., Sun, X., Liu, C.: Coverage and Detection of a Randomized Scheduling Algorithm in Wireless Sensor Networks. IEEE Transactions on Computers 59(4), 507–521 (2010), doi:10.1109/TC.2009.170

[32] Peng, M., Xiao, Y., Wang, P.: Error Analysis and Kernel Density Approach of Scheduling Sleeping Nodes in Cluster-Based Wireless Sensor Networks. IEEE Transactions on Vehicular Technology 58(9), 5105–5114 (2009), doi:10.1109/TVT.2009.2027908

[33] Hu, F., Xiao, Y., Hao, Q.: Congestion-aware, Loss-Resilient Bio-monitoring Sensor Networking for Mobile Health Applications. IEEE Journal on Selected Areas in Communications 27(4), 450–465 (2009), doi:10.1109/JSAC.2009.090509

[34] Du, X., Guizani, M., Xiao, Y., Chen, H.: A Routing-Driven Elliptic Curve Cryptography Based Key Management Scheme for Heterogeneous Sensor Networks. IEEE Transactions on Wireless Communications 8(3), 1223–1229 (2009), doi:10.1109/TWC.2009.060598

[35] Du, X., Guizani, M., Xiao, Y., Chen, H.: Secure and Efficient Time Synchronization in Heterogeneous Sensor Networks. IEEE Transactions on Vehicular Technology 57(4), 2387–2394 (2008)

[36] Du, X., Guizani, M., Xiao, Y., Chen, H.: Two Tier Secure Routing Protocol for Heterogeneous Sensor Networks. IEEE Transactions on Wireless Communications 6(9), 3395–3401 (2007)

[37] Liu, C., Wu, K., Xiao, Y., Sun, B.: Random Coverage with Guaranteed Connectivity: Joint Scheduling for Wireless Sensor Networks. IEEE Transactions on Parallel and Distributed Systems 17(6), 562–575 (2006)

[38] Ozdemir, S., Xiao, Y.: Secure Data Aggregation in Wireless Sensor Networks: A Comprehensive Overview. Computer Networks 53(12), 2022–2037 (2009), doi:10.1016/j.comnet.2009.02.023

[39] Xiao, Y., Zhang, Y., Peng, M., Chen, H., Du, X., Sun, B., Wu, K.: Two and Three-Dimensional Intrusion Object Detection under Randomized Scheduling Algorithms in Sensor Networks. Computer Networks 53(14), 2458–2475 (2009), doi:10.1016/j.comnet.2009.05.002

[40] Wu, K., Liu, C., Xiao, Y., Liu, J.: A Delay-Constrained Optimal Data Aggregation Framework for Wireless Sensor Networks. ACM/Springer Mobile Networks and Applications (MONET), special issue on advances in mobile ubiquitous computing and wireless multi-hop networking 14(5), 571–589 (2009)

Bayesian Framework for Automatic Image Annotation Using Visual Keywords

Rajeev Agrawal[1], Changhua Wu[2], William Grosky[3], and Farshad Fotouhi[4]

[1] Grand Valley State University
1 Campus Drive, Allendale, MI 49401
[2] Kettering University
1700 West Third Av, Flint, MI 48504
[3] The University of Michigan
4901 Evergreen Road, Dearborn, MI 48128
[4] Wayne State University
431 State Hall, Detroit, MI 48202
agrawalr@gvsu.edu, cwu@kettering.edu,
wgrosky@umich.edu, fotouhi@wayne.edu

Abstract. In this paper, we propose a Bayesian probability based framework, which uses visual keywords and already available text keywords to automatically annotate the images. Taking the cue from document classification, an image can be considered as a document and objects present in it as words. Using this concept, we can create visual keywords by dividing an image into tiles based on a certain template size. Visual keywords are simple vector quantization of small-sized image tiles. We estimate the conditional probability of a text keyword in the presence of visual keywords, described by a multivariate Gaussian distribution. We demonstrate the effectiveness of our approach by comparing predicted text annotations with manual annotations and analyze the effect of text annotation length on the performance.

Keywords: Visual keywords, Bayesian probability, image annotation.

1 Introduction

The metadata available with the images has been in the past for image retrieval. This metadata may be in the form of text annotations or any information associated with the image. The challenge here is to have the metadata available. In social networking environment, users are encouraged to annotate image is the form of tags, which can be used later to search or browse images. Many techniques have been proposed to automatically annotate the image using the available text annotations. In [1], it is proposed to describe images using a vocabulary blobs. Each image is generated by using a certain number of blobs. A co-occurrence model is proposed in [2], in which co-occurrence of words with image regions created using a grid is examined.

An image, represented as sequence of feature-vectors characterizing low-level visual features such as color, texture or oriented-edges, is modeled as having been stochastically generated by a hidden Markov model, whose states represent concepts [3].

G.S. Tomar et al. (Eds.): UCMA 2010, CCIS 75, pp. 142–157, 2010.

A multimodal image keywords approach is used in [4], which takes the advantage of both low level features and available text annotations. It has been shown in [5] that models trained on rectangular partitions outperform those trained on object-based partitions. Therefore, we do not apply any complex segmentation algorithm to create tiles. In addition to this, most of the segmentation techniques are very subjective and do not always extract the relevant segments/objects. They need manual intervention to select the domain specific objects.

How to define the term *visual keyword* in the context of image? One simple answer is to consider each pixel a word, but this method is the same as using the low-level contents of an image. Therefore, we need a proper definition of a visual keyword that is simple and independent of context and content. The number of visual keywords can vary depending on the chosen template size of a tile. The idea of using visual keywords or a visual thesaurus, first appears in [6]. This works with images, not words, and helps in recognizing visually similar events, so-called "visual synonyms," using both spatial and motion similarity. Visual keywords can be based on color, texture, pattern, and objects in the image or any other user-defined features, depending on the domain. Visual keywords are created by cropping domain-relevant regions from sample images. These regions are then assigned labels and sub-labels to form a thesaurus and a vocabulary, respectively [7]. In a highly simplified form, even a pixel can be considered as visual keyword, but it does not really provide any meaningful semantic concept.

The rest of the paper is organized as follows: Section 2 describes the related work in the area of image annotation and visual keywords. An overview of creating visual keywords is given in Section 3, and Section 4 presents the Bayesian framework of image annotation. Section-5 has experiments and results. Finally, in Section 6, we offer some conclusions and discuss future work.

2   Related Work

In automatic image annotation, the first step is the representation of an image by extracting low level features and their associated text keywords. In [8], an image is represented by three 1-D color histograms in the red, green and blue channels, while a histogram of the directions of edge points is used to represent general shape information. A, so-called, blobworld representation [9] is used to retrieve images. This approach recognizes the images as a combination of objects, making both query and learning in the blobworld more meaningful to the user. In all these works, color is the fundamental unit used to represent an image, which is very similar to the keywords in a text document. However, the representation of the color features may vary in the different systems, ranging from histograms to indexing. A keyblock-based approach [10] encodes each image as a set of one-dimensional index codes linked to the keyblocks in the codebook, analogous to considering a text document as a linear list of keywords. For each semantic class, a corresponding codebook is generated. However this approach does not have any invariant properties and requires domain knowledge while encoding the images. More recently, the visual keyword approach has been used for visual categorization using support vector machines (SVM) and naïve Bayes classifiers [11]. Objects and their image locations are discovered, by using a visual analogue of a word, formed by vector quantizing low-level features [12], and extracting a large number of overlapping, square sub-windows of random sizes, at random positions from the training images [13].

To establish the relationship between image regions and text keywords, a statistical model is used. A cross-media relevance model is introduced in [14] that learns the joint distribution of a set of regions and a set of text keywords rather then looking the direct correspondence between a single region and a single keyword. A Complement Components Analysis based Bayesian model to estimate the class conditional probabilities is proposed in [15]. A heuristic greedy iterative algorithm to estimate the probability of a keyword subset being the caption of an image uses the *Automatic Local Analysis* of text information retrieval [16]. we explore solutions to the problems of large scale concept space learning and mismatch between semantic and visual space. Before assigning multiple labels for unlabeled images, first higher level semantic concepts are clustered into topics in the local neighborhood and then these topics are used to as lexis [17]. The Automatic Linguistic Indexing of Pictures - Real Time (ALIPR) system is developed to fully automate online pictures at high speed. In particular, the D2-clustering method is developed to group objects represented by bags of weighted vectors using a generalized mixture modeling technique [18].

3   Visual Keyword Image Presentation

In our proposed approach, the visual keywords are obtained by classifying the MPEG-7 features of the tiles in the training image set. In this section, we will give a introduction to the MPEG-7 descriptors and the process of obtaining the visual keywords.

3.1   MPEG-7 Descriptors

MPEG-7, formally called the Multimedia Content Description Interface, is a standard for describing multimedia content data that supports some degree of interpretation of semantics determination, which can be passed onto, or accessed by, a device or computer code. MPEG-7 is not aimed at any one application in particular; rather, the elements that MPEG-7 standardizes support a broad range of applications [19]. MPEG-7 compatible data include still pictures, graphics, 3D models, audio, speech, video, and composition information about how these elements are combined in a multimedia presentation. In this work, the MPEG-7 color descriptors are extracted using a software tool based on MPEG-7 Reference Software: the eXperimentation Model [20]. There are seven color descriptors in MPEG-7 standard: color space, color quantization, dominant colors, scalable color, color layout, color structure, and GoF/GoP color. In the current description of MPEG-7, the following six color spaces are supported: monochrome, RGB, YCrCb, HSV, HMMD, and monochrome (intensity only).

Here is a brief overview of those descriptors which are used in our work:

Scalable color descriptor: The scalable color descriptor (SCD) is a global color histogram, encoded by a Haar transform. The SCD is defined in HSV color space. It has been found to be useful for image-to-image matching and retrieval based on color features. Retrieval accuracy increases with the number of bits used in its representation. The number of bits can be 16, 32, 64, 128 or 256.

Color layout descriptor: The color layout descriptor (CLD) represents the spatial color information in an image or in an arbitrary shaped region in YCrCb color space. Being very compact and resolution-invariant, this descriptor provides a matching functionality with high retrieval efficiency at very small computational costs. The default number of coefficients is 12.

Color structure descriptor: The color structure descriptor (CSD) captures both color content and the structure of this content. It is used for image-to-image matching and still image retrieval. An 8x8 structuring element is used to extract color structure information instead of using each pixel individually. This descriptor can distinguish two images in which a given color is present in identical amounts but the geometry of these pixels is different. The color values are represented in HMMD color space. The number of bins can be 32, 64, 128 or 256. The CSD provides improved similarity-based image retrieval performance compared to ordinary color histograms.

3.2   Visual Keyword Generation

Figure 1 shows our approach to generating visual keywords from the low-level features. Let $\{I_i \mid i = 1 : n\}$ be a set of n images. Each image is divided into non-overlapping tiles, after which we extract various features from each tile resulting in T, k-element feature vectors, where T is the total number of tiles in all images I. Let V be the desired number of visual keywords. We then cluster this set of feature vectors into V clusters, each cluster corresponding to one of the V visual keywords. Our approach treats each tile like a word in a text document, counting the number of times tiles from each bin appear in an image. Tile-feature vector can be formed using simple low-level features, such as color histograms, textures, etc., or the more sophisticated features such as Scale Invariant Feature Transforms (SIFT) descriptors [21] or MPEG-7 descriptors [22]. SIFT is a transformation that transform images into scale-invariant coordinates relative to local features. SIFT generates a large number of features that densely cover the image over the full range of scales and locations. In SIFT, keypoints are detected by checking the scale-space extrema. The descriptor of each keypoint is based on the gradient magnitude and orientation in a region around the keypoint.

The procedure to create visual keywords is completely unsupervised and does not involve any image segmentation. Another important parameter to consider is the selection of template size to create tiles, since this size has a direct effect on the computation costs. A small template size will result in a large number of tiles and, hence, higher computation costs. We find that a template size of 32 x 32 pixels is appropriate [23], which extracts important information from an image and still doesn't create a very large number of tiles. We use the scalable color descriptor (SCD) with 64 coefficients, which are good enough to provide reasonably good performance, the color layout descriptor (CLD) with 12 coefficients, found to be the best trade-off between the storage cost and retrieval efficiency, and the color structure descriptor (CSD) with 64 coefficients, sufficient enough to capture the important features of a tile. Hence, a tile vector has 140 coefficients. We note that all three MPEG-7 descriptors have different sizes in different feature spaces as described in section-3.1; therefore they are normalized within their own feature space using the following simple normalization technique:

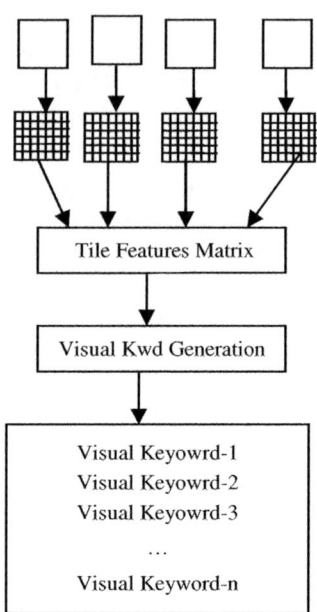

Fig. 1. Visual keyword generation process

$$f_i^{'} = \frac{f_i - \min_i}{\max_i - \min_i}$$

where f_i represents the ith feature in the feature space, $\min_i$ is the minimum possible value of the ith feature, $\max_i$ is the maximum possible value of the ith feature, and $f_i^{'}$ is the normalized feature value. The tile matrix is then created using the normalized tile vectors as its column vectors.

After obtaining the normalized MPEG-7 descriptors, we use the high-dimensional clustering algorithm, *vcluster* [24], to cluster all the tile vectors into the desired number of clusters. Each cluster will represent a visual keyword. The vcluster routine uses a method called *repeated bisections*. In this method, the desired k-way clustering solution is computed by performing a sequence of $k - 1$ repeated bisections. In this approach, the matrix is first clustered into two groups, and then one of these groups is selected and bisected further. This process continues until the desired number of clusters is found. During each step, a cluster is bisected so that the resulting 2-way clustering solution optimizes a particular clustering criterion function. Note that this approach ensures that the criterion function is locally optimized within each bisection, but in general, it is not globally optimized. The cluster that is selected for further partitioning is the cluster whose bisection will optimize the value of the overall clustering criterion function. The following criterion function is used to find the membership of a tile with a cluster:

$$\text{maximize} \sum_{i=1}^{k} \sqrt{\sum_{v,u \in s_i} sim(v,u)}$$

Where $sim(v,u)$ is the similarity between vector v and u, and it can be computed by the dot product of v and u. The above criterion function is used by many popular vector space variants of the K-means algorithm. In this method, each cluster is represented by its centroid vector and the goal is to find the clustering solution that maximizes the similarity between each vector and the centroid of the cluster to which it is assigned.

After this step, an image is then described by a vector, whose size is equal to the number of clusters (visual keywords). Each cluster is described by a mean vector and a covariance matrix. The j-th element of this vector is equal to the number of tiles from the given image that belongs to the j-th cluster. The visual keyword-image matrix is then formed, using the image vectors as columns. Finally, we normalize each column vector to unit length and generate the normalized visual keyword-image matrix.

3.3   Text Keywords Extraction

There is a variety of information associated with the images in addition to low-level features. They may be in the form of content-independent metadata, such as time stamp, location, image format or content-bearing metadata, which describes the higher level concepts of the image, such as animal, pet, male to describe a dog image. This semantic information, however, cannot be extracted directly from the visual contents, but represents the relatively more important meanings of the objects that are perceived by human beings. These conceptual aspects are more closely related to users' preferences and subjectivity. Concepts may vary significantly in different circumstances. Subtle changes in the semantics may lead to dramatic conceptual differences.

The algorithm for this step is very straightforward. We first create an initial term-document matrix. To reduce the effect of the morphological variations of words, we use Porter's stemming algorithm [25]. The minimum and maximum term (word) length thresholds are set as 2 and 30, respectively, which are reasonable for our experiments. The term-document matrix is then normalized to unit-length.

3.4   Creating Co-occurrence Visual Keyword and Text Keyword Matrix

In our training set of images, each image is already annotated with one or more text keywords. Since we can know for each tile in an image, which visual keyword it falls into, we can build a visual keyword and text label matrix M. An element M (i, j) in the matrix shows how many times visual keyword v_{ki} and text annotation t_{kj} show up in the same image. The larger an element M (i, j) is, the high is the correlation between visual keyword v_{ki} and text annotation t_{kj}. The visual keyword v_{ki} is described by $(mean_i, cov_j)$.

4 Bayesian Probability Framework

The proposed approach is based on a Bayesian probability model. Bayesian methods view the parameters as random variables having some known prior distribution. Let us assume ω is a set of classes and x are the training samples. The Bayesian approach allows us to compute posterior probabilities from the prior probabilities $P(\omega_i)$ and the class-conditional probabilities $P(\omega_i \mid x)$. Let γ denote the set of test samples, the posterior probability $P(\omega_i \mid x, \gamma)$ can be calculated as follows:

$$P(\omega_i \mid x, \gamma) = \frac{p(x \mid \omega_i, \lambda)P(\omega_i \mid \lambda)}{\sum_{j=1}^{n} p(x \mid \omega_j, \lambda)P(\omega_j \mid \lambda)}$$

Now, we apply the Bayesian concept in image annotation.

The problem for annotating a new image can then be described as follows.

Problem Statement: Given a new image I with multiple tiles $\{ t_i \mid i=1:n\}$, a set of visual keywords descried by $V = \{ (mean_j, \mathrm{cov}_j) \mid j = 1 : m \}$ and an integral co-occurrence matrix $M(i, j)$ obtained from the training images, find the probability of text keyword T_i to be a valid text annotation of image I.

Since an image is composed of tiles, the task is to find the following conditional probability $p(T_k \mid (t_1, t_2, ..., t_n))$. If we assume that the tiles are independent of each other, then $p(T_k \mid (t_1, t_2, ..., t_n))$ can be computed using the following equation:

$$p(T_k \mid (t_1, t_2, ..., t_n)) = 1 - \prod_{i=1:n} (1 - p(T_k \mid t_i)) \tag{1}$$

where $p(T_k \mid t_i)$ is the conditional probability of having T_k as the label given the existence of tile t_i in an image. This conditional probability can be rewritten as:

$$p(T_k \mid t_i) = p(T_k, t_i) * \; p(t_i) \tag{2}$$

Where $p(T_k, t_i)$ is the joint probability of T_k and t_i. Since t_i is a tile in the new image, then we can assume $p(t_i)$ is 1. Then we have

$$p(T_k \mid t_i) = p(T_k, t_i) \tag{3}$$

$$= p(t_i \mid T_k) * p(T_k) \tag{4}$$

$p(T_k)$ is the probability of text keyword T_k. Since there is no easy way to tell which text keyword is more likely to occur than others, we assume all text keyword have the same probability. By setting $p(T_k) = 1$, we have

$$p(T_k \mid t_i) = p(t_i \mid T_k) \tag{5}$$

$$= \sum_{j=1:m} p(V_j \mid T_k) * P(t_i \mid V_j) \tag{6}$$

where $p(V_j \mid T_k)$ is the conditional probability of visual keyword V_j given the existence of text keyword T_k. To simplify the problem, we can approximate $p(V_j \mid T_k)$ in the following way:

$$p(V_j \mid T_k) = M(k, j) / \sum_{j=1:m} (M(k, j)) \tag{7}$$

The probability computed using the above equation determines the probability of the visual keywords based on the co-occurrence matrix M. If a visual keyword appears with a text keyword more frequently than other visual keywords, the conditional probability of this visual keyword given the text keyword is, of course, higher than the conditional probabilities of other visual keywords. $P(t_i \mid V_j)$ is simply the probability of t_i belonging to visual keyword V_j, which is described by a multivariate Gaussian distribution. In the proposed approach, we use the density at t_i to approximate the probability of t_i belonging to V_j.

5   Experiments and Results

5.1   Data Set

We conduct experiments using the LabelMe image collection downloaded from the MIT AI Lab [26]. There are 658 images selected from 15 categories. The collection has been annotated by online users, and therefore has a wide variety of annotations. They do not conform to any fixed annotation list. In this collection, many classes have very few training samples; on the other hand there are classes with many training samples. In addition to this, we have to deal with partially labeled training images. We use a template size of 32 x 32 pixels to create non-overlapping tiles. The original images in the collection have different resolutions, varying from 2560 x 1920 to 300 x 205. The images are resized to 640 pixels x 480 pixels if they are larger to restrict the number of tiles to a fixed limit; however the smaller images are left in their original sizes to extract all available semantic information in them. The MILOS software [27], which is based on the MPEG-7 XM model, is used to extract the color descriptors SCD, CSD, CLD. The total number of descriptors used is 140, in which we have 64 of SCD, 64 of CSD, and 12 of CLD. The maximum number of tiles an image can have is 300; the total number of tiles is 165750. Table 1 lists the image categories, the number of images in each category, and the number of keywords used to annotate the images in each category.

Table 1. Details of Image dataset

Image category number	Image category	Number of images	No. of text keywords
1	Boston street scene	152	539
2	cars parked	39	159
3	kitchen	14	117
4	office	24	130
5	rocks	41	80
6	pumpkins	58	129
7	apples	11	67
8	oranges	18	68
9	conference room	28	128
10	bedroom	14	79
11	dining	63	266
12	indoor home	59	127
13	home office	19	109
14	silverware	81	248
15	speaker	37	123

5.2 Performance Evaluation

To evaluate the quality of predicted text annotations using the Bayesian framework, we calculate the average *precision* and *recall* statistics. For a test image I, the precision and recall are defined as

$$\text{Precision} = \frac{T_w}{T_p}, \ \text{Recall} = \frac{T_w}{T_g}$$

where T_w is the number of correctly predicted annotations, T_p is the number of predicted annotations and T_g is the number of ground truth annotations. Conceptually, precision and recall value should be less than 1. In our results, we find that the correct predicted annotations are more than what are in the original annotated list, therefore

Table 2. Precision, recall and F-measure

Image category number	Average number of keywords	Average precision	Average recall	F-measure
1	3.54	**0.49**	2.18	**0.80**
2	4.08	**0.71**	2.17	**1.07**
3	8.36	**0.66**	0.90	**0.77**
4	5.42	0.33	0.81	0.48
5	1.95	0.29	1.80	0.51
6	2.22	**0.44**	3.03	**0.77**
7	6.09	**0.41**	0.89	**0.56**
8	3.77	0.31	1.05	0.48
9	4.57	0.27	0.72	0.39
10	5.64	**0.51**	1.30	**0.73**
11	4.22	0.38	1.53	0.61
12	2.15	0.24	1.51	0.42
13	5.74	0.29	0.59	0.39
14	3.06	0.17	0.83	0.29
15	3.32	0.24	0.96	0.38

recall is more than 1 in many cases. We also calculate a single performance measure called F-measure, which considers both precision and recall. F measure trades off precision versus recall, and is the weighted harmonic mean of precision and recall.

$$F = \frac{2 * precison * recall}{precision + recall}$$

We also analyze the performance of our results against the number of text keywords in each category and draw some useful conclusions.

5.3   Evaluating Performance of Predicted Text Annotations

We use the same set of images for training and testing to see the effect of Bayesian learning on predicted text annotations. We create 1500 visual keywords, which is approximately 1% of the total number of tiles. We conducted experiments with different number of visual keywords and this percentage was found to be good enough to represent the semantic concepts of our image collection. Table 2 includes average precision, average recall and the F-measure values along with the average number of keywords in each image category. We have considered only the first 10 text annotations predicted by the Bayesian model to calculate precision, which is reasonable. As we mentioned earlier, the average recall and the F-measure in our case are different and can be more than 1. The average precision values are in the range 0.17 to 0.71 (Figure 3). These results are much better than the results reported in [1]. The six categories *Boston street scene, cars parked, kitchen, pumpkins, apples and bedroom* have average precision values more than 0.40. The six categories *office, rocks, oranges, conference room, dining* and *home office* have average precision values more than 0.25. Only the three categories *indoor home, silverware,* and *speaker* have the precision values less than 0.25. The worst performance, we get is for *silverware* category. On closer inspection, we observe that the image sizes of this category are smaller than those of the other categories. Therefore, the number of tiles extracted before creating visual keywords is smaller than in other categories. In other words, the semantic concepts embedded in *silverware* tiles could not be represented by the visual keywords as well as those in other categories. The concept of creating visual keywords is to identify the hidden inherent semantic concept from the images, which gets diminished with few tiles in this category. Figure 2 shows the F-measure values for all the image categories.

Table 3. Sample images with ground truth (GT) and predicted text annotations (PA)

No.	Image	Ground truth and predicted text annotations
1		GT: building car fence ladder occluded rear tree window PA: ladder streetlight rear pedestrian fence lampost personsitting onewaysign sailboat bridge
2		GT: building carSide door wheel window PA: streetlight trafficlight abstergent do not enter bedandframe sidewalk stop pole
3		GT: Box car license plate PA: carnumberplate rearviewmirror licenceplate cardboardbox bumper pipe pillar tire sprinkler pillarpartition
4		GT: Cabinet Dispenser Door Faucet Mug Paper Sink Towel bottle box coffeemachine microwave trash PA: dispenser laundry coffeemachine open towel faucet plug kettle sink cabinet
5		GT: books desk keyboard pole screenfront PA: pole streetlight screenfront journal cpu desk carnumberplate pillar keyboard pipe

Table 3. (*Continued*)

6		GT: Shoe pumpkin shadow toolbox PA: toolbox shadow shoe tube drainpipe abstergent pumpkin squash corridor wood
7		GT: Stone trunk PA: treepart trunk fallenleaves stone rock boulder foliage dry jacket lawn
8		GT: apple bottle glass milk plastic plate water PA: cookinggas milk plastic ketchup butter wood sauce knob mouth easel

Visual keywords are constructed to extract the inherent concepts hidden in the images using low-level features. Given the low-level features in an image category, K-means clustering algorithm is able to identify the similar clusters. In other words, the full or partial objects in the images fall into the same cluster. Now, the visual keywords combined with partial text annotations can predict the objects in the test images using Bayesian learning. Table 3 shows some sample images and their ground truth text annotations as well as our predicted text annotations. In image-1 ground truth information, there was no *onewaysign* and pedestrian annotations, but the predicted list has them. Image 5 has *CPU, pole, journal, pillar* in the predicted list, which are not in the ground truth list. We note that pole and pipe may refer to the same object. But, the predicted text annotations can only be as good as its training dataset. In image 7, there are only two annotations in the ground truth, but our model could successfully predict other annotations like *fallen leaves, rock, boulder, lawn,, dry, and foliage*.

5.4   Effect of Text Annotation Length on Performance

Figures 3 and 4 show the effect of the number of annotations on the average precision and F-measure. What emerges from the comparison is that the number of annotations during training play a crucial role while predicting annotations for a new test image. If an image category has more text annotations, the Bayesian model is able to predict good quality text annotations for that category. Since the image collection in our training dataset doesn't restrict text annotations to any limited vocabulary, the annotations are not homogeneous. Identical words are even spelled differently. We use Porter's algorithm to create stems from the annotations and the final vocabulary is created. For example, *organize, organizer, organization* will have the same stem.

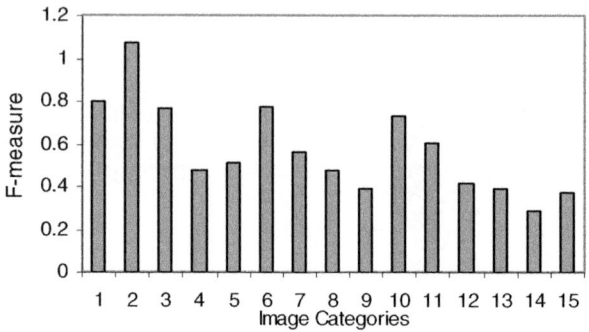

Fig. 2. F-measure

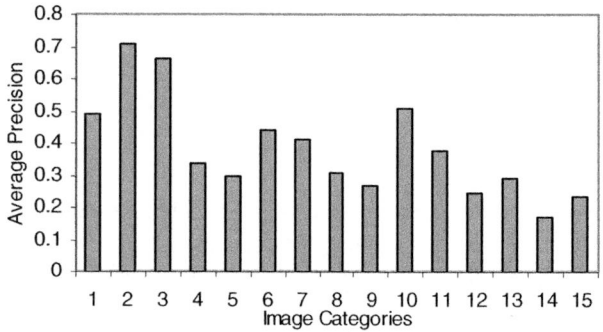

Fig. 3. Average Precision

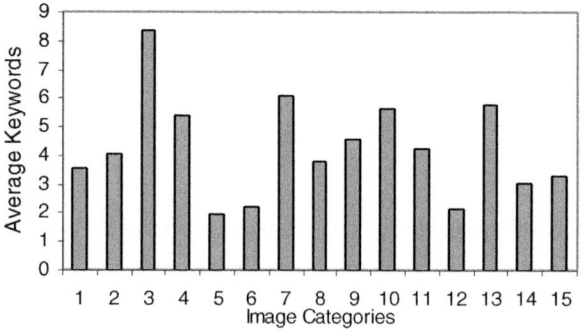

Fig. 4. Average number of keywords

The average number of keywords in *cars parked* (category 2) are more than in *Boston street scene* category-1), increasing the average precision and F-measure for *cars parked*. This is evident in *conference room* (category 9) and *bedroom* (category 10), in *silverware* (category-14) and *speaker* (category 15), and in others. Note that this is not the only factor improving average precision. Image size and the number of images in the category also play a role. An illustration of this is *cars parked* (category 2) and *kitchen* (category 3). The *kitchen* category has an average number of keywords almost double that in *cars parked*, but the F-measure and average precision decreases instead of increasing. This is due to the fact that the number of images in *kitchen* is only 14, whereas, *cars parked* has 39 images. The same is true for indoor home (category 12) and home office (category 13). We can draw the conclusion that the quality of predicted text annotations is a function of the number of training images, average number of text keywords, and the number of visual keywords or the size of the image.

6 Conclusions

We presented a Bayesian framework for automatic image annotation using the visual keywords concept. We analyzed the performance using average precision and F-measure. We also looked the effect of the number of keywords on the annotation performance. We concluded that the quality of predicted text annotations is a functions of the number of training images, average number of text keywords, and the number of visual keywords or the size of the image. The visual keyword approach makes it possible to extract the semantic concept hidden in low level image contents. The results were remarkable considering the heterogeneous image data set, which has vastly different number of images in various categories. The framework is completely unsupervised and doesn't depend on any complex segmentation techniques. Once a Bayesian learning model is trained, it is easily scalable and not very expensive to large image collection.

It is possible to identify the objects and their location in an image using the knowledge of the location of the tiles. This can be done by indexing tiles belonging to a visual keyword to their locations in the images. We can improve the performance of our model by first improving and extending the quality of original text keywords of the images using WorldNet [28]. We have used only three MPEG-7 color descriptors for our experiments. There are other color and texture descriptors, which can also be used to extract low level features from an image.

References

1. Duygulu, P., Barnard, K., Freitas, J., de Forsyth, D.A.: Object Recognition as Machine Translation: Learning a Lexicon for a Fixed Image Vocabulary. In: Heyden, A., Sparr, G., Nielsen, M., Johansen, P. (eds.) ECCV 2002. LNCS, vol. 2353, pp. 97–112. Springer, Heidelberg (2002)
2. Mori, Y., Takahashi, H., Oka, R.: Image-to-word transformation based on dividing and vector quantizing images with words. In: Proceedings of the International Workshop on Multimedia Intelligent Storage and Retrieval Management (1999)
3. Ghoshal, A., Ircing, P., Khudanpur, S.: Hidden Markov models for automatic annotation and content-based retrieval of images and video. In: Proceedings of the ACM SIGIR Conference on Research and Development in information Retrieval, Salvador, Brazil, August 15 - 19, pp. 544–551 (2005)

4. Agrawal, R., Grosky, W., Fotouhi, F., Wu, C.: Application of Diffusion Kernel in Multi-modal Image Retrieval. In: Proceedings of the Ninth IEEE International Symposium on Multimedia Workshops, December 10-12 (2007)
5. Feng, S.L., Manmatha, R., Lavrenko, V.: Multiple Bernoulli Relevance Models for Image and Video Annotation. In: IEEE Computer Society Conference on Computer Vision and Pattern Recognition, vol. 2, pp. 1002–1009 (2004)
6. Picard, R.W.: Toward a Visual Thesaurus. In: Workshop in computing. In: MIRO 1995, pp. 35–48 (1995)
7. Lim, J.H.: Building Visual Vocabulary for Image Indexation and query Formulation. Pattern Analysis and Applications 4(2-3), 125–139 (2001)
8. Jain, A.K., Vailaya, A.: Image Retrieval Using Color and Shape. Pattern Recognition 29(8), 1233–1244 (1996)
9. Carson, C., Belongie, S., Greenspan, H., Malik, J.: Blobworld: image segmentation using expectation-maximization and its application to image querying. IEEE Transactions on Pattern Analysis and Machine Intelligence 24(8), 1026–1038 (2002)
10. Zhu, L., Rao, A.B., Zhang, A.: Theory of keyblock-based image retrieval. ACM Trans. Inf. Syst. 20(2), 224–257 (2002)
11. Csurka, G., Dance, C., Fan, L., Willamowski, J., Bray, C.: Visual categorization with bags of keypoints. In: ECCV Workshop on Statistical Learning in Computer Vision (2004)
12. Sivic, J., Russell, B.C., Efros, A.A., Zisserman, A., Freeman, W.T.: Discovering Objects and Their Location in Images. In: IEEE International Conference on Computer Vision, vol. 1, pp. 370–377 (2005)
13. Maree, R., Geurts, P., Piater, J., Wehenkel, L.: Random Subwindows for Robust Image Classification. In: Proceedings of the IEEE Conference on Computer Vision and Pattern Recognition, June 20 - 26, vol. 1 (2005)
14. Fan, J., Gao, Y., Luo, H., Xu, G.: Automatic image annotation by using concept-sensitive salient objects for image content representation. In: Proceedings of the 27th Annual international ACM SIGIR Conference on Research and Development in information Retrieval, SIGIR 2004, Sheffield, United Kingdom, July 25 - 29, pp. 361–368. ACM, New York (2004)
15. Yang, C., Dong, M., Fotouhi, F.: Image content annotation using Bayesian framework and complement components analysis. In: IEEE International Conference on Image Processing, September 2005, vol. 1, pp. 1193–1196 (2005)
16. Zhou, X., Wang, M., Zhang, Q., Zhang, J., Shi, B.: Automatic image annotation by an iterative approach: incorporating keyword correlations and region matching. In: Proceedings of the 6th ACM International Conference on Image and Video Retrieval, Amsterdam, The Netherlands, July 09 - 11 (2007)
17. Wang, M., Zhou, X., Chua, T.: Automatic image annotation via local multi-label classification. In: Proceedings of the 2008 International Conference on Content-Based Image and Video Retrieval, Niagara Falls, Canada, July 07 - 09 (2008)
18. Li, J., Wang, J.Z.: Real-Time Computerized Annotation of Pictures. IEEE Transactions on Pattern Analysis and Machine Intelligence 30(6), 985–1002 (2008)
19. http://www.chiariglione.org/MPEG/standards/mpeg-7/mpeg-7.htm
20. MPEG-7: Visual experimentation model (xm) version 10.0. ISO/IEC/JTC1/SC29/WG11, Doc. N4062 (2001)
21. Lowe, D.G.: Object Recognition from Local Scale Invariant Features. In: Int. Conf. on Comp. Vis., vol. 2, pp. 1150–1157 (1999)
22. Manjunath, B.S., Salembier, P., Sikor, T. (eds.): Introduction to MPEG-7 Multimedia Content Description Interface. John Wiley & Sons, Indianapolis (2002)

23. Agrawal, R., Grosky, W.I., Fotouhi, F.: Searching an Appropriate Template Size for Multimodal Image Clustering. In: International Conference on Multimedia Computing and Systems, ICMCS 2009, Ouarzazate, Morocco, April 02-04 (2009) (accepted)
24. Karypis, G.: Cluto: A clustering toolkit, release 2.1.1. Technical Report 02-017, University of Minnesota, Department of Computer Science (2003)
25. van Rijsbergen, C.J., Robertson, S.E., Porter, M.F.: New models in probabilistic information retrieval. British Library Research and Development Report (1980)
26. Russell, B.C., Torralba, A., Murphy, K.P., Freeman, W.T.: LabelMe: A Database and Web-Based Tool for Image Annotation. Int. J. Comput. Vision 77, 157–173 (2008)
27. Amato, G., Gennaro, C., Savino, P., Rabitti, F.: Milos: a Multimedia Content Management System for Digital Library Applications. In: Heery, R., Lyon, L. (eds.) ECDL 2004. LNCS, vol. 3232, pp. 14–25. Springer, Heidelberg (2004)
28. Miller, G.A.: WordNet: a lexical database for English. Commun. ACM 38(11), 39–41 (1995)

Author Index

GPSR Compliance

The European Union's (EU) General Product Safety Regulation (GPSR) is a set of rules that requires consumer products to be safe and our obligations to ensure this.

If you have any concerns about our products, you can contact us on ProductSafety@springernature.com

In case Publisher is established outside the EU, the EU authorized representative is:

Springer Nature Customer Service Center GmbH
Europaplatz 3
69115 Heidelberg, Germany

Batch number: 09490872

Printed by Printforce, the Netherlands